CIVIC CENTER

I Left It on the Mountain

Also by Kevin Sessums

Mississippi Sissy

I Left It on the Mountain

Kevin Sessums

ST. MARTIN'S PRESS • NEW YORK

Some of the content, reporting, and scenes in this book are based on the author's previous reporting for *Interview*, *Vanity Fair*, *Parade*, *Los Angeles Confidential*, and *The Daily Beast*.

The author's interview with Brigid Berlin was originally published in *Interview* magazine, February 1989. Courtesy of BMP Media Holdings, LLC.

Excerpts from *The Andy Warhol Diaries* by Andy Warhol, edited by Pat Hackett. Copyright © 1989 by The Estate of Andy Warhol. Reprinted by permission of Grand Central Publishing and The Estate of Andy Warhol. All rights reserved.

"The Pruned Tree" from *Selected Poems*, published by Atheneum. Copyright 1971 by Howard Moss. Reprinted by permission of The Estate of Howard Moss.

www.stmartins.com

The Library of Congress Cataloging-in-Publication Data is available upon request.

ISBN 978-0-312-59838-9 (hardcover)
ISBN 978-1-250-02317-9 (e-book)

St. Martin's Press books may be purchased for educational, business, or promotional use. For information on bulk purchases, please contact the Macmillan Corporate and Premium Sales Department at 1-800-221-7945, extension 5442, or write to special markets@macmillan.com.

First Edition: February 2015

10 9 8 7 6 5 4 3 2 1

for
Perry Moore

CONTENTS

Do you not see how necessary a world of pains and trouble is to school an intelligence and make it a soul?

    —an excerpt from a letter dated May 3, 1819, and written to George and Georgiana Keats by poet John Keats

I've met some friends of yours. In fact, you seem to be known by everyone, and I have a whole new idea of your life. You were born and instantly flown to New York, where, like a Commissar of Culture, you proceeded down a long receiving line that included major and minor figures in the worlds of dance, drama, poetry, sculpture, architecture, and so on. The only thing you missed is alchemy.

    —an excerpt from a letter dated July 22, 1983, and written to me by poet Howard Moss

I Left It on the Mountain

ONE

The Starfucker

Still in bed, I realized it was my fifty-third birthday. My next thought was about the adventure I was going to have in a month. As a kind of birthday present to myself I had decided, as suggested by my friend Perry Moore, to walk the Camino de Santiago de Compostela. The Camino is a spiritual pilgrimage of over five hundred miles across northern Spain that pilgrims have walked for over two thousand years. Maybe that was why I was having so much trouble getting out of bed that birthday morning—not that I was another year older, but that my body had already begun to rebel at having to walk those five hundred miles of a trek my depleted spirit was demanding of it.

I cracked open an eye: another hotel room. Down the hill outside my window, Los Angeles, like me, lolled and continued to wake. I have awakened in many such overly conceptualized hotel rooms in Los Angeles since becoming known as a writer uninhibited by fame. I cracked open my other eye in that one six years ago and focused on it all. The low-slung sofa a sloe-eyed decorator, no doubt, deemed, "Divine!" before demanding an assistant buy it in bulk at the Pacific Design Center out there down that same hill outside my window so he, the sloe-eyed one, could then speed off to Melrose to make a tattoo appointment, his bicep finally big enough to have Emily Dickinson's entire two lines

"'Hope' is the thing with feathers / that perches in the soul" inked across it. Next to the sofa was a rather tatty red repro Saarinen chair. But the thing I recall the most from that immobile morning I turned fifty-three is my featherless solitude. They were—the sofa, the Saarinen, the solitude—the same somehow: each carefully chosen, precisely placed, all elements of an acquired aesthetic.

Many of my assignments over the years have taken me to LA to interview the phalanx of movie stars over whom I have mostly fawned. "The Impertinent Fawner" could have been printed on my business cards if I had ever thought myself in need of any. I had—I have—chosen a life free of business cards. That alone, I tell myself still, is accomplishment enough.

Or has it been? Is it?

Is it enough for a man to interview Madonna?

Is it man enough?

She was the first person about whom I wrote a cover story for *Vanity Fair* during my fourteen years there as a contributor after my stint as executive editor at Andy Warhol's *Interview*. This was, however, the once-upon-a-time Madonna, the one during *Dick Tracy* and Warren Beatty, before Malawi and Lourdes and alleged face-lifts, the one who has found a way, unlike me so far, to inhabit her fifties. Back when I first met her she had, through her first surge of real wealth, an aesthetic that could also be described as an acquired one. Her pride at her good taste outweighed her need for privacy at that point and she invited me to her home.

It was January 1990. Time Inc. and Warner Brothers were about to merge. The Leaning Tower of Pisa needed repair and was suddenly closed to visitors. A few days before, the Dow Jones reached a record 2,800 points. Jim Palmer and Joe Morgan were to be inducted into the Baseball Hall of Fame that month and Panama's Manuel Noriega was to surrender to American forces. Moscow was getting its first McDonald's. *The Simpsons* was ready to premiere on the fledgling Fox Network. And I was sitting in the back of a black sedan being driven high into the hills overlooking all of Los Angeles, a kind of city-state replete with

valet parking, huevos rancheros, and replication. I stared out my window. On one side, down below, was the gnarl of Sunset. On the other,
looming even larger, was the Valley in a city that states: This is what
a valley is.

The sedan pulled into Madonna's drive. I waited a bit before getting
out, because I was early for the interview. It is a trait of mine—arriving
early—ingrained in me by my grandfather, who made sure, back in my
Mississippi childhood, that ours was the first car each Sunday morning in the parking lot of Trinity Methodist Church. He would then make
all of us, my grandmother and brother and sister and me, wait until the
second family drove up for the worship service before we could get out.
Then on his cue—an exaggerated groan as he opened his door and unfolded his body—we all climbed from the car.

Madonna's house up in those hills that day was as far from Trinity
Methodist's parking lot as I had ever traveled. With an exaggerated groan
I unfolded my own body and, climbing from the car, climbed from the
life that had brought me to such a place.

I rang Madonna's bell and readied myself for one of her assistants to
answer it. Wrong. "Ready or not, here I come!" could, since her own
childhood, have been her mantra, the mantra of a woman who has never
hidden from but always sought herself. Why had it surprised me—she
could not disguise her satisfied grin when I gasped a little at the sudden sight of her—when it was she who swung open the door to greet
me?

She wore no makeup at all that day except for lipstick that had been
applied to the now-reddest lips allowed in town. On her tiny, exqui-
sitely toned legs she was wearing black fishnet stockings beneath black
cutoff jeans. She had not buttoned the top three buttons on a studded
black denim shirt. A black leather cap was cocked atop her head. Black
pumps were on her feet. Even the straggly strands of dirty hair streaming from under that cap were surprisingly dark, for she had planned,
slyly so, to end our time together that day in her kitchen as I watched

her eat a big bag of barbecue potato chips and feign bemusement at the trashy tabloids she purposefully had waiting for her perusal, all the while getting her hair washed in the kitchen sink, then dyed yet again back to the blond color that was her showbiz shade.

The house, like her, was surprisingly small, startlingly white, all modern angles and hard edges. Everywhere there was an exquisite incongruity. Outside, a black Mercedes 560SL was parked next to a coral-colored '57 Thunderbird; inside, twentieth-century art hung above eighteenth-century furniture. Candles, embossed with Catholic saints, dotted the house's sophisticated rooms. On a kitchen counter, audiotapes of Joseph Campbell's *The Power of Myth* lay stacked beside tapes by Public Enemy.

Atop her work desk was a beautiful portrait of her mother, who died of cancer when Madonna was six. "My memories of her drift in and out," she admitted to me. "When I turned thirty, which was the age my mother was when she died, I just flipped because I kept thinking I'm now outliving my mother."

I didn't gasp this time, but I did noticeably blanch. My mother had died at the age of thirty-three from cancer when I was eight and I, having already outlived her by several months, was about to turn thirty-four in a matter of weeks. The fact that I had also by then outlived my father, who had just turned thirty-two when he was killed in a car crash before my mother's illness, didn't lessen the odd panic I had been experiencing. It only served as the panic's foundation. Fed it. It was a heady feeling. Addictive? Perhaps. I only knew I was ironically growing to depend on such panic to feel alive.

I told Madonna of this shared panic of ours when she asked if I was all right. I had planned to match her brashness that day but had not anticipated just how brash we would instantly be with each other. It threw me. Where do I take the conversation from here? I was thinking, but there was no need to worry. She remained firmly in control.

"I thought something horrible was going to happen to me when I turned thirty," she said, reaching down and straightening the frame that contained her mother's image. Had the woman in that picture known already that she had cancer? Had she sensed something awful was about to happen? I stared into the eyes of Madonna's mother, eyes that a long-ago camera lens had caught in an unguarded moment. I saw the anger that had embedded itself there, the sorrow, peering back at me from beneath my own reflection.

"I kept thinking, like, this is it, my time is up," said Madonna, cutting her eyes defiantly my way after they had caught mine there in the glass atop her mother's face. Madonna's defiance somehow gladdened me. It was, in essence, her allure. She continued to straighten her desk. "It was a tough year last year. I was going through so many things . . . and my divorce . . . ," she said, mentioning Sean Penn without mentioning his name.

An ornately gold-framed Langlois, originally painted for Versailles, was as large as the entire ceiling in the house's main room, and that is exactly where Madonna had hung it, Hermes's exposed loins dangling over our heads as we headed that way. Boxer Joe Louis, photographed by Irving Penn, pouted in a corner across from May Ray's nude of Kiki de Montparnasse. Above the fireplace was a 1932 Léger painting, *Composition*. Across from it was a self-portrait by Frida Kahlo.

Earlier, in the entrance foyer, I had walked by another Kahlo. I stopped following Madonna about the house long enough to walk back toward it all by myself. She now followed me. I asked her the painting's name. "*My Birth*," she told me, coming to stand close beside me and gaze also at the image. It depicted Kahlo's mother in bed with the sheets folded back over her head. All that could be seen of the mother were her opened bloody legs, the head of the adult Kahlo emerging from between them.

Madonna touched my arm.

"If somebody doesn't like this painting," she said, "then I know they can't be my friend."

I did like the painting—it haunts me still—but I did not become her friend. We became, as one does so often where I reside just outside the frame of fame, heightened acquaintances. It's the kind of public relation-ship that can so easily flow from the intimacy that a good interview engenders when it veers into a conversation performed as a private one. Madonna and I, veering, talked a lot that day about abandonment be-cause of the deaths of our mothers from cancer when we were children. "I don't know if going to a shrink cures the loneliness caused by such abandonment," she'd confided, "but it sure helps you understand it."

Would I ever truly understand it? I wondered the morning of my fifty-third birthday as I continued to lie in bed, feeling as if I had even aban-doned myself in a way I had yet fully to comprehend. Noon arrived. I had to be at lunch in a matter of an hour over at the Peninsula hotel in Beverly Hills to interview Hugh Jackman for the cover of *Parade*. A siren outside my window was the day's first wail as I considered the arc of my career. Andy Warhol's *Interview*. *Vanity Fair*. *Parade*. Yep: fifty-three.

I thought back to an earlier birthday. It was the night of the *Vanity Fair* Oscar party at Morton's—March 27, 1995. Courtney Love was at my table, since she had also requested that I be her escort that night. We had already been spending a lot of time with each other leading up to a cover story for *Vanity Fair* that was scheduled to run in its upcom-ing May issue and were by then heightened acquaintances of our own.

A couple of months before the *Vanity Fair* party I had flown out to Seattle, where she lived on the shores of Lake Washington. It was to be our first meeting and she had kept me waiting for well over an hour down in the living room of the house she had shared with her late hus-band, Kurt Cobain. I became bored going over my interview notes by the fourth or fifth time and began to inspect what appeared to be a kind of Buddhist altar set up on a side table. I opened a tiny box posi-tioned there. What exactly could it contain? I picked up a bit of its con-tents with my fingers and felt the coarseness of the crinkled thread-like stuff I was holding. As I more closely inspected it—even giving it a whiff—Love entered the living room behind me and I heard, for the first time, a voice. Low. Hoarse. Hers. "What are you doing with Kurt's pubic hair?" she asked.

I ended up conducting most of the interview with her that day as she lay naked in her tub and scrubbed her own pubic hair while I sat on the toilet with the seat down. I also spent many more hours with her on the road as she toured with her band Hole. I swigged vodka from the bottles she offered me both backstage in Salt Lake City and at New York's Roseland. And I accompanied her to New Orleans to look at real estate. She wanted to own a haunted house, as if the one back in Seattle weren't haunted enough.

Like Madonna all those years earlier, Love had graciously given me a tour of her home. She'd even unlocked a kind of inner sanctum where Cobain had committed suicide in the studio above the garage, which she'd had converted to a hothouse filled with row upon row of orchids. It was the last thing we did together at the end of a very long day there on the shores of Lake Washington. She walked me into it. Not the studio exactly. Not the hothouse. But the silence Cobain had left there. The light refracted from Lake Washington gilded it all with a silvery grayness. She too touched my arm. We talked about the orchids.

Love had asked me to pick her up at her room at the Chateau Marmont the night of the Oscar party. When I arrived she was not alone but had paired up with a kind of dollish doppelgänger, Amanda de Cadenet, who was then the wife of Duran Duran's bassist John Taylor. The women were wearing matching dime-store tiaras and were dressed in what appeared to be long, lacy satin slips, as if they had tried on their gowns but then decided to discard such a bourgeois concept as clothing.

"These are the cheapest wedding dresses we could find," Courtney had insisted when I asked if she and de Cadenet were indeed wearing undergarments to the party. "We are gorgeous lesbians in twenty-dollar dresses," she grandly stated, then stated it again later, less grandly, with more of a put-upon rock 'n' roll moll in the mix, when we got to the party and she was interviewed outside by a cadre of roped-off reporters.

The flashbulbs went into a frenzy at the rope line outside Morton's. The satin from the slips or wedding dresses or whatever it was she and de Cadenet were wearing shimmered in the shock that even those cameras seemed to be registering at such attire, the tacky gimcrackery of their tiaras exposed by the chum of paparazzi. Forget her faux-lesbian pal de Cadenet; this was the real chum for which Love was ravenous. All their posing—chins just so, those chintzy tiaras becoming precariously unpinned—churned the chum even more. Me? I happened to be the bald gay guy who remained completely still between them in the midst of it all, which is an apt description of a certain swath of that town, perennial, patient, that has always been there, dead center.

One of the *Vanity Fair* cover stories that had run before that imminent one on Love was one on Jessica Lange, who was nominated for Best Actress that night for her performance in *Blue Sky*. Madonna, Lange, and Love—they were the three blond muses I thought about the morning of my fifty-third birthday as I lay in bed unable to move. Unbeknownst to Lange—the truest of these muses—she had even been the person who inspired me to embark on the adventure I was about to attempt in a matter of weeks.

There have been times in my job as a chronicler of celebrity that I thought I owed it to an actor or actress to write more than an impertinent puff piece. In those incidences I have tried to mine the ore of stardom, if not art, and find its seam and, in so doing, perhaps discover the very essence of that person. Yet even mining metaphors seemed lacking when dealing with Lange. Her allure—her own gravity, if you will—went deeper than any ore, any seam in it. She had recently returned at that point to live much of the year back on her family farm in Minnesota and by rediscovering her roots she had also rediscovered the gravity one attains from the land itself, the ever-onward trudge atop it, its hold on us all as we walk. There was, she had insisted to me, a mystical grounding one encountered when one was alone with one's own undergrowth.

"That's all I do anywhere is walk. Walking for the sake of walking," she told me when surprising me with a phone call one morning after I thought our interviews had been completed. "But none of that silly walk-ing," she warned. "That power walking."

She was piddling around in her kitchen with the phone to her ear, so I asked what she had taped to her refrigerator. The piddling stopped and she read aloud the two quotes I assumed she read silently to her-self every time she reached for a carton of milk or some leftovers.

The first was from T. S. Eliot:

"'We shall not cease from exploration,'" she read, "'and the end of all our exploring will be to arrive where we started and know the place for the first time.'"

She paused, seeming to gather herself before she could go on. "Then there's this," she said. "It's from Kierkegaard. 'Above all, do not lose your desire to walk. Every day I walk myself into a state of well-being and walk away from every illness. I have walked myself into my best thoughts and I know of no thought so burdensome that one cannot walk away from it. But if sitting still—and the more one sits still—the closer one comes to feeling ill. If one just keeps on walking everything will be all right.'"

Lange was allowing herself some silly walking on the red carpet when I watched her arrival at Morton's after the Oscar ceremony. She clutched her Academy Award in one hand, then the other, its familiar heft—this was her second one after winning for *Tootsie*—something she could handle with a deftness that did not feel foreign to her. Falling leaves, appliquéd onto her sheer bodice, continued in an autumnal tumble down the rest of her gown. I had not noticed that leafy tumble on the TV screen when, in her acceptance speech, she thanked her children for their love and understanding, as well as those who had rescued the film. *Blue Sky* had been completed in 1991 but not released until 1994 because of the bankruptcy of its studio, Orion. She especially thanked Tony Richardson, the film's director, but seemed careful not to men-tion his death in 1991 soon after the film was completed. She had spo-ken of him in the past tense, but that could have been construed as a reference again to how long it had taken the film to be released. If one weren't an insider in Hollywood one would have never known that this most dashing of men had actually died. Richardson had been the husband of Vanessa Redgrave and the father of Natasha and Joely before he left Redgrave to be able to continue openly his love affair with Jeanne Moreau. He did not become open about his bisexual nature and his other, longer love affair with men until he contracted HIV. He died of AIDS.

Tom Hanks, who had won his Oscar the year before for not only dying of the disease but also humanizing it, had just won his second in a row a few hours earlier. The one he now held was for *Forrest Gump* and a scrum of admirers over there in the middle of Morton's was trying to make eye contact with him. Over by the bar, Anthony Hopkins was shouting a whisper into Nigel Hawthorne's cocked ear as if they were on some stage planning the murder of Caesar instead of standing in a din of after-dinner guests. Sharon Stone glided through the throng toward a twenty-year-old Leonardo DiCaprio. Over against the wall Tony Curtis was checking me out yet again after telling me earlier that he'd once had a crush on Yul Brynner. "I think that's why you're making me feel so odd. You kinda look like him. I haven't slept with a man in decades, but the night is young," he'd flirted.

I had wanted to greet Lange at the door, but Pat Kingsley, her PR rep, was insisting she linger a bit longer on the red carpet. Kingsley was the toughest of a tough lot and had at one time or another represented Natalie Wood, Frank Sinatra, Al Pacino, Candice Bergen, Jodie Foster, Richard Gere, Sally Field, Will Smith, and Tom Cruise. I had a grudging respect for Pat and even liked her in spite of our adversarial roles in Hollywood. She was a liberal from the South like me, and though she had the gangly grace of a woman who once perhaps could have been a basketball star with the meanest of hook shots, she was a rabid baseball fan who liked to attend Dodgers games with another of her clients, Doris Day. I marveled at how Kingsley maneuvered Lange with the guileful patience of a major-league manager, a patience so guileful, in fact, that what she was feeling—what Pat seemed to be feeling at that very moment—was not patience at all but a perturbed restraint while taking the measure of the other team on the field.

I had already downed more than my requisite two vodkas and decided Lange and not my bladder would have to wait. When I returned from the bathroom, she had finally been allowed by Kingsley to enter the party and she and Hanks were having a private little laugh, which seemed to gather strength as it rippled through the room until the roar that surged around them—the preening of the privileged herd—had as its source the sound the two of them were making at that very moment when the party itself knew to crest. I huddled at the bar with a few *Vanity Fair* colleagues and reached for another vodka. ". . . very . . ." was all I heard Lynn Wyatt say to Betsy Bloomingdale as they passed by me before pausing long enough with George Hamilton to bask, along with him, in his handsomeness.

Was it Hamilton's overly debonair demeanor that began to depress me so in that instant? Or was it the smell of vomit on the well-upholstered Anna Nicole Smith who had just thrown up in the ladies' room yet sashayed right past me back into the party, one of her hips hitting me with such unacknowledged force I spilled a bit of my vodka? Whatever the reason, the frivolity of the night began to detach itself from me— fall away—just as that foliage on Lange's dress was falling away from some unseen tree that began to cast its shadow on the night. I looked at Lange across the room, who seemed to have been feeling the same way. Our eyes met and we smiled wanly at each other. She waved her Oscar-less hand at me and then her Oscar itself, trying to cheer us both up.

Michael J. Fox made his jaunty way through the crowd—nothing wan about him—and stood beside me there at the bar. I had interviewed Fox for a cover story at *Interview* during my Factory days. We remarked on the party and reminisced about my visit to his house years earlier. "But after that interview you left behind a piece of paper with some words on it. My dog Barnaby found it a few days later between the sofa cushions and I took it from him before he could chew it up. I've been wanting to tell you this for a long time," said Michael. "It was a litany for a word association game."

I downed the rest of my vodka.

"Yeah," Fox said, laughing. "Every word was sexual. 'Pussy.' 'Dick'. 'Cock.' 'Fuck.' . . ."

I moaned, hearing the litany itself lend even more noise to the party, muddying the laughter of a neighboring starlet. With each word Michael had fun flinging back at me I heard how I not only sexualized my own life but tried to do the same thing to others. Sam Shepard had found it so alarming during the conversation I had with him down in a horse stable in Charlottesville for his own *Interview* story that he would have bucked himself if he had not said something. "Everything is sexual to you," he had stated quietly with a stare so steely it had stopped our conversation for a moment. Where was Shepard? I wondered. Where was that steely stare of his I now so suddenly longed for in this crowd of anxious glances? His absence next to Jessica's side that night went unmentioned but not unnoticed.

After Michael J. Fox had cornered me with my own coarseness, I looked around for a lifeline. Even Courtney Love would have served the purpose if she and her doppelgänger hadn't dumped me after dinner to disappear into the party's swarm. Jessica Lange finally—even sweetly—headed toward me just in the nick of time. As she walked up to Michael and me, I gave her a big hug, more in relief than congratulations, and as I did I caught a glimpse of my wristwatch. "It's after midnight," I said in Lange's ear. "That means it's March twenty-eighth. My birthday. Shit. I totally forgot. Guess it's not about you anymore, Jessica. It's all about me now."

"Seriously?" she asked. "It's really your birthday? Okay. Here," she said, handing me her Oscar as if it were some last-minute gift she'd gotten for me. "Happy birthday. Hold this. It's getting much too heavy anyway."

She asked Michael and me if we wanted to be her dates to the *Pulp*

Fiction party over at Chasen's, since a certain segment of the crowd had already begun to make a mass exodus over there from Morton's. She grabbed my wrist and looked at my watch herself. "Pat is commandeering the limo and I'm supposed to meet her out front in just a couple of minutes now. Come on, boys. Be my dates."

Michael and I shrugged and followed her out to the limo. We climbed in the back with her. Michael took a jump seat. I sat next to Jessica and put her Oscar between my legs. Pat Kingsley sat on the other side of her and looked over at me with an expression of confusion and disgust. How had she been so lax as to allow someone like me in the limo with her client? The limo swerved abruptly for some reason—it was hard to know why through all the tinted glass—and we all fell silent for the ride over to Chasen's, as if in a show of respect for its impending demise. The *Pulp Fiction* party we were headed toward was more than Chasen's last hurrah. It was its wake. The restaurant, by closing its doors forever in just a few days, was proving that a certain sort of Hollywood was not just dying out but finally dead.

Only the year before at *Vanity Fair's* first Oscar party Dominick Dunne had used Chasen's as a kind of parable to illustrate our place in its world. I had been standing at that same spot at the bar at Morton's feeling the same odd despondency and smiling wanly or glancing anxiously at anyone who'd smile or glance back when Nick, as he was known to his friends, noticed me hanging out all alone. He came over and gave me a nudge. "What's wrong, kid?" he had asked.

I shrugged and shook my head at it all. I tried to pretend I wasn't feeling what I was feeling. But the pretense was too much—not the party's but my own. "I was just thinking of something John Keats once wrote in a letter," I told Nick, sounding even more pretentious than I was feeling. Yet Keats has always been a comfort to me. "'Who would wish to be among the commonplace crowd of the little famous,' he wrote, 'who are each individually lost in a throng made up of themselves?' This is kind of a commonplace crowd of the overly famous, but it still holds true, huh. They are each individually lost in a throng of themselves. I know I'm lost in it. I feel like I'm just visiting my own life."

Nick put his arm around me. "Fuck John Keats," he said. "You know Chasen's?" he asked me. "It was the Morton's of its day. Not sure how long it can hang on. So glamorous yet so homey when Hollywood itself was both those things. There's a great waiter who's still working over at Chasen's. He's hanging in there. His name is Tommy. Tommy Gallagher. He's a real character. Doesn't take guff from anybody. Much wiser than John Keats. Some of the stars used to come in just so Tommy could take their measure. See Nancy Reagan over there," Nick said, nodding toward the former First Lady who had attended the party that year. "She and I were talking earlier about Chasen's. She and President Reagan loved to dine there. They go way back with the place. She told me that when she was in the hospital having both her children Tommy sent over food from Chasen's so she wouldn't have to eat that hospital grub. She also told me that 'Ronnie' had even proposed to her there in his favorite booth and that Tommy had overheard their plans to be married at the Little Brown Church in the Valley with Bill Holden as their best man. Nobody else was invited but Bill and his wife—I forget her name. Nancy told me that Tommy never breathed a word to anyone. Never told a soul. Never tipped off the press. And the day of the wedding he came and stood across the street from the church in order to pay his respects. That's who we are—you and I, Kevin—we're Tommy the waiter from Chasen's standing silently across the street all alone. You just have to find a way to feel lucky about that. I've got to get back to Nancy now. She's looking over here. Sometimes we get to cross the street."

He touched my arm.

"Happiness is a choice, kid," he said. "Choose to be happy."

If happiness is a choice, is sadness one also? I only know on my way to Chasen's that night in the back of that limo I could have pretended it was the greatest birthday I'd ever had—filled with famous guests, a date who had just won the Oscar for Best Actress—but I realized it was far from it. I don't mean for that to be interpreted in any way against Jessica Lange. She only showed me kindness that night, generosity. But I didn't really know her, nor she me, and yet there we were—the night of her Oscar win, the wee hours of my birthday—in the back of a limo together. The moment itself wasn't exactly the saddest moment of my life—there's been too much competition for that—but it was the exact moment that I became aware of how sad I really was, so sad I could not breathe and cracked a window to get some air. I tried to find the absurdity in the situation later and, in my diary, labeled Kingsley "The Peeved Publicist" and Fox "the town's latest iteration of Jimmy Cagney, who sat rather irritably at that point himself on the jump seat." And yet as I remember it now, the absurdity subsides and all that is left is how rational the sadness was.

"Roll that window up," Pat ordered me as we pulled into Chasen's parking lot and the paparazzi pushed toward us. She reached across Jessica and took the Oscar from between my legs and handed it back to her. Then on Pat's cue—a groan as exaggerated as my grandfather's as she made sure to be the first to unfold her own body before confronting a room full of people as worshipful as any in a small Methodist church sanctuary back in Mississippi—we all climbed from the car.

Pat put on her best game face and ran interference, confronting the flashing bulbs of the paparazzi with a combination of fearlessness and feigned indifference. Soon after our entrance, she cleared a space in one of the booths. Was it the one where Ronnie had proposed to Nancy? It really didn't matter. That night it was Lange's as she settled into it and received those who fell into her line of vision.

I resumed my spot next to her and, sitting there, allowed the night to befall mine as well. Sculpted profiles, perfected, formed taut bas-reliefs of flesh against the room's dark knotted paneling. Courtney Love, who'd already made her way over there, loomed largest, her loudness, her dishabille beauty, causing a bit of the crowd to puddle like standing water about her. She gave me a withering stare, then winked at me before throwing her head back and laughing with too much abandon.

In another cluster, Quentin Tarantino, his back to me, more than spoke. He was spinning a yarn o   his spray of spittle in evidence there in the deep glow of   n's chunky heavily shaded lamps. I watched some of it sett   ad of his own Oscar he'd won for Best Original Screenp   g it with little blisters of moisture as if it were beginning   like everybody else in the overcrowded room. Martin L   had won the award for Best Supporting Actor for his   the movingly creepy Bela Lugosi in *Ed Wood*, kept letting   his spittle-less Oscar's head for luck.

Landau's own head was topped off with a toupee. With all the congratulatory jostling throughout the evening, it had become a bit untethered and listed to the left as he too now listened to Tarantino, whose sour joy at having only won the Best Original Screenplay Oscar permeated the room until the whole venue took on the surly swank of *Pulp Fiction* itself. Samuel L. Jackson, who was so brilliant in *Pulp Fiction* but had lost the Oscar to Landau, stared sourly, joyfully, at the man's left-listing toupee. John Travolta's hairpiece held tight. Sharon Stone shook an old man's hand. Love got bored with throwing back her head at the horror of herself and came pushing through the party toward Lange's booth. She knelt and paid homage. Lange was visibly tiring but still had enough in her to give that gimcrack tiara now there in front of her a couple of gentle taps, the last gesture of amusement she would allow herself that evening. I looked away from Love. I thought of the orchids.

I still thought of those past orchids as I sat staring at a present one, tastefully potted, there on my hotel room's desk, a lone labellum clinging to its own life. I noticed the message light blinking on my phone and wondered if someone had called to wish me a happy fifty-third birthday. I punched in the code and heard instead the voice of Hugh Jackman's publicist telling me that his photo shoot for the cover of *Parade* was running late out in Malibu so our lunch had to be pushed back by an hour. I shrugged at the message and focused on the job at hand. The extra hour gave me just enough time to shower and peruse my notes concerning Jackman's juggernaut of a career as well as his disciplined adherence to a twice-a-day meditative practice that such a career conversely engendered in him.

I'd been up late the night before, in fact, reading about his devotion to the School of Practical Philosophy, upon which his meditative practice is based. Having already memorized most of the information, I only gave my notes a perfunctory fifteen minutes. I then folded them and stuffed them into my back pocket before having the hotel doorman hail a cab from the queue of five or six at the ready for East Coasters like me. To be seen in a cab is anathema to a Los Angelian. It's almost as bad as lowering one's price or losing to the Celtics. When I've pulled up in one out there I've seen some people roll their eyes. Others grow quiet. All recoil.

Once I got to the Peninsula hotel, I had to wait still longer after Jackman's publicist called yet again to tell me that they were stuck in freeway traffic. I read my notes once more, then sat and watched the swirl of tourists in the lobby—a bevy of bejeweled Arab women arguing about something in a language that lifted and fell in a kind of ancient flyting ritual, a couple of towheaded children telling each other secrets, a bride-to-be from Brentwood, I surmised, sweeping in with some garishly dressed girlfriends for the shower they were throwing for her over in the Verandah Room.

Jackman suddenly came bursting through the front doors looking around for someone who had been described to him, no doubt, as bald and short with a tape recorder at the ready. He spotted me and I laughed at his harried state, thankful for it. I had worried I was the one who would be slightly rattled that day. My dark mood that morning had scared me, making me think I really might be as mad as a March hare. Hugh, who hated being late, appeared rather mad and hare-like himself as he hurried toward me. We were, around 3:00 P.M., the only ones left in the Peninsula's Belvedere restaurant.

I relaxed into the resulting privacy and was prepared for another coy give-and-take with a carefully coached celebrity. I was also prepared to ask him any question I felt compelled to ask. What I was not prepared for was the one question he felt compelled to ask me.

"I turned forty last year and it didn't bother me at all," Jackman said when I told him it was my birthday. "Life has only gotten better."

"Yeah, well, forty didn't bother me either," I said. "But turning fifty sure did. When I moved to New York back in 1975 there were old coots like me now—well, gentlemen of a certain vintage, the art world's Henry Geldzahler and the poet Howard Moss—who told me, 'You should have been here in the 1940s and 1950s, kid, when New York was New York.' I'm at that age now when I hear myself talking to young guys about how great New York was in the seventies when Times Square, like sex back then, was dirty. But it's our youth we miss, not any earlier version of the city. What we miss is that earlier version of ourselves when we ourselves could be dirty and innocent at the same time."

"Have you seen *American Swing?*" Jackman asked. "It's that documentary about the sex club Plato's Retreat during the seventies. I really want to see that."

"I never wanted to see the real place that much when it was around," I told him. "The one or two times I went there I couldn't get the smell of it out of my nostrils for a day or so. Somebody gave me my first hit of poppers there."

"Yeah, I read about something called the Mattress Room they had there," he said. "Sounded kind of . . . ah . . . redolent."

"I don't like public sex," I heard myself confessing to him. "But I'll do anything behind a locked door. If I don't like it then I don't do it again."

"That's brilliant," Jackman said, laughing as if I were joking. "My favorite play I studied in drama school was *The Bacchae.* It's about King Pentheus, who gets eaten alive by all the women in a kind of orgy," he said, his eyes widening in anything but a steely stare, and I suddenly had an image of my three blond muses—Lange and Madonna and Love—devouring him in the role of the king. "I love that idea of animalistic chaos and following our desires," he continued. "I think the Wolverine character I've played a couple of times now kind of represents that. He's a man who battles between the animal and the human in him, between the chaos in him and the self-control he must have. We all deal with this to some extent every day. At what point do we let go and do what we want to do when we should submit to rules? This is a man who is terrified of the blind fury he gives in to. It's when he's at his most glorious and at his most devastating—and yet at his most destructive."

I certainly understood battling the animalistic side of myself, which usually ended, however, in a destructive bacchanal of sex and drugs instead of blind fury. And yet for the first time I realized in that very moment that is exactly the way my blind fury unfurls itself: sex and drugs.

I cleared my throat and asked a prepared question. "Isn't your adherence to the practice of the School of Practical Philosophy all about acknowledging the duality in our natures and yet finding the unifying element in us all? There is a sentence in Sanskrit . . . ," I said.

". . . Tat Tvam Asi . . . ," he said.

"Thou art that," we said together.

Jackman and I finished our meal as well as our interview, touching on all the topics that *Parade* readers wanted to know about—not Greek kings being devoured by three blond muses, but his adopted children, his own parents and childhood in Australia, his love for his wife, his hosting of the Oscar telecast, his stage and movie career. The waiter, surprising me, brought out a piece of mocha-frosted cake with a lone lit candle stuck atop it. Jackman must have told him to do it when he excused himself earlier, saying he had to make a quick phone call. The waiter made an elaborate ritual out of it all and then Jackman serenaded me with "Happy Birthday."

"Do you know about the Camino in northern Spain?" I asked him as the waiter handed us two forks. "It's a spiritual path that people have walked for two thousand years. I'm doing it in a month. I'm walking from France. Over the Pyrenees. And, if I make it, all the way across Spain to Santiago, where Saint James is said to be buried in the cathedral there."

"And what do you hope to find once you start walking?" asked Jackman.

"I don't know. I'm hoping it finds me," I said. "I feel somehow I'm already walking the Camino, having decided to do it. Coincidences are becoming even more heightened. Everything is beginning to connect. I just finished Shirley MacLaine's book *The Camino* about her own walk along the path. She talks about her inner spiritual journey in it as much as the trek itself. There are even astral projections in it. Things like that. But all these heightened coincidences did begin to happen to me while I was reading her book."

"Yeah? I'm listening. This kind of stuff fascinates me," said Jackman.

"I was in Starbucks reading Shirley's book when the door opened and I looked over and saw the most beautiful boy I think I've ever seen," I told Jackman. "He kind of looked like an astral projection himself. He was backlit by the sun and his blond wavy hair seemed to be encircled by a halo. I guess he looked more like an angel than an astral projection, but angels like that don't look at me anymore now that I'm past fifty, so instead of cruising him I turned back to Shirley's book. A few minutes later, the angel tapped me on the shoulder and said he couldn't help but notice what I was reading and asked if I was going to walk the Camino. He told me that he had walked it the year before but had to stop before he made it all the way because one of his knees blew out when he reached Burgos. We talked for a while about his experiences walking it and he gave me his name and number and e-mail in case I wanted to talk some more. His last name was Amore. He was an angel named Love. Can you believe that?"

"Yes. I can," said Jackman. "I do."

We sat in silence for a moment. "Have you seen Geoffrey Rush on Broadway in Ionesco's *Exit the King*?" I then asked him.

"Yeah. I did. It was amazing," he said.

"Yeah. It was," I agreed. "Did the play speak to your own fear of death like it spoke to mine?"

"Of course," said Jackman, taking a final bite of cake. "Not at the time, particularly, because I was so engrossed in Geoffrey's performance and the virtuosity of it. But I woke up the next morning to meditate and the first thing that came to my mind was that brilliant . . . well . . . not a description so much as a showing, a sharing of that oblivion, the casting off of everything in that last monologue when the queen is talking and he, as the king, physically, silently, did what he did. That's what meditation is. It's that natural shedding of all this stuff. It was a completely different meditation for me the next morning after seeing *Exit the King* and I've been meditating for fifteen years. But it somehow changed my view, my perspective, what they call in Sanskrit your *bhavana*, which means what you bring to something, what you feel about something. I realized anew what a gift meditation is. It's dying twice a day. I'd never thought of it that way. It is a practice of dying—what it's like to get rid of the ideas, the desires, the body even. There is a part of meditation that is a feeling of bodilessness."

Jackman turned and now looked right at me. There was no steeliness in his stare, no accusatory cast, as there had been years earlier in Sam Shepard's, just utter stillness that, in turn, stilled me with its stern regard. He touched my arm. "I want to ask you a question, Kevin," he said. "I hope you don't mind. But I feel I must, in all seriousness, ask you this. Have you fucked the angel?"

And with that, I had the sensation of leaving my own body by burrowing down to its deepest desire, the seam in its ore. Jackman had just summed up my whole dilemma. It was the journey—the trudge—I had been on my whole life. How do I fully combine the spiritual with the carnal? Was this why the Camino beckoned me so? "Not yet," was all that I could answer.

TWO

The Climber

Because my 1960s Mississippi boyhood was bracketed by the deaths of my parents I became lost in the wilds of an overgrown sorrow, a place even scarier and darker than Mississippi was in 1963 and 1964. It was, I have since come to realize, the tragic unruliness of my life and all that surrounded me that caused me to seek refuge in the world of celebrity even then. Kennedy was assassinated in the same year both my parents died. Medgar Evers was gunned down. Freedom Summer occurred, the decomposing bodies of Schwerner and Chaney and Goodman found in an earthen dam up in Neshoba County where my uncle Doots owned the hardware store off the town square in Philadelphia.

It was not the make-believe quality of show business that attracted me. It was instead that one could exert such control over that make-believe. I hovered closer and closer to the TV screen because happily-ever-after only happened, as far as I could figure out, there inside it where narrative after narrative came to nest. Sitting in front of that TV screen is where, in 1965, I built my own nest after my parents died. I would not only seek it out—narrative in all its forms—but begin to look on my own life as narrative as well.

Andy Griffith's make-believe life in Mayberry was what I longed for mine to be and found comfort not only in the show but also for the first time in longing itself. Yet I could only visit Mayberry on Mondays after Lucy with her latest made-up last name had helped me laugh. Sundays were for Ed Sullivan and the Ponderosa and the pearled blindfold of Arlene Francis. Tuesdays were for Red Skelton and *Petticoat Junction*. Wednesdays, *The Beverly Hillbillies*. Thursdays, *Bewitched*.

But after yet another long week in fourth grade, Friday night was the one I lived for. That's when my favorite two Wests would stir me with an unseemly appreciation for inseams and pet ocelots. Robert Conrad starred in *The Wild Wild West* and his tightly tailored nineteenth-century secret agent trousers barely hid the treasures buried beneath them. I'd sit in front of the TV screen and try to get just the right angle to catch the best view of the preening Conrad. Anne Francis, a half hour later, was the star of *Honey West*, a twentieth-century sleuth in possession of the pet ocelot that almost made her as exotic to me as that beauty mark beneath her lower lip. I'd skip *The Addams Family*, which came on during the half hour between those two shows—the idea of family macabre enough that first year I was without parents—and take a hurried bath before carefully pointing a Bic pen (my Honey West ritual) beneath my own lower lip, inking on a beauty mark as perfect as a period, the punctuation on a sentence my flesh kept trying to write.

On Saturday I chose *The Hollywood Palace* over Rod Serling's western, *The Loner*, starring Lloyd Bridges. I tried *The Loner* once—the name appealed to me even then—when Brock Peters starred as a black Union soldier going home to see his father, who had been lynched by the Klan the night before Peters arrived, which proves just how surreal the world was for me back then, for it was Rod Serling who gave me my one dose of reality on the TV screen. I quickly turned the channel back to *The Hollywood Palace* and saw for the first time three other black people who blended more smoothly into the happily-ever-after world I was creating for myself. I stood and mimicked their movements—these women who dared to deem themselves the Supremes—and surprised myself with the ease with which my hips, my hands, my head mirrored their rhythms, my grandfather peering in from the hallway door and ducking quickly back behind it when I did a pivot identical to Diana Ross's and caught his disdain at such a display.

On Saturday afternoons I made sure to have the old Zenith turned to yet another rerun of Johnny Weismuller in one of his twelve Tarzan movies that the local CBS station in Jackson would air as a weekly double feature with one of the twenty-six episodes of *Jungle Jim*, Weismuller's follow-up 1950s TV series. My younger brother and sister would be running about the yard playing their usual Saturday afternoon games while I, sitting inside, would sink deeper and deeper into the sadness about our parents' deaths. I would be wondering if my mother and father were together in heaven, as I was told they were in both dismissal and comfort by the adults always hovering about that first year, or whether death had made them disappear altogether. Obliterated them. Blown them away like the dust the preacher on both occasions had said they'd become.

Mostly, however, I'd wonder if it had turned them into bits of the darkness that I stared into when refusing to fall asleep. My fear that year was a second abandonment as they purposefully slipped together further and further away, death the place where they had escaped me. I'd lie awake trying to memorize their faces or how different their flesh felt when I'd tug at them, touch them, parenthood still tactile when they were taken away from me. I'd even try to conjure their different smells. But it was the sounds of their voices I missed the most when they'd talk down the hall on other nights when they were still alive and the low hum of their presence lulled me to sleep, how they'd overlap each other, laugh, then lower their laughter before laughing some more. I even missed the troubled sighs that would invariably slip from them in my sissy presence. I lay in bed that first year of their absence as their combined sigh-less silence grew louder and louder, louder than the crickets, louder than the creak of my mattress, louder than my grandfather's snores in the next room that goaded me to stay awake if he so easily could not. It was not that I was scared of the pitch-blackness of a Mississippi country night. Just the opposite. I welcomed it, for I could then be a sentinel, staring straight into it, if prayers were answered and my parents were sent back to me to be discerned in such utter darkness.

Some nights I'd pretend that darkness was the chalkboard at the beginning of the hospital show *Ben Casey*, on which symbols were written and a man's voice intoned, "Man, woman, birth, death, infinity." I'd lift my hand toward the darkness left in front of my face by my parents' deaths and pretend to trace the symbols into it and intone in my tired little whisper, "Man, woman, birth, death, infinity," trying to keep myself awake.

Each night I traced those symbols in the darkness I'd remember that awful day I drew them for my mother on a piece of paper when she was in her real hospital room and I had pointed out what each had meant, trying to impress her and cheer her up and take her mind off the pain with which her by then brittle, brutally thin body, nothing but cancer cells sheathed in the flimsiness of a hospital gown, was wracked. I had memorized the names of the symbols especially for my visit that day because she loved *Ben Casey* and I'd overheard her complain to my grandmother during my last visit that her own real doctors weren't as cute as he was. Dr. Casey had the swarthy good looks of my already dead father and I knew somehow what she was really saying was that she missed my father as much as I did. "Is that why you like Ben Casey, Mama, 'cause he looks like Daddy did?" I asked her when I was left alone with her that day to draw those symbols while my grandmother took a break to get some lunch.

My mother started to say something but then screamed out in pain and grabbed her bony body beneath the hospital bed's tightly tucked sheets. "Kevin, I'm sorry!" she moaned, then screamed out again. Another scream. Another. Then another. I backed up against the wall as far away from her screams and her pain and her writhing as I could get without leaving her alone in the room. A nurse came bustling in, her brogues screeching on the well-waxed tile floor sounding almost like my mother's screams, which kept on coming. The nurse had a bottle with her and hung it from the pole next to my mother's bed. A tube and needle dangled from the bottle and swayed to and fro, its shadow like an agitated snake appearing suddenly in the room along with the nurse. I pressed my body against the wall and whispered "Man, woman, birth, death, infinity, man, woman, birth, death, infinity" to calm my fear as I watched the nurse find a vein in my mother's arm. Another nurse then entered to hold my mother down so the first nurse could stick that dangling snake-like needle in her vein. Whatever was in the bottle they had hung from the pole filled the needle and then my mother's vein and then her body, instantly calming her writhing. The second nurse left, never having looked my way, but the first nurse stopped and cupped my face in her hand and asked if I wanted a Popsicle. I shook my head no, freeing myself. My mother moaned behind her. The nurse left and I walked over to the bed and asked my mother if she wanted to drink some water. She nodded yes with her eyes closed and, on tiptoe, I put the bent straw from a glass of water into her mouth. A bit dribbled down her chin and I wiped it off with my finger. I stared at the needle in her arm. I looked at the veins in my own arm. I wanted a needle in one of mine so I could feel what my mother was feeling. I was tempted to pull the needle out of her arm and stick it into me so I too could feel that instant calm. Instead I watched the liquid in the bottle—something I'd heard the nurses call morphine as they walked away down the hallway moments before—slowly empty into my mother's stilled body. A smile creased her dry lips. She moaned again and sighed, but not out of pain. Something else seemed to cause her moans now, her sighs, something much like what could elicit such moans and sighs from her when I'd hear them in happier times as I hid in her closet with her clothes and shoes, back when my father was still alive and lying with her on their bed. Her eyes still closed, she reached up with her hand toward the utter darkness my father's death, her husband's, had left in front of her own face. She traced in the air the symbols that I had just drawn for her. "Howard," she then said my father's name instead of intoning the names of the symbols. "Howard, you're here. Do you see him, Kevin? Say those symbols again for Daddy. Your son's so smart, Howard. Kiss me. Ben Casey. Howard. Hold me. You're here." I stared at the needle sticking in her arm. Was that what was making her so happy so suddenly? Was that all it took to take her pain away when I could not with my recitation of symbols from some silly TV show? She stopped talking to my father. She stopped talking to me. She was completely quiet. An indecipherable bliss had settled over her. I stood in her silence and watched her drift away.

Often, there in my nest in front of the TV screen back at my grand-parents' home, I'd lose myself in just such indecipherable silence the deaths of my parents had put in my head and drift away myself within it. I have often thought that my impulse to write is a way to solve all the silence they left me with. Even the dialogue on the TV screen could not interrupt it when, as a child, I'd sink into it. Words were useless against it back then. Yet on those Saturday afternoons, Johnny Weiss-muller, the Banat Swabian émigré in possession of the swellest pair of pecs I'd ever seen, could let loose his ululating Tarzan yell and always jerk me back to earth, to Mississippi, to myself, a nine-year-old boy al-ready guessing that death, not a symbol at all, had many guises.

Later in my television-centric youth, I watched a wizened Weissmuller on *The Mike Douglas Show* describe that Tarzan yell as a recording of three combined voices: "a soprano, an alto, and a hog caller." But back on those afternoons of an earlier childhood I had no idea the yell was faked. I thought Tarzan actually did let loose like that. It was the tru-est sound I'd ever heard and seemed to be making the maddening noise my heart itself longed to make to warn me of the danger that was ap-proaching like some beast Tarzan was warning Jane and Cheeta and Boy about in their televised version of Africa. The beast that was stalk-ing me, however, was my own adult self—sex crazed, excessive, HIV positive—there already in the low brush of such a childhood.

A buddy of mine e-mailed me a few summers ago to see if I would be interested in going to Africa with him to climb Mount Kilimanjaro with a group of friends in January of the next year. I had always dreamed of visiting Africa ever since I spent those lazy Saturday afternoons in Mississippi with Weismuller and his way with a vine, his loincloth, the same few lions in every episode. If I really did go to Tarzan's homeland and do something so anomalous for me—in my fifty years I had never slept in a tent or a sleeping bag or taken a hike any place other than Central Park—would I be able to shake myself out of this new form of mourning I found myself in once I was diagnosed with HIV? If I submitted my body to an experience as unforgiving as the climb up Mount Kilimanjaro would I be able to find a way to forgive myself for the predicament I had caused by behavior far more dangerous than any mountain climb could prove to be?

In the three years since my doctor had first sat me down and said these simple words, "You are HIV positive," I had grieved for my HIV-negative self, a beloved person, like a dead parent I knew I must someday place in the past if I were to live in the present. I had dealt with the societal shame of my diagnosis by not allowing myself to deny it by keeping it from my friends and family or pretending I was not HIV positive when the subject came up in conversations. I had coped with the initial side effects of my medical regime. And had attempted— unsuccessfully—to deal with the drug abuse that was the linchpin to the real fix in which I now found myself, death no longer something to guess about in its many guises but to count on.

I had even grappled with a grand sort of anger, so grand it at times surfaced as rage. And its surfacing happened in the most surprising moments, as when I received a note from Tom Cruise. During that first year of my diagnosis no one had sent me a note about it. That, in itself, struck me as odd, formal, more thoughtful than friendly. It was postmarked "Los Angeles," a place as tribal as any in Africa. And Cruise was indeed thoughtful. But sitting there on the heavy grain of his monogrammed stationery this word, among many others, was the one that stared back at me: "illness." I read that note several times when I received it, each time lingering over that one word, my rage growing at the sight of those seven little letters. My heart raced. I reeled. Tears stung my eyes. From that moment on I resolved that though others might now perceive me as ill, I would not allow my self-perception to be readjusted in such a way. Semantics, always important to me as a writer, had taken on an added significance as words and their meanings had become lifelines to which I clung.

But I could not—no matter how hard I tried—forgive myself for what I kept concluding was a suicidal act: becoming infected at such a late date in my life with HIV. This climb up Kilimanjaro just might help me find that forgiveness I still had not found. I was determined to find it. I could not go on living a life that awaited rage.

I retrieved Cruise's note from its hiding place beneath the felt lining of the wooden deco box that held my tarnished silverware and read it for the first time since receiving it. I had hidden it there because I didn't want to throw it away, but I also didn't want it lying around to serve as a kind of certification for my "illness." Once I retrieved it—it had been in that box untouched for over two years—I did not pause over those seven letters. Most important, I did not put it back into its hiding place but threw it into one of the drawers of my desk where I kept unpaid bills and drafts of magazine articles and sharpened pencils and a couple of pornographic DVDs, the detritus of a writer's life. I then e-mailed my friend back that he could include me in the climb up Kilimanjaro. I looked at my calendar and began the countdown of days until I could board a plane and head for Africa, a place that once upon a time held that sound my heart still longed to make.

The group my friend had put together for the climb up Mount Kilimanjaro was a diverse one. He was a consultant for Médecins Sans Frontières and his boyfriend, who also helped organize the climb, was then the director of treatment and advocacy for Gay Men's Health Crisis in New York City. His sixty-five-year-old father and his father's sixty-nine-year-old best friend, two flinty old gentleman-farmer lawyers from New Hampshire who had never left the United States, also wanted to come along. Others in the group included an internist who was a professor at Columbia University; a Mexico City–based social services consultant; a Web site developer from Boston along with his Massachusetts husband, an editor in textbook publishing; and a product production director for Martha Stewart, who had e-mailed Stewart to tell her that he was making the climb having known that she had made it once herself. Within seconds, Martha had e-mailed him back: "DON'T TAKE THE ALTITUDE FOR GRANTED!!!!"

I certainly wasn't going to. I had done my research. I read many blogs about the climb in which those who had successfully made the summit on the six-day Machame Route we were taking claimed that the last forty-eight hours of their ascent were the hardest two days of their lives. I read, of course, Hemingway's *The Snows of Kilimanjaro* and one of his stark sentences stuck out to me among all the other stark ones. I read it over and over as I had the sentence Cruise had written me with "illness" in its own stark predicate. "You can't die if you don't give up" was Hemingway's proposal to me.

The tour company one chooses and the guides one is assigned are the difference between a successful climb up Kilimanjaro and a less successful one. Mauly Tours, run surprisingly for such a male-dominated continent by three Indian women (two daughters and their mother), was the Tanzanian company we chose not only for the testimonials of its former customers but also for our smugly enlightened politics. Our guide, Adam Ringo, and his two assistants—Bernard Lucas and Anthony Mtui—could not have been more professional. To lead a bunch of grumbling gay city slickers and two crusty old heterosexual Live-Free-or-Die-ers up an African mountain takes the carefully attuned emotional skills of a psychiatrist, the inspirational aptitude of an athletic coach, and the bedside manner of a medical professional.

Our first day of the climb consisted of hiking up the steep rocky steps embedded in the two levels of rain forests that circle the foot of Kilimanjaro where most of the members of the mountain's Chaga tribe live in their hidden villages and work so diligently to protect their tree farms from poachers. The forest's jungle-like canopy shielded us from the heat of the sun but also created a steam bath effect as, sweating profusely, we climbed steadily upward. The nervous excitement I had been feeling as we began the day quickly gave way to the calming concentration that overtook me when my body experienced the steady exertion that such a climb required. The jungle here receives over seventy-eight inches of rain per year—three times the rainfall of London—which results in the vast array of vegetation: the latched branches that serve as a home for the ever-scurrying blue monkeys and the thousands of species of birds, the colorful *Impatiens kilimanjari* that blooms nowhere else in the world but here, and the abundance of usnea (old man's beard) that hung from so many of the gigantic trees hovering about our path.

Seven hours later we finally reached our first camp. I stared at the small tent I was to share that night with my friend from Martha Stewart's company and found the breath, there at around eight thousand feet, to blow up my air mattress to put beneath my sleeping bag. During that first night, however, I discovered the mattress would not retain the air I had blown into it, and for the next four nights of the trek I would be sleeping flat against the sharp, rocky ground.

I awoke the next morning with an aching sacroiliac and a scowl on my face, wondering what in the world I had gotten myself into. But the scowl—if not my aching back—slowly began to disappear when I looked above our tents as the morning clouds parted and I got my first real look at the mountain's snow-covered peak. I had put on my iPod earlier in the morning and Blossom Dearie was now singing, incongruously, "I Walk a Little Faster." "Can't begin to see my future shine as yet / . . . rushing toward a face I can't divine as yet," she sang there on a slope covered in heather as I tried to fill my lungs with the air that was becoming as seductively thin as Blossom's voice. The sun hurried the rest of the clouds away and I stood in the oddly chilly warmth provided by both it and Blossom's sophisticated plaint. I stared at the distant peak. Would I really make it up there? I wondered. Would I find that evasive bit of self-forgiveness I had come seeking? Or would I just wake up every morning with additional back pain? I silenced Blossom— she was going on now about building herself a stronger castle in the air—and set forth on the second day of the climb.

The moorlands at this altitude became, at first, dense with even more heather—rhinos once lived here among all the groundsel and lobelia, as our guide Bernard, an expert on plant and animal life, had informed me when spotting the now-infrequent flowers along our increasingly rugged route. As we approached the alpine desert that jutted up before us, I hung back with my friend who had initially e-mailed me about joining him on Mount Kilimanjaro and confessed to him the main reason I had decided to come along was that I considered this a trek for self-forgiveness. I knew that he had been HIV positive himself for twenty years, which was now more than half his life. He first found out when he donated blood to the Red Cross through his fraternity at Dartmouth and got the fateful call that amounted back then to a death sentence. He had been nineteen.

He greeted my confession with silence.

I pressed him further and asked him the one question I had always wanted to ask him. "How have you stayed alive?"

He didn't break his stride but motioned at the view below us. "This," was all he said, shrugging as he gestured at the rough beauty of the world in which we now found ourselves. "This," he said again, "this," and moved steadily onward.

At the next campsite on the Shira plain I wanted some after-dinner Blossom Dearie, but my iPod's battery was already running too low. I had to listen instead to nearby German climbers gabbing away all at once, a cacophony of guttural enthusiasms competing with an even nearer group of hippie progeny from Northern California listening to one of their members play an odd assortment of tunes on his too ably fingered fipple flute: "Climb Every Mountain," "How Do You Solve a Problem like Maria?" and "Moon River." I had visions of Andy Williams and Julie Andrews in matching lederhosen waltzing toward the Barranco wall, our next day's destination, while I tossed and turned on the Shira's shards of gravel beneath my flat sleeping bag.

In the morning, barely having slept, I trudged down to the latrine to stand in line for my turn inside the foul wooden shed with the tiny hole carved into its floor that had served as the unmet target for the man with stomach problems who had been in line in front of me. I held my breath and took better aim. By the time I exited the shed the campsite had become overrun by white-necked ravens that roamed the place like rats attempting to scavenge what they could from our breakfast leftovers.

When traversing the twenty-six miles of the journey up and down and across Kilimanjaro one experiences climate changes that are the equivalent of a six-thousand-mile trek. That morning, there at the 11,500-feet altitude of the Shira camp, I began to cope with how cold the next few days were going to be. I bundled up for the misty climb toward the Machame Route's famous Shark's Tooth, a tower of lava we were aiming to reach in the afternoon after making our way through the rocky terrain that reminded me of the starkest of NASA's images of neighboring planets.

Though I had been taking my Diamox pills as a prophylactic against altitude sickness, this was the day that I became frightened that I just might be the first member of our group to turn back. I began to experience the first signs of nausea and could feel the pressure inside my head as my brain had begun to swell. My headache was so bad—I was feeling so sick—I could barely chew what lunch I was able to choke down. By the time we reached the lava tower at 14,300 feet, I was really worried. Self-forgiveness was the last thing on my jumbled mind. I only wanted to breathe more steadily and calm my wildly skipping heart.

Was I making myself physically sicker here in Africa instead of finding the deeper healing for which I yearned? It was a bit selfish of me anyway to come to Africa, the place on this planet most decimated by AIDS, to seek some bit of inner peace instead of turning my gaze outward and finding a way to help others who suffered much more than I. I looked over at the sixty-five- and sixty-nine-year-old codgers from New Hampshire who stayed with me at the bottom of the cloud-enshrouded Shark's Tooth as the other seven in our group excitedly set out to climb its bouldered ridges. I felt, at that exact moment, older, more feeble, closer to death, than I had ever felt in my life.

When the group returned, exhilarated by their extra feat of physical daring, we slowly made our way down toward our next camp beneath the Barranco wall, which, in turn, we would go straight up the next morning at 6:00 A.M. sharp. The acclimatization worked as we went lower and lower into the welcome lushness of a valley we approached through a concatenation of gigantic cacti. My headache disappeared. My appetite returned. Dinner that night was so rollicking that we even made the two old codgers "honorary homos" because they were cracking jokes as sexually risqué as the rest of us. It wasn't until we heard a deafening whoop come from their tent later in the evening that we had to renege on their new titles. The sixty-nine-year-old had brought a hand-cranked radio on the climb for what we all thought were his nightly BBC news updates. Instead, he was trying to find out the score of the NFL play-offs and that night he finally heard that his beloved New England Patriots had made it into the Super Bowl. The rest of us emerged from our tents to find the two men anxious to tell us of the Patriots' achievement.

We all, however, quickly fell silent with the sight that was before us. The moon, one night shy of its fullness in what could only be called a firmament at this altitude, was slowly rising over Kilimanjaro's peak and whitening it even more. We all contemplated whatever thoughts were passing through our minds after the arduous success of the climb so far: tomorrow's final ascent to the summit, our newfound camaraderie, the Patriots' chance at a three-peat, Tom Brady's ass.

For my part, I said a silent prayer of thanks for being right there on that mountainside and nowhere else on earth. For the first time since my diagnosis, I did not simply want to run out the clock on my life. I knew—knew with all my heart—that I wanted to live. As I watched the rising of that moon, I believed more strongly in God than I had ever believed before. I felt a divine forgiveness. But I still did not feel my own.

The next forty-eight hours were, as those blogs I had read predicted, the hardest of my life. We climbed for nine hours during the day—up that Barranco wall and down and up and through the Karanga Valley in a constantly spitting rain until we reached the Barafu camp-site at the base of Mount Kili's highest peak. We filled up on pasta that evening in our dinner tent before lying down for three hours. After I popped a Sustiva tablet—one of my HIV meds that should not be taken on a full stomach—my altitude sickness suddenly combined with the dizzying disorientation that Sustiva can sometimes cause. I began to panic, worried that it would be my HIV medication that would stop me from going any farther. I lay on the hard, sharp ground and begged the God in whom I newly believed to make the Sustiva cease causing its side effects. Was this a form of prayer, this begging I had been brought to? I finally fell asleep for an hour, too exhausted to beg any longer.

We were roused precisely at midnight by Ringo, our lead guide, to begin our ascent to the summit. I sat straight up and checked for any Sustiva signs. No, I concluded, all I was feeling was altitude sickness, which, believe it or not, was preferable to my HIV meds' vertiginous side effects. Relieved, I strapped on my headlamp and layered on my clothes, grateful that all ten of us in the group had made it this far.

The scree though which one had to maneuver for the final steep four thousand feet up the mountain made it difficult to gain one's footing in the six hours of darkness required to make it to the top. For every three steps I took forward, I slipped back one step, sometimes two. And as I climbed higher and higher, the altitude sickness became more pro-nounced. Suddenly those Sustiva side effects didn't seem so bad com-pared to what the thinner and thinner air was now doing to my body. The frigid temperature made my teeth chatter. My heart raced faster and faster. My breath became more labored. My head began constrict-ing around my brain—or was my brain swelling? Whichever was hap-pening—I was too disoriented to reason it out—I had the sensation of my skull scraping against whatever was inside it until I feared for my cranium.

I hit many walls that night of the ascent and fought through all of them—the utter fatigue, that blinding headache, the recurring nausea, even hallucinations. I thought I saw small animals scurrying around my feet at several points, but as long as I could tell myself they were not real I knew I was still okay, still lucid. I was quite literally brought back to earth when the ground rumbled ferociously, then rolled beneath us. A small avalanche crashed down by us on the right. Ringo turned, more than slightly shaken himself, and remarked that in ten years of guiding groups up the mountain he had never experienced an earthquake or a volcanic reminder or whatever it was that had just happened.

Such an occurrence, however, did not scare me. I felt instead newly energized. I picked up one of the rocks that had rolled at my feet to put in my pocket as proof I had been on that mountain heading for its summit. I climbed onward with a new vigor. I looked up and saw the moon, now full, hanging close over our heads in the crystal-clear sky. The Southern Cross seemed to rest weightlessly atop my left shoulder. I saw a falling star. But I did not wish upon it. Wishes seemed an affront on such a night, when sheer will was all that seemed to matter.

The first to turn back that night was the married couple from Boston, the youngest two members of our group. They had made a pact that if one were to have a problem then both would return to camp. After one of them began to have trouble standing without passing out, they decided to head down. The next to follow them was my friend's partner from GMHC. He feared edema was setting in. The rest of us were saddened by their departure but climbed steadily upward. I was third in line right behind the sixty-five- and sixty-nine-year-olds. As long as they were making it up, I was determined to follow. About seven hundred feet from Stella Point, the first milestone one reaches on the final ascent at 18,800 feet, the sun rose around us. I turned to see the morning's rays hit the gigantic glacier I did not know had been looming right above me, its glittering beauty blinding me for a wondrous moment. I was finally certain I was going to make it to the top and began too excitedly to scramble in the scree. "Pole, pole," said Ringo, the Swahili word—pronounced "poelee"—meaning "slowly."

At Stella Point, as we marveled at Kilimanjaro's crater, our friend from Mexico City collapsed in an exhausted heap and refused to keep climbing toward the summit at Uhuru. He turned back and, after taking a short break, the rest of us found what reserves of energy we had to keep climbing. A kind of comforting delirium had set in with me and I began to carry on a speedy conversation with Bernard, who had been assigned to accompany me to the top. I told him about being HIV positive and how this whole climb had been a journey toward self-forgiveness. Unlike many Africans, who still feel uncomfortable with the subject, he sweetly listened without seeming to judge me as I told him about the last three years of my life. "But time is running out on this trip," I said as the summit came into view. "As happy as I am to make it all this way, I feel a little disappointed that I haven't had . . . well . . . the epiphany I came seeking," I said.

"What does this word mean?" he asked. " 'Epiphany.' "

"It's when something dawns on you that you've really known all along," I tried to explain to us both. "It's a secret that tells itself."

Tears stung my eyes caused by the wind as it whipped across the glacier within Mount Kilimanjaro's deep and dangerous snow-filled crags right into my face. I looked out at the world below and all that I had left behind—my fear of death and yet my longing for it. I shivered in the unrelenting wind and heard that howl my heart had finally found. I turned and reached the summit.

The descent was even more difficult.

Bernard left me and assisted Babu, as the guides, using the Swahili word for "grandfather," had nicknamed the sixty-nine-year-old. He and his sixty-five-year-old buddy, my friend's unerringly reserved father, had also both made it to the summit through pure Yankee grit. But Babu's knees were now killing him and the walk down on the scree would prove to be quite painful. My friend and the Columbia internist and the Martha Stewart stalwart started down ahead of them. I soon was falling behind, only a little ahead of Babu, my own knees finally giving me trouble.

My friend's father, at one point, found himself next to me. It was easy to see where my friend had gotten his resoluteness, his pluck, for his father, head down most of the time, taciturn, had walked steadily, single-mindedly, without complaint for the last five days. "I bet when you heard about your son's HIV diagnosis you never dreamed you would be climbing Mount Kilimanjaro with him twenty years later," I said to him after we had walked a while in silence.

He did not take his eyes off the path ahead of us. "Yep," he finally said. "We thought we were going to lose him in two or three years." He dug his walking sticks deeper into the scree. "We even joined a support group of parents whose sons had just been diagnosed. Out of everybody in that group, my wife and I are the only ones who still have a son who's alive."

He paused.

"Is that a hawk?" he suddenly asked, motioning toward the sky with one of his walking sticks as the bird reached its pitch.

We stood for a moment.

We caught our breaths.

We stared at the hawk's soaring grace.

"Did you have to forgive him for getting infected?" I finally asked.

"I'm religious—not as religious as I should be, perhaps—but I do believe God put my son in my life to teach me tolerance," was all that he said, the steady clicks of our walking sticks hitting the mountain the only sounds that were left between us.

I was the last to make it to Barafu. Both old men had even made it back there before I had. We were allowed to rest for one hour—it had taken me three hours to make it back down—before descending for five more hours to our final camp. I had crossed over from the heady spiritual high of making the summit to the dour state when the body begins to recoil from such punishment. I had gotten through the whole climb without blisters on my feet and in those eight hours of our descent my two big toes had become encased in them. This was not what I had come to the mountain for. I wanted to be enlightened, not laid low. I was now truly suffering from exhaustion. I could barely look at the food at dinner that evening and headed for my sleeping bag at 7:30.

The next morning after duct-taping moleskin to my feet, I felt a bit better but still felt oddly depressed, having physically accomplished what I had come to do yet still not finding the one spiritual answer I had come seeking. I focused on the rain forest we were now walking back through and let go of any hope of conjuring my own forgiveness. Of all the sensations I had felt in the last few days, that was the final one that pulled at me and caused the most pain: the letting go of hope.

"Kevin!" I heard Bernard call my name from where he was now leading the group while Ringo stayed in the rear with Babu and his own pair of painful knees. "Come up here. I have something to show you."

I limped up to Bernard's side and he pointed to a large green plant by the path we were on. It didn't look like anything special to me. It certainly wasn't beautiful. Just a big green leafy thing that I had ignored in its abundance as we'd started our climb five days before.

"See this?" Bernard asked. "Every Chaga household has this plant in it. It is dry *Cena afrimontana*—more commonly known as *masare*," he said. "But we Chaga call it the Forgiveness Plant. If we have a fight with someone in our family or a neighbor, we take a cutting from one of these plants and give it to the person that has angered us and in that way they know that all is forgiven. This is the secret that I think I am to tell you," he whispered close to my ear. "Is this the secret you came to hear? Is this the secret that must tell itself to you?"

I watched him walk back to the front of our group. I then bent down to take a cutting from the plant in order to give it to myself. That is when I finally heard it, the sound of love itself, the low laughter of it, the overlapping of its two voices, its presence no longer a sigh of confusion but of comfort. "Kevin, honey, what are you doing?" I heard my mother's voice. And then my father's: "Son, there's nothing to forgive."

I stood.

I moved on.

I did not touch the plant.

I left it on the mountain.

THREE

The Role-Player

It was January 2009. Nineteen years had passed since I'd been on Madonna's doorstep. It had been three years since I'd made the summit of Mount Kilimanjaro. The same glow from the TV screen that would lull away all the pain that life had dealt me when I was a child in Mississippi was, however, still in my life. Honey West? She no longer walked her pet ocelot before me on the screen, but a naked man did have a leash around another naked man's neck there in a pornographic DVD. I turned my eyes away from the image and watched the overaged urchin sitting at my desk in front of my MacBook aglow in his own kind of light. He had stopped long enough clicking through the Manhunt sex site online—where I had earlier found him; twenty-two, he'd said, versatile, he'd said, into role play, he'd said—to focus on the glass pipe he now put to his chapped lips. He lit the torch beneath the pipe's bulb into which he had just dropped two big crystals of meth. The meth melted, then sizzled, the torch's flame flickering shadows across the planes of the youth's drawn beauty. His concave cheeks collapsed even farther as he sucked the resulting smoke down into his ready lungs. He put down the pipe, cooling it on a wet paper towel, and walked over to me where I lay on my bed watching him. His body knew how to be naked, how to be watched, how to walk toward me. I could not resist him as he bent down to give me the only kind of kiss he had left, puffing those sallow cheeks of his out as far as they would go and exhaling into my mouth, down into my own throat, my own lungs, as he locked his lips on mine, their chapped roughness like the loveliest of razors, until I was forced to swallow the smoke inside him he allowed now to ooze deeply down into me, the very sinew of it seeking the depths of my body. "Fuck me some more," he whispered as the delirium hit.

It was already past 4:00 A.M. In eight hours I was expected at the Algonquin Hotel to have lunch with another overaged urchin—the then nineteen-year-old Daniel Radcliffe—to interview him for The Daily Beast about his latest Harry Potter movie as well as his Broadway run as Alan Strang in *Equus*. That latter role was one I had played myself when I was an actor. The daily beast, I thought, that's a good name for drug use once it becomes an addiction. Had mine? Had it yet? Had it really?

I faked a yawn.

"I'm going to have to wind this down," I told the kid, who shrugged and returned to the pipe. I turned off the porn and visited the bathroom, first stopping to pet my dog, Archie, where he lay taking it all in from his staked-out patch on the room's increasingly stained white steer skin rug. When I returned, the boy was lying on my bed on his stomach with his ass arched toward me, his hands spreading its cheeks. He raised his butt higher in the air in both surrender and defiance. There was too much meth in me to get an erection, so I grabbed a dildo from the bag of sex toys he had brought along with him and inserted the giant head of it into his widening hole. Archie watched the boy's butt arch higher toward me as I rammed the dildo deeper into him. I thought not of Madonna or Kilimanjaro or the boy's moans there below me but counted, with each thrust of the dildo into him, the one-two-three-four months until I was to walk the Camino and escape all this. I had put my iPod on shuffle to shut the boy up when he complained of my music selection earlier and my one Doors download gave way to an aria from *Fidelio*. Archie barked once, as he always did at Beethoven. I no longer looked at the boy's beautiful ass but over at Archie. "Shshsh," I hissed at him. "Deeper," begged the boy. ". . . deeper . . ." And on that fifth deep thrust of the dildo into the overaged urchin who lurched, then seemed to flutter, float for a second, then fall flat again against the filthy sheets, I thought of the five months hence when I'd do it, when, at the end of the Camino I'd walk into Santiago. I pulled the dildo out. There was only Beethoven now. Archie refused to bark.

I made it to the Algonquin a half hour before Radcliffe was scheduled to arrive in order to gather myself and go over the extensive notes I had made. I had convinced the boy, with an offer of the remaining meth that I had bought for us, to leave my apartment with his bag of toys, his pipe, his ass issuing its commands of surrender. I had then showered. Drunk a protein shake. Sipped the two ounces of wheatgrass juice I had put in the refrigerator when I knew I would be getting high. Eaten one banana. Lots of yogurt. Poured three cups of coffee. Downed some Gatorade. A bottle of water. Gargled. Brushed my teeth. Gargled again. All of this as much of the ritual for me as seeking out the sallow beauty of yet another boy with a pipe to pack, to light, to lift to our lips in an attempt to obliterate, for a few hours, the rest of the hours in my life.

I hadn't had a wink of sleep and my mouth still tasted of the boy. There was a metallic leftover methness mixed up with him in there. I slumped down in one of the overstuffed chairs in the Algonquin's lobby. I watched the muffled wheeling of suitcases atop the carpet, which, like me, had become a bit too threadbare for such a place. I looked away from the rug's threadbareness, from mine, and focused on the whistle hanging from a fat doorman's neck. I flinched at my reflection when he moved away from the mirror hidden behind him. I thought of the Vicious Circle, who had once had their own lunches there. This lunch I was about to have proved I was in my own version of a vicious one. The wordplay itself—the fact that I was still able privately to partake in it—calmed my racing heart with proof that my brain was still functioning and, therefore, so was I. I reached into my pocket for my trusty vial of Visine and put the umpteenth drops of it into my eyes. As the blur of Visine cleared, I saw Radcliffe standing in front of me.

He looked a little shocked at my condition as we settled into a back corner booth. "I was up all night with a stomach bug," I heard the lie too easily scrape some of the meth-ness from my mouth. "I wasn't about to cancel this lunch, though," I told him, then asked the waiter to bring me a ginger ale. "You're really nice to have scheduled it. I know how tiring a run in *Equus* can be."

"Yes, I heard from Sam—our production's press rep—that you played the part of Alan Strang. Back in the 1970s, was it?" he asked.

"I played it with Tony Perkins in a production down in Philadelphia and in a tour or two," I said, using the memory to focus my thoughts. "I almost got the part on Broadway when Richard Burton took over the role of the psychiatrist, Dr. Dysart, but my experience with the show's director, John Dexter, wasn't the best."

"What was Dexter like?" Radcliffe asked.

"Well, I was never directed by him except at my callbacks. I auditioned for him several times but finally had to deal with the 'dirty old man' side of him," I said, hearing the term for the first time as a description that could just as easily be used now for me. Yet, hearing it so clearly, I had also found almost immediately "the nest" in the conversation, as I'd come to think of such a moment over the years when I interviewed celebrities. So much of my childhood had been taken up with seeking the comfort I felt nesting in the presence of such creatures on the television or in the movies. I carried on secret conversations with them even then, imagining they were the ones who understood how trapped I felt in my otherness, in the Mississippi countryside, in my grief. At the very moment when I alighted in the nest that a conversation with a celebrity created, I became that comforted child once more. Even, on that day, when I had felt so strung out on meth, it could sober me up, if only momentarily, with a deep-seated solace. I was no longer dirty. I was no longer old. I was no longer even a man. I was that child comforted in a nest of his own making. With someone famous, I could be my truest self. With someone famous, I could be alone.

I had brought along a copy of my memoir, *Mississippi Sissy*, and inscribed it to Daniel as we began to talk about playing the boy in *Equus*, whose sexuality had been warped by religion. Radcliffe raved about Richard Griffiths, who was playing Dysart opposite him, an actor so entombed in flesh that an elegiac carnality was his appeal, because Dysart, as written, is stuck in a sexless marriage.

"That's what I think is sort of fantastic about Richard as a piece of casting," Radcliffe told me. "If you see someone like Burton or Tony Perkins in that part—if they weren't fucking their wife, if they had gotten to that point in their marriage—you'd have a hard time believing that they wouldn't leave to find somebody else to fuck like a secretary or a nurse or whomever. But you almost got cast to play the part with Burton? What happened?"

"Keith McDermott, who did play the part, was amazing in it. I don't know what his experience with Dexter was. I can only speak of mine," I said, sipping at the ginger ale that had just arrived. "Dexter asked me to come out to his home in Atlantic Highlands, New Jersey, one Saturday for a lunch, with a couple of other boys who were up for the role. Keith wasn't a part of that threesome, all of us overaged urchins," I said, smiling at my private joke. "We were picked up at the stage door of what was then the Plymouth Theatre, where *Equus* was playing. Dexter had sent his tall black male secretary to drive us out to Atlantic Highlands, but we got stuck in traffic. I was still going to the Juilliard School of Drama then. I was just about as cute as you are now, though my shag haircut might have made me cuter. We all had shags back then. At least the three of us boys in the car with that tall black secretary did. 'Shag' is a verb over in England, huh. I think Dexter wanted to use it in such a way when we got out there to Atlantic Highlands. He wanted to shag all us boys with our shags," I went on. My words were picking up too much speed. I was aware of it but could not stop the careening. My voice also had all the hoarseness to it that a night of smoking meth could cause, the consonants all sanded down to husks of themselves where they stayed lodged in the back of my throat to be stammered free. Was the stammering giving me away? Did I still smell of sex? "Do you really want to hear all this?" I finally asked when I stopped to take a breath and gesture toward the waiter for another ginger ale.

"Yes. Please. Carry on," said Radcliffe, seemingly relieved not to have to keep up his part of the conversation just yet.

"Well, we were almost an hour late for lunch," I continued when that next ginger ale arrived. "Dexter's first words when we entered the house were, 'You're late, you black cunt!' You Brits say 'cunt' more than we do over here, I take it."

Radcliffe stared at me. He decided to giggle. "Go on," he said.

"Well, there were three huge goblets of red wine poured at the ready and, after a bit of conversation, Dexter asked me if I would be the first to accompany him into his study. He locked the door behind him and told me to strip because he said he needed to see if I could pass for a naked seventeen-year-old boy. I was already twenty by then and I wanted the part more than anything I'd ever wanted in those twenty years. So I took off my clothes. Stood there in my underwear.

"'No, no,' he said. 'I must see everything. You have to be comfortable being nude because you must be nude in the play. Do it.'

"I did as he said and then watched him take a big gulp of his Burgundy as he took me in. Blushing a color close to that of the Burgundy, I stared down at his desk. Atop it were the blueprints for the stage design of Leontyne Price's upcoming production of *Aida* at the Met, which Dexter was also directing. I had placed my own goblet of wine next to the blueprints. I reached for it to take a few needed gulps myself.

"'No, no,' he said again. 'First turn around for me. Let's see how hairy your bum is.'

"Again, I did as he said, but as I turned my hand grazed my goblet, spilling the wine all over the blueprints for *Aida*. I grabbed my underwear and was about to mop it up.

"'Don't worry,' said Dexter, waving me away, though he was obviously pissed. 'Whatever the wine blotted out I wasn't supposed to see. I'll just pretend I didn't approve these plans and demand the designer draw up a revised set.'

"I don't know what happened when the other two went in there. But we had a mostly silent lunch." I paused to take a breath. I sipped at my ginger ale.

Radcliffe giggled again. "Nothing like that ever happens to me. Should I be insulted?" He studied my eyes. "You should put that story in your next book," he said.

I kept the ginger ales coming as he and I wished each other a Happy Martin Luther King Jr. Day, the "Happy" seeming even more appropriate since the very next day Barack Obama was going to be sworn in as the country's forty-fourth president. "We happen to be meeting at a very American moment," I told Radcliffe. "Does it make you feel overly British to be here right now?"

"I feel privileged to be here for Obama's inauguration. But I do tend to go doubly British when I am away from home. I have picked up certain phrases while here in America that I plan to eradicate as soon as I get back home. I've begun to say 'I know—right?' That phrase and its little rhythm there is very American and not really used in England. I've started saying that and people are picking me up on it when they come over to visit."

We turned our attention to other differences between America and Britain, though we agreed that America's class structure was becoming as ingrained as Britain's has always been. "Your mother is Jewish. Do you identify as Jewish yourself?" I asked.

"Yeah yeah yeah yeah. Absolutely. I actually really do. My dad is Northern Irish and my mum is Jewish," he told me.

"Talk about a half-blood prince," I said.

"Well, that's working blood for certain. Though I am not religious in the least, I am very proud to be Jewish."

"What's it been like working in the small-bower world of the theater?" I asked. "It's a very different environment from film. Much more collegial and camp and . . . well, let's face it: gay."

"For a lot of straight guys, and I know I'm guilty of it sometimes," he said, "when you know a gay guy has a crush on you it is the most flattering thing."

"I've seldom met a straight actor who isn't a fag hag. Are you?"

"Oh, probably. Yeah, I'm a fag hag, to use your term," Radcliffe said. "I know I definitely caught it. Absolutely. My mom was a casting director and my dad was a literary agent and I was surrounded by gay men from a very young age. And I was the only boy in my class at school who had that kind of relationship with gay men. Most of my friends had parents who had proper jobs in banks and law firms, so none of them had been exposed to homosexuality in the way I had—as a normal course of things. So they had a rather different attitude toward it than I."

"After lights-out, they'd just bugger each other, then ignore it the next day in class," I said.

"Well, I didn't go to a boarding school if that's what you're getting at," he said. "That's one thing Harry Potter has done if nothing else. It has restored the reputation of the English boarding school. It has made it something other than a hotbed of homosexuality."

A hotbed of homosexuality. It sounded as if he were describing my apartment. "We all play roles in life," I said. "I finally decided my truest role, even more than The Sissy, even more than The Homosexual, is The Orphan," I said, wondering at that very moment if The Addict would one day override even that. "Harry Potter is perhaps the most famous orphan now in all of literature," I said, still able to focus on the conversation at hand. "But there is a whole genre that centers on the orphaned. Your first role at nine was the young David Copperfield. You are now the personification of the most beloved of orphans. It is the thing about you, Daniel, that moves me the most."

"I suppose they make good heroes—orphans do—because we love the underdog," he said. "For an orphan, from the earliest, most basic, most primitive part of your life, things have gone against you. So in that sense an orphan is the ultimate underdog. Everything we know about how people work and are successful, in the conventional sense, starts with family. So the notion is for that to be taken out of the picture one has to work doubly hard to achieve things."

"You're not an orphan, but you are an only child who attained worldwide fame at a very early age," I said. "Has fame become a kind of a sibling to you?"

"It's not so much the fame thing as it is the person you are when you are in front of an audience," Radcliffe said. "Or . . . well . . . being interviewed like right now."

"So you've had to become your own sibling?" I asked.

"In a way, yeah, because you develop two personas. It's not even a conscious thing. Something happens. That's what fame does to you. You acquire another self."

That's what drug addiction does to you, too, I wanted to say. Instead, I said, "You're a big fan of John Keats."

"Exactly. The biggest," said Radcliffe.

"I'm a fan too. He was also an orphan. I was wondering if his theory of negative . . ."

". . . capability . . . ," said Radcliffe, finishing the term.

"Yes. Exactly. Do you use Keats's theory of negative capability in your approach to acting, in your approach to life? In it he states—I think I'm getting this right—that the deepest truths are to be found in uncertainty and doubt and mystery and not in the 'irritable reaching after fact and reason.'"

"Absolutely! Absolutely! You've found me out!" he said excitedly. But then his voice grew quiet once more. Again he stared right into my tired and bloodshot eyes.

"The truth is to be found in the things that are not certain, Kevin," he said. "And not solid. And not easy. And not simple." He touched my arm. "That's the secret."

The secret to what?

Alchemy?

"I like this sibling of yours, Daniel," was all I finally had to say. "It was nice meeting him."

"I know—right?" he softly said.

And it was then, in that moment, I realized it was I who was still the overaged urchin. Not that boy with his bag full of toys the night before. Not Daniel Radcliffe. Not Harry Potter. Not even John Keats. I was the one who was still trying to play that role.

FOUR

The Brother

My younger brother, Kim, an obstetrician and gynecologist, is also an artist and a sculptor. I didn't need to delve into the teachings of the School of Practical Philosophy, as Hugh Jackman had, to learn about the duality so inherent in all our natures. All I needed was to share a Mississippi childhood with such a brother. It was a bit later that I learned this kind of duality could be described as Keatsian from listening to poet Howard Moss. He was talking about having seen Marlon Brando in *A Streetcar Named Desire* on Broadway, which somehow led to a story about how Howard met our mutual friend Edward Albee, which led Howard, through some path known only to him, to discuss with me John Keats for the first time. Howard's voice was more like a low hum, a thrum of sound I had to lean in to hear more clearly and then decipher. As he offered me a quick discourse on Keats I began, in that twentieth-century poet's generosity toward the nineteenth-century one, to see my younger brother more generously as well.

I relaxed that day in Howard's thrum and, as I so often found myself doing, followed somehow the thread of his thoughts by sinking more deeply into my own. As he explained Keats's "negative capability" to me I began to conjure an image of Kim as a little boy carrying his pellet gun out into our yard. Such a sight always bothered me, for I knew that what often followed was his killing the cardinal or blue jay or occasional robin that alighted above him in the grove of pine trees. I would hide wrapped in a curtain that first autumn my brother became obsessed with the killing of birds and would spy on him through the window as he took careful aim. The pinecones and straw around him on the ground had fallen from the trees, leaving the limbs bare above him, so that when the birds perched there they would stand out more starkly and would enable him to get a better shot. I'd stand at that window waiting for the moment my brother, his little cheek puffed out with a mouthful of pellets, removed one from his mouth, which allowed him to lodge the thing, lubricated with his saliva, more easily into the gun. Often he'd get the kill in one shot and the stunned creature would fall to the silent thud of its death on all that freshly fallen pine straw carpeting our country yard.

My brother had begged my grandparents to let him take a correspondence course in taxidermy and they had relented. After he'd shoot a bird, he would bring it into the house and gently lay it on a kind of plinth-like altar he had made back in his room so that he could more easily follow the instructions from the course manual opened up beside it. I hated it with all my heart when he shot a bird. It was just more death to be dragged into our lives. But he was trying to have dominion over death. I had suddenly realized it as it all came together for me that day when Howard Moss first held forth on negative capability and John Keats, the sound of Moss's low incessant mumbled thrum mixing with the soundless straw that broke a shot bird's fall. Kim, so lost after our parents' death, so alone out there in the yard, longed to find a way to preserve life. But in his longing he had to kill something to learn how to do it.

"You know what finally stopped me from killing those birds?" my brother asked me when I was talking with him about his taxidermy days. "I looked through the sight of that pellet gun one day and a red-winged blackbird turned and looked right back at me. It was the first time a bird had done that. I felt seen."

Kim and his wife had stopped in New York on their way to Maine, where he was going to check in with the Farnsworth Museum and its Wyeth Center, which had purchased a bust of Andrew Wyeth that he had sculpted. It was the only bust Wyeth had ever sat for and in his flinty way he had developed an affection for my brother and a respect for him as an artist, so much so that Wyeth had stated in his will that he would furnish the endowment to purchase the bust for the Farnsworth's collection. Andy Wyeth had been my brother's idol when he became interested in art after his detour into the details of taxidermy, so this was a kind of completion of a circle in his life.

Before he headed up to Maine he wanted to see the Willem de Kooning retrospective at MoMA as well as a grouping of Cy Twombly sculptures he'd read about. My brother's art had once been realistic. Lifelike. He had recently, though, freed himself from the strict boundaries of sculpting busts and begun to move in a more abstract direction, using found objects and utilizing collage in his art. Twombly now inspired Kim as much as Wyeth once had.

The galleries opened and we headed upstairs. On one of the upper floors we turned a corner together and I saw my brother stop in awe to find the Twombly sculptures suddenly before him instead of his having to study them in photographs. "You can't get the feel of it, the scale, without seeing the real things," he said, a reverence in his voice he usually saved for church, for my brother is also a religious man. Born again, he'd claim. Kim is comfortable talking about God's grace in a way I feel a bit awkward being around. And yet I often feel the need to broach the subject with Kim as a way of justifying myself to him.

One Twombly sculpture's worn patina reminded me of the wooden crucifix—an altarpiece—from the 1840s that I had bought at a flea market the weekend before. I had responded to the crucifix's own sculptural qualities, not its religious ones. The long, thin Christ figure no longer had its arms and had been worn to a soft tannish hue that animal hides often have. There were grooves carved in its sides where Christ's ribs would have been. The only color was the faintest bit of pink in two of the grooves to symbolize the blood of his wounds. The long, thin, worn figure had been in a booth filled with religious relics, but I was drawn immediately to it alone and had picked it up. It had fit perfectly atop my forearm as I had stood staring at it for several minutes, unable to put it down. It was from a Catholic church in the Philippines, I was told by the booth's purveyor, yet it felt as if it had always belonged to me.

I mentioned all this to my brother, whose brow furrowed a bit as he looked more closely at the Twombly. I knew that familiar furrow. Kim was disguising it as an appreciation of Twombly, but it was the furrow that creased his brow when he prepared himself for another of my justifications.

"I then went across the street from the flea market to an antique store to pick up a vase I'd bought," I continued, following him as he studied more of the Twomblys. "I go there a lot. The woman who runs it and I are kind of friendly with each other without really knowing one another. I told her about the armless Christ figure and she asked, 'Are you a believer in Jesus?'

" 'Yes. I believe there was such a person,' I said.

"Her whole demeanor changed," I told my brother. "She grew stern. 'But do you believe he rose from the dead?' she asked me.

" 'I'm not so sure,' I told her."

My brother sighed.

I found an odd satisfaction in the sound of my brother's troubled sigh, which was so like that sigh my father could make at my presence. It was one of the ways Kim resembled my father without even knowing it. I continued. " 'It's a historical fact,' she said, pointing her finger in my face."

I then abruptly pointed my own finger in my brother's face to demonstrate how adamant the woman had been, but he just as abruptly pushed it away to get a closer look at the most elongated of the Twombly sculptures.

"'He rose from the dead,' she wouldn't let up." I wouldn't let up either and followed my brother to the next Twombly. "'There's no denying it. It's a historical fact,' she kept saying as if that were all the argument she needed to make. But when I got home I couldn't get our conversation out of my mind. So I went back."

"Oh, brother," my brother said.

"When I walked back in the store she wouldn't look at me. But I told her I came back to tell her what bothered me about her making the resurrection simply a historical fact was that she took something wondrous and made it dry and commonplace. I told her that, yes, I had my doubts about it. But without doubt one doesn't have faith. Faith without doubt is really just blind obedience. The deepest truths are to be found in uncertainty and doubt and mystery and not in the 'irritable reaching after fact and reason,'" I said, and heard myself wrapping myself in Howard Moss quoting John Keats and remembered how I had once hidden wrapped in that curtain so far out in the country in Mississippi and watched a much younger brother take aim at a helpless bird before it could turn and look back at him. He turned in that moment away from the last Twombly and looked back at me. Our eyes met, but they didn't see; they aimed. My brother and I longed to find a way to preserve life. But in our longing we had to kill something in each other to learn how to do it.

My brother and his wife headed for the de Kooning exhibit. "When Andy Wyeth was sitting for me we talked about a lot of stuff," Kim said. "We started off talking about ears," he said as he absentmindedly reached down to run a finger along one of his wife's in the gentle offhand way that husbands flirt with their wives after years of marriage. "'You've given me big ears,'" Andy told me, admitting that his were big but not quite that big. 'Don't you think you should make them more delicate?' he suggested. 'Ears are a delicate thing.'

"'You know ears can be portraits themselves,' I told Andy. 'They can reveal as much as the eyes or the mouth as far as I'm concerned.'

"'You know I feel the same way,' he said. 'Edward Hopper and I once had this conversation and he told me that Eakins didn't feel that way,'" my brother quoted Wyeth, pronouncing "Eakins" as "Aikens." "'Eakins' ears were all the same,' Andy said, 'sort of put in only to finish the head.'"

"I always thought it was 'Eakins,'" I said, using the long *E*.

"Well, as Andy insisted when I told him I thought it was pronounced that way too, 'Hopper always pronounced it "Aikens" and if pronouncing it "Aikens" was good enough for Edward Hopper it's good enough for me.' As I put the finishing touches on Andy's own head we talked about other American artists and his place among them. We talked about our families and the family tragedies we'd each had to live through. We talked a lot about what goes into a painting or a piece of sculpture." Kim kept talking as we passed an assortment of each lined along the walls of MoMA. "I finally told him that I hoped that all of his work now owned by Japanese collectors would someday return to America.

"'That would be nice,' he said. 'But I won't be here to see it.'

"'Maybe not,' I told him. 'But if I'm still here when it happens I'll tell you when I get there.'

"'Awwh, I'll be down there,' Andy said, pointing toward hell, then turned his finger up toward heaven. 'And you'll be up there.'

"'What makes you say that?' I asked Andy.

"'Oh, I'm just an old scoundrel,' he said. 'I'm not a very nice person, you know.'

"'Well, I believe the outcome isn't based on what we did here,' I told him. 'We're all scoundrels We're born that way. I believe it's based on what somebody else did for us.'

"'Nobody's ever said that to me,' Andy told me."

We turned into the de Kooning exhibit and I stared at one of his earliest portraits of a woman, the low cut of her dress revealing but a glimpse of a nipple, as faint and pink as the lone wound on that armless altarpiece that had finally found a home with me.

———

In 1962—when I was six years old, my brother was four, and our new little sister was two—our big-eared father quit his job as a basketball coach at a small Mississippi high school to accept the job as the track coach at Hinds County Junior College and we moved from Clinton, Mississippi, a few miles down the road to Raymond. "I'm just a professor of P.E.," he'd often crack the same deprecating joke when some of his fellow coaches with a bit of seniority on him would visit us where we had taken up residence in Raymond in one of the faculty houses built by the junior college in a circular street just off campus. Mississippi was a violent and scary place in the summer of 1962. It was the cusp of the Civil Rights Movement and the air was already fetid with the feel of forced change. But if one lived in a cosseted neighborhood where the picket fences and faculty families all were white there was, even in the Mississippi of 1962, a sense of comfort and safety. The only progressive thing about the place was the Saturday night dinners that would travel course by course from faculty member house to faculty member house, parents taking their ice teas and children in hand to cross yard after freshly mown yard. We'd eat fried chicken at one dining table, butter beans and corn bread at another, potato salad and deviled eggs at a third, barbecued hamburgers slathered with mayonnaise at a fourth, meringue-slathered lemon icebox pie at a fifth.

We would all then end up on those lazy Saturday summer nights at a designated final home and watch our fathers take turns churning the ice-cream makers all lined up in a row as each of the kids waited his or her own turn to help them sprinkle the rock salt on the ice packed about the ice-cream canister to make the ingredients our mothers had concocted freeze more quickly. We children would then eat as many bowls as our parents would allow us of the sweet, soft, luscious stuff that was finally spooned out.

The next morning we all went to church in the clothes our parents told us to wear and then started kicking off our shoes on the car ride home so we could be barefoot before we arrived in our driveways. We walked to and from the elementary school every Monday morning without any parent concerned enough to accompany us on our twice-a-day trek across town. I can't recall any door ever being locked when I'd run up to it and walk right in. I knew every mother's name on that circle of faculty homes and knew exactly which fathers I should avoid just as I knew when to avoid my own.

I was certainly avoiding him that first Sunday I told him that I had decided to go with my mother and my little sister to the Methodist church and not with my little brother and him to the Baptist one. It had been an unspoken rule in our family that the "men" were Southern Baptist and the "women" were Methodist, since the latter was considered by my father somehow a less masculine form of religion. I never understood the distinction, but I did understand wanting to be less masculine in any form it took when I turned six years old. That morning—after I fed our two Chihuahuas in their pen in the backyard, which was the one chore I loved to do around the house—I had made my father momentarily mad at me when I told him I wanted to go to the Methodist church with my mother. I had already practiced what I was going to say to him by telling it to Chico and Coco, the Chihuahuas who had become my confidants since my father had purchased them several months earlier. My father, to my surprise, did not put up a fight when I told him my decision. He even seemed a bit relieved not having me tag along with my little brother and him, who were much more of a team together as a pair than we ever were as a threesome. When he had first brought the Chihuahuas into our family, he and I had surprisingly bonded over our love for the little creatures, but that now seemed so long ago, months being eons when one is a child. My father and I both knew that I—after each having confused our shared love for the family's dogs for a renewed father/son bond that no coach and his sissy son could ever maintain—had taken sides for good that morning. Not the Methodist's. Not my mother's. But the women's.

After a lunch that day of baked potatoes and a green bean casserole and a roast, which filled the house with the scent of the powdered French onion soup that my mother had sprinkled atop it to melt into a muddy beefy crust, we changed into our summer shorts and shirts. My brother and my father went outside with the plastic bat and baseball I had no interest in and I, carrying my little sister back to my parents' bedroom, helped my mother put her down for her nap. I placed my parents' pillows from their bed around my little sister to protect her from rolling off the bed, then went back to the kitchen. I cleared the table and put the dishes in the sink for my mother to wash. I went out to the backyard to play alone with Chico and Coco in "our pen," as I'd come to think of it. I fed them some of the table scraps left over from our lunch and told them about what the Methodist church looked like and how nice all the women had been to me when I arrived there with my mother. I even sang them a bit of the song we had sung from the Cokesbury hymnal—"The Church Is One Foundation"—for I was amazed at how the pronoun references in the hymn were all feminine ones, how it confirmed to me that the Methodist church was more welcoming to women. I sat and read the first verse over and over during the sermon attempting to memorize it knowing I would try to sing it to Chico— and especially Coco—when I got back home. "The church's one foundation / Is Jesus Christ her lord; / She is his new creation / In water and the word," I softly sang. I stroked Coco. "From heaven he came and sought her / To be his holy bride; / With his own blood he bought her, / And for her life he died."

I hummed the song a bit more and gave Chico a few strokes he too was insisting on having from me, then went back into the house and picked up the two bulletins from the Baptist and Methodist churches left on the kitchen counter. I took a pencil and a notebook with "Hinds County Junior College" emblazoned on its cover from the top of my father's old oaken rolltop desk that stood like a sentinel—stolid, unmovable—next to the dining table. I sat on the kitchen floor and opened the notebook to a blank page. I placed the bulletins precisely side by side on the floor by me. I held the pencil the way my first-grade teacher, Miss Bridges, had taught me and on the blank page wrote the words "BAPTIST" and "METHODIST" in capital letters as they had appeared on the covers of the bulletins. I tried to decipher why one was for men and one was for women. I studied each letter that made up each of the words. Listening to the plastic ball hit the plastic bat outside mixing with my mother's soft soprano singing "Love Me Tender" to my sister in the back in her bedroom, I began to transform the capital Ts in both the words before me into people. The Ts in "BAPTIST" I made into men with muscles and baseball gloves. The Ts in "METHODIST" I made into women wearing bracelets and earrings and whose gloves were not big-fingered leather ones used for baseball games but dainty and laced and looked like the gloves my mother had worn that past Easter, the ones she had let me try on when my father wasn't looking.

I suddenly heard the laughter of a neighboring coach and his two rambunctious boys who were a few years older than I as they came bounding into our yard to say hello to my brother and my father. I stopped my drawing and went outside. The other coach had a small baseball uniform that his boys had outgrown and was offering it to my father. I assumed it would be mine because I was the older child and had first dibs on such things but my father took the bat out of my brother's hand and stripped him down to his underwear and put the uniform on him right there in front of all of us. The uniform was pin-striped and had the word "YANKEES" written across it. My father was a New York Yankees fan and I had heard him often argue with that other coach about two men named Maris and Mantle who played for the Yankees. My father was a staunch Maris man. The other coach always stuck up for Mantle.

"Turn the kid around," the other coach told my father once he had gotten the uniform on my little brother. There it was—Maris's number 9 on the back. My father laughed and picked up my brother, Kim, and held him to his chest and kissed him all over his laughing face.

The other coach then reached into his back pocket and retrieved a little Yankees baseball cap and plopped it on Kim's little head. I pouted at all the manly bonhomie about me and sat down on the driveway next to our father's new pale blue Volkswagen he loved so much. I dug my finger in the groove of the tire that I leaned against and watched the rubber darken beneath my fingernail. "Don't do that, Kevin," my father scolded me, which I knew he would since he hated when I touched the odd little car and smudged it with my fingerprints, which I had already planned to do once my fingers were blackened with the rubber.

My father put Kim down and then turned to the other boys, who always picked on me when we were alone. "You kids want to have a race?" he asked, and pulled me up from where I sat. He led us all down to the circular street and lined us up. He and the other coach taught us all how to get into a crouched position as if we were in our starting blocks and on the junior college track team ourselves. I looked over and realized my brother and the other two boys had on sneakers, but I had not put any on when I came outside. I was still barefoot, but I knew my father would get mad if I asked to go inside to put on a pair of sneakers myself because I'd be making everybody wait for me and interfering with his own excitement of finding a way to combine yet again his love of coaching with his role as a father.

"Nan!" he shouted to my mother inside. "Bring me my starting pistol! We got a race on our hands here! Kimbo there is raring to go."

The other boys and I sat down on the hot pavement, but my brother would not move from his crouch, so ready was he to race and gain my father's approval. The front door opened and my mother carried the pistol in one hand and a magazine in the other. "Don't shout so loud," she told my father. "I just got your daughter—remember you have a daughter—down for her nap." My mother had gotten up late that morning so had to rush to get us all ready for church and had complained about having to skip her shower. She had even put her unwashed, unbrushed blond hair under a Sunday hat, which she said made her feel oddly old. She was now hatless, however, and her hair lifted in the sudden breeze about her head. By taking off that Sunday hat and her sedate flowered dress that went with it, she looked no longer odd nor old. She effortlessly looked like a movie star to me. Indeed, it was when she put no effort into her appearance at all that she was the most beautiful to my six-year-old eyes. She wore red shorts and a white blouse. She too was barefoot and her toenails were painted the exact same red as her shorts. I looked at the magazine she held and deciphered the word

"REDBOOK" on it. It thrilled me that I had begun to make out the flow of letters more easily now that I was six and I could combine them into words and then the words into sentences. I smiled at my burgeoning knowledge—how it could remain so silent inside me—and how the magazine's deciphered name matched my mother's toenails and shorts. She handed my father his pistol. When she turned to walk back into the house my father slapped her on her butt in front of the other coach, who laughed with too much bluster. My mother turned back around and slapped my father on his own butt with her *Redbook* magazine. He grabbed her in his arms and kissed her on her mouth. The boys next to me giggled, but I was accustomed to seeing such displays between my parents. It was a natural and regular occurrence. After the kiss my mother's hips had an extra little wiggle in them in those red shorts as I watched her walk back through the door. The other coach winked at my father, who grinned his lopsided grin back at him before they shared a chuckle. A lawn sprinkler came on next door.

"Okay, boys, back into your starting positions like Kimbo there," my father ordered us, and raised his starting pistol. We obeyed and readied ourselves like my little brother, who had still not moved from his crouch. "On your mark," my father said. I looked down at the toenails on my bare feet. "Get set." I wondered what my toenails would look like painted red like my mother's. "Go!" The report from the gun startled me and I fell backwards from my crouch. When I looked up, the other boys and my little brother were already rounding the first bend of the circular street. "Goddamn it, Kevin. Get going. Go! Don't let Kim outrace you, boy. Go, Kim!" shouted my father. "Kimbo, go! Go!"

I scrambled to stand as quickly as I could and began to run. But the faster I ran the more I knew my arms flapped about in a way that the other boys' arms did not. I then focused on my little brother and tried to catch up with him and match my arm movements to his as he pumped them by his sides, but I couldn't make my movements match. I could not. I couldn't. The pavement was growing hotter and hotter beneath my bare feet and the gravel in the roughly paved road was embedding itself into my soles. A sharp pain began to throb in my side the more I exerted myself. My arms became more frantic. My wrists were wrong. This was not the way a boy should run. I could see that by the three examples in front of me. But I could not mimic what I saw. In my panic, I could not right myself. I couldn't. I began to cry.

The other two boys went straight into their yard when we rounded the third curve where they lived and began to play with their dog. They weren't even going to finish the race. If they were not then I decided I wasn't either. I sat on the next lawn over and watched my brother hit the finish line and race right into my father's waiting arms. The other coach shaded his eyes and looked past me at his sons playing with their dog. He walked past me on his way home without acknowledging my presence. I looked at the bottoms of my bare feet. They were pink from the heat of the pavement. I scraped the loose gravel from them. I limped home, thankful for the cooling green feel of the grass from yard to yard, careful to avoid the summer stickers, until I reached my father, who would not acknowledge my presence now either. I stared at the pistol sticking out of his pocket as he handed my brother back the plastic bat and began again to pitch him the plastic ball to hit.

I went inside the house and stood at a window and for the first time enfolded myself in a curtain to hide and watch my brother be a boy and wonder why he had such ease at it when I did not. I heard my mother turn on the shower back in her bedroom and I tiptoed back to her bathroom. My sister was sleeping amidst the pillows I had carefully arranged about her little body. I stood in the bathroom's doorway and stared at the shadow of my mother's naked outline behind the shower curtain as she soaped up her small breasts. Her red shorts and white panties were on the bathroom floor. Her white blouse was hanging from the doorknob. I saw her tiny bottle of red nail polish on the bathroom counter. I quickly grabbed it and put it in my pocket. The tiles on the bathroom floor felt so cool beneath my still-burning feet.

My mother pushed back the curtain and for a moment I caught a glimpse of her glistening body. There was a flash of nipple. She gasped at my presence and pulled the curtain around her like I had only moments before pulled another curtain around me at the window in the living room. "Kevin, honey, what are you doing?" she whispered.

I shrugged.

"Is the race over?" she asked. "Did you win?"

I shook my head no and, shrugging again, tried not to cry.

"That's okay, honey. That's okay," she said. Her hair was slicked back and wet, the steam from the shower encircling her face. "Would you hand Mommy that shampoo over on top of the lavatory there?" she asked. I handed it to her and when she reached for it the shower curtain slipped. For the second time I saw a glimpse of her nipple. It was as pink and dimpled as the soles of my feet had been when I had scraped the gravel from them earlier. "Let me finish my shower," my mother said from behind the curtain.

I walked back into the kitchen and found my father and my little brother sitting on the floor with the Hinds County Junior College notebook in front of them in which I had earlier written the words "BAPTIST" and "METHODIST" and made the Ts into men and women. I looked down by my father's side. He had torn out that page of the notebook and wadded it up where it lay next to his pistol on the floor. He handed my brother and me a pencil each he had taken from his desk, then gave us each a new blank piece of paper he tore from the notebook. He opened it to a blank page for himself and pulled another pencil from a pocket of his shorts. He took the Yankees cap from my brother's head and plopped it on mine.

"I'm sorry, Daddy," I said.

"Sorry? For what?" he asked. I wanted to say for being a Methodist now, for quitting the race, for being a sissy. Instead, I once more shrugged. He gave me a hug. "Son, there's nothing to forgive," he whispered in my ear. He turned and studied my handiwork. "I see you've been in here spelling and drawing today, Kevinator," he said. "I thought maybe Kimbo and me would join you. Let's see. What do you want to draw now? How about a landscape? Do you know what a landscape is?" he asked me, and pulled me down to the floor close to him, holding me on one side and my brother on the other. I shook my head no. "It's a pretty picture of a mountain scene or something like that. Let's all draw a mountain. I'll go first and you boys can copy me."

My little brother and I watched my father draw two mountains with a river running through the valley between them. He then drew some trees around the river.

"Draw some birds in the sky," my mother said, entering the kitchen and smiling at the landscape of the men in her family before her on the floor. Her freshly washed hair was still wet from the shower and she was wrapped in a towel. She held my little sister, who was just waking up. "Go on, draw some birds. A sky is not a sky until there are birds in it."

"Birds . . . ," my father said, staring at the blank part of the paper above the mountains he had drawn. "How do I draw some birds? . . ." With a flourish, he marked the sky with three or four of the creatures with the simplest of strokes of his pencil. "See that, Kevin? Daddy made birds by just making a flattened-out M. Who knew an M could have wings, huh? What words start with an *m*?" he asked me, sensing how much I loved my new knowledge of language. "What words have wings?"

" 'Mommy,' " said my mother.

" 'Methodist,' " said my Baptist father, smiling up at her.

" 'Maris,' " I said, trying to please him.

"That's right, Kevinator," he said. "Attaboy."

"And 'me,' " I said. " 'Me' starts with a *m*."

"You," my father said, shaking his head at the very thought of me and kissing me on my cheek. "Yep, you do," he said. " 'Me' does, I mean. You're my little bird boy, I guess. Go on, draw one like I just did."

I obeyed him as he watched me draw a flattened M all by myself in his version of a sky. We watched it fly on the page before us there in the midst of the flock of Ms he had drawn. " 'Man' starts with an *m*," I softly said.

"Yes, it does," my father said. "Yes, it does."

I reached into my pocket and felt the bottle of red nail polish I had hidden there. I knew that later—before I painted the nail on just one of my little toes red to see how it looked, how it felt, before I returned the tiny bottle to my parents' bathroom—that I would take the polish and paint some red flowers on my own landscape. I would then give it to him the very next Sunday as his Father's Day gift.

A few weeks before Kim had arrived in New York for our MoMA visit he had sent me some photos of his latest art. I was rather shocked at how different it was from his earlier sculptural work. I just always assumed that he would stick to the calm of realism. But this work consisted of a kind of cacophony that began to harmonize as you viewed it. Many of the pieces were about the juxtaposition of objects. One consisted of a grid of letters on which some were circled and I thought of those flattened-out Ms our father had fashioned into birds on that Sunday when the concept of conjured landscapes came into our combined life.

I looked at those e-mailed photos for a long time—to appreciate not just the art but also the artist—the brother—who could still surprise me, who could still run circles around me with his accomplishments.

This is what I wrote in my e-mail to him in response:

Kimbo:
I love that you are continuing to explore what being an artist means to you. I think a lot of your early work was all about the very frightened little boy inside you who saw the world as a chaotic place—so chaotic it could kill one parent in a moment and move on to claim another one just in case you didn't grasp how cruel and chaotic it could be. Somehow though that little boy peering out from your man's eyes could stare at a canvas or a lump of clay and create order. Your early work was all about healing yourself. Your gift to translate so precisely what you saw was God's answer to a little boy's prayer: a way to preserve life without killing it. This new work is not an answered prayer. You have evolved

enough maybe—do any of us really ever heal in life?—so that the work itself is now the prayer.

My little brother—the one in that Yankees uniform who could so effortlessly please our father—grew up to be a father of four children. Kim created a life for himself in Mississippi that I could never create for myself. He always felt at home there. I never did.

He has his successful medical practice and lives in a beautiful antebellum home. He built himself a tennis court. He put in a pool and a pool house. He even expanded one of his guesthouses into a modernist studio and gallery to create and display his art. The gallery/studio stands now, a sleek rebuke to the main house, which was built in 1840, with its antebellum specifics—the portico, the porches, the columns.

Is that studio standing to the side of his home what I have become? Am I but a gallery? Is my life the sleek rebuke to his?

FIVE

The Mentor

In many ways Andy Wyeth was my brother's mentor even though Wyeth only spent a couple of days sitting for Kim. Once my brother as a boy had been shown a book of Wyeth's work by a family friend he had studied everything he could about the man and his art. Wyeth was as much a phantom presence around our childhood home as our parents were. My brother had written a letter to Wyeth—one he'd been in a way composing his whole life—when he sent him the photos of the preliminary studies of the bust he had been working on. He really just wanted the man to know what he had meant to him. But even before he read that letter and had only looked at the photos of the studies, Wyeth must have instinctively seen with his keen eye that the man who had shaped him with so much feeling and understanding had somehow been shaped in return by Wyeth himself in some deeper way. I've always thought that had been—more than the artistry he saw in the bust itself—what had triggered his impulse to issue such an invitation to my brother to pay him a visit and put those finishing touches on the sculpture.

My first mentor when I arrived in New York City, Henry Geldzahler, was not an artist, but he was certainly a part of the art world. Once the curator of twentieth-century art at the Metropolitan Museum (where he had been no fan of Andrew Wyeth), Henry, when I met him in 1978, had recently been appointed New York City's commissioner of cultural affairs by Mayor Koch. I had been having lunch with a mutual friend of Henry's at One Fifth Avenue when Henry joined us. Henry was bearded and jovial and was wearing a bow tie made of porcelain, which he proved by grabbing my fork and tapping the bow tie's sculpted knot. I knew the moment the fork's tine took clinking notice of that bow tie that he was someone I needed to know. He took my measure as well to see if I, all of twenty-two years old, could keep up my third of a One Fifth lunchtime conversation. Would I get his jokes? Make a few of my own? Take his handoff of some offhand cultural reference and run with it? All curators and art world arbiters have the instincts of sheepdogs as, sniffing about, they tend to the talent they gather around them. That day Henry decided to cut me out of the herd so I could be a part of his much smaller, more finely honed drove.

Henry didn't think of himself as a mentor to me, even though I certainly did. I even mentioned how grateful I was that he was playing such a role in my life when I stopped by his place on West 9th Street one Sunday on our way to brunch and waited for him to finish the crossword puzzle in *The New York Times Magazine*. "I've never met a boy in less need of mentor than you, Miss'sippi," he told me, having nicknamed me that when I told him that was the way we pronounced it back home, my Mississippi roots, which I had always been rather embarrassed by in New York, making me exotic in his discerning eyes. "In many ways you have mentored me," he said. Never looking up from the puzzle, he reached over and cupped my face in his hand, which had become his sign of affection for me. An important part of it was his not having to look at me when he did it, as if he were presenting his latest discovered exotic treasure for the world's edification so that it could see what he had already seen. "You'll understand one day when you're my age," he said.

Even though Henry was only forty-two when we met, he did have the appearance of someone much older. His perfect little paunch, the enthusiasm his beard had for its grayness, his bald pate, his signature cigar, and the resulting redolence that nested right along with the gray in that beard, the fedora that often crowned the dandyism below—it all combined to give him the costume of age even as it gave him the image he more desired, that of the Poo-Bah. His pen poised, he peered down intently at the taunt of the remaining tiny empty squares before him, then worked the crossword puzzle some more. "The young mentor the old," he said. "You? You, Miss'sippi, have taught me that 'goodness' can be an eight-letter word for 'guile.' But mentor? No," he said, putting down the pen with a flourish and finally looking my way. "Think of me more as your passport."

New York did cease to be a big city with Henry by my side and became instead a small town. I gained entry into the Manhattan of private screenings, gallery openings, uptown parties, downtown dinners at Odeon, and many more lunches at One Fifth. It was with Henry I spent my first Christmas Eve away from home in 1979 and it was he, whose family emigrated from Belgium when he was five years old, who made me feel that "from this night forth you are an honorary Jew."

He took me for a meal at Sardi's that Christmas Eve, then to see a preview of the Broadway production of Harold Pinter's *Betrayal* starring Blythe Danner, Raúl Juliá, and Roy Scheider. Afterward Henry and I wandered around Times Square and ended up at the Hay Market bar on Eighth Avenue, which was frequented by male hustlers and their clientele. Henry had an appreciation for such bars and, conversely, I think part of his attraction to me was its chasteness. Just as he cured me of any lingering embarrassment of my Southernness by pointing out to me how it was a large part of my appeal, my presence in his life as a boy he could adore without the need to bed alleviated any guilt he might have had about the ones he bedded but didn't adore. He seemed to be known by several of such boys that Christmas Eve at the Hay Market who looked me over as their latest competition. That would have normally made me uneasy, but not that night. Let them look at me as the newest boy in their midst, I thought, as I stared them down and stood my ground. Little did they know that this was the night, as the last Christmas of the 1970s approached, I was leaving any semblance of my boyhood behind.

At midnight, the Hay Market bartenders began to shout, "Merry Christmas! Drinks on the house!" and a rash of hustlers rushed the bar, elbowing Henry and me out of the way. Suddenly, as if they'd been waiting for their cue, through the front door of the place burst a bunch of caroling drag queens singing "Hark! The Herald Angels Sing!" We all joined in. When Henry and I made it back to the bar, the bartender did a double take my way and asked, "Who's this new little present, Henry, ya found under the tree? I'd like to unwrap this one myself."

Henry, without looking my way, reached out and lovingly cupped his hand around my face, reassuring me that I was not only treasure but also treasured. "This is Miss'sippi," he said.

The bartender leaned in closer. "And what did you get for Christmas, Miss'sippi?" he asked me. "Lips?"

Henry roared with laughter and for a few weeks afterward my nickname was no longer Miss'sippi. "Lips!" was now what heralded my arrival on West 9th Street before Henry and I would head out to another night on the town for a society function or an arts benefit. One such dinner event concerned the saving of Grand Central Station when it was threatened with being demolished. It was the first time I was in the presence of Diana Vreeland, who was seated on one side of Henry at the dinner. It speaks to what a presence hers was that it barely registered with me for several moments that on the other side of him was Jacqueline Kennedy Onassis. God knows who and what those two women thought I was, there at their table. A waiter who had the audacity to take a seat? A waif who had walked in off the street? Henry, however, made sure to include me in the conversation, but I was so in awe of my tablemates I barely recall what was said. I do recall his talking to Mrs. Onassis about the "Landmark Express" train they were planning to take to D.C. in support of the Grand Central landmark designation case going before the Supreme Court. They made plans to sit together.

Henry had to get up at one point to work the room in his relatively new role as commissioner. When he got up, Vreeland leaned over to where I was seated and motioned me over to sit between Jackie O and her. I'll never forget the orders Vreeland issued to me that night. "There is a chasm here, young man, between Jackie and me. Henry's dutiful departure has left a chasm. Your lot in life tonight is to be a chasm filler. Come keep the couloir warm," she said, and patted the seat beside her. I did as I was told even though my vocabulary back then wasn't sufficient enough to understand the pun she had just made. I did instinctively know enough, however, to just keep prompting her and let her talk. Mrs. Onassis kept smiling enigmatically at all that Vreeland had to say. That seemed to be Vreeland's own duty that night, as official as any Henry was performing around the room: to keep Jackie smiling.

When Henry returned I started to give him back his seat, but he shook his head and sat where I had been sitting. Mrs. Onassis, at that point, finally asked me a few questions about myself and my life and I began to stutter out some answers. I was obviously nervous to be talking to her. When I am nervous my boyhood stammer often returns to haunt me. Beneath the table I felt Vrreeland's hand reach over and gently give my knee a few reassuring taps as the "M" in "M-M-Mississippi" was having a hard time m-m-making it past M-M-Miss'sippi's lips.

On another occasion, Henry took me to a benefit honoring director Harold Clurman, who, along with Cheryl Crawford and Lee Strasberg, founded the Group Theatre. When we arrived Henry saw that he was seated next to Kim Stanley at our table and he switched his place card with mine so I could be her tablemate. Stanley and I hit it off and she wanted to hear all about my southern gothic past and teared up when I told her about the deaths of my mother and father when I was a child. She told me her own mother was an interior decorator and her father was a philosophy professor and she teared up even more when telling me about her brother Kenny, who was a pilot during World War II and "never came back home to be my brother." She all but ignored Arthur Miller, who was on the other side of her at the table, thankful, it seemed, to talk about anything other than theater and the lore of her own talent at such a dinner. When Clurman got up to make his rambling acceptance speech, Stanley, like Vreeland at that earlier dinner, reached over and patted my knee. Stanley then grabbed my hand and clutched it with such force, such feeling, it seemed as if, in that moment, it was the last tether left her.

"I knew you and Kim would get along," Henry told me as we rode home from the party that night. At first I had heard my brother's name when he said it and not Miss Stanley's. At the sound of my brother's name in such a sentence I felt my throat tighten. Tears, confusingly, came to my eyes. "You're wounds of a feather, you and Kim," Henry said, yet sensed the moment he said it the comment itself had wounded me. It had. I heard not only pity in it but also derision. "Sorry, Miss'sippi," he said. But he was wrong. It wasn't just Mississippi I had fled in my move to New York. It wasn't just my brother and all he stood for in his ease at living all his life in such a place. It was the pity I felt back there as an orphan, a sissy one at that, and the derision the pity had deformed itself into once I came out of the closet as a teenager. Henry's presence in my life up until that moment had been a kind of banishment of such pity, such derision. His acceptance of me helped me to accept myself. He reached out to cup my face in his hand—for the first time as a form of apology—and for the first time I turned away from him.

The next month or so he invited me to even more events and more parties as a kind of "apology tour," I see now as I look back on it. Then the invitations—indeed, his very presence in my life—began to taper off until one night at a society function up on the East Side that had to do in some way with the Metropolitan Museum of Art, we became bored—or maybe that was when he finally decided it was I who bored him and not the party. Whatever the reason, when such a feeling of social ennui at such a party began to nudge at us we played a game of his devising called spot the doyenne. That night I beat him at spotting his adored Lily Auchincloss, whom he had once deemed "the doyenne's doyenne," and I even laughed at my having beat him at beckoning her to our side. After a bit of conversation, as we watched Mrs. Auchincloss walk away toward others at the party, Henry reached over and cupped my face in his hand. Surprising me, he turned it toward him and looked right at me. His eyes were welling as mine had in the car that night he'd said my brother's name when he was talking about the saddest woman I'd ever met. He willed them however, to stop their welling. I watched his will at work. "You no longer need a passport," he said, revoking himself, I know now, from my life. "You have attained your citizenship."

I was to see Henry only a few more times before his death in 1994 from liver cancer when he was only fifty-nine. But I never stopped loving him in the way we loved each other—tentatively, platonically, totally. I went to his memorial service at the Metropolitan Museum, at which his dear friend David Hockney spoke so movingly. Hockney was one of the many friends of Henry's who became, for a while, a friend of mine. I went up to David afterward, each of us welling up the same way Henry had when he knew before I did that we weren't going to be seeing each other anymore. David and I hugged. We, unlike him, could not will our tears away. We reminisced about Henry.

"He cut me out of the herd at the exact moment I was ready," I told David. "He knew that need in me. He was the first to really know it."

"He cut me out of it too," David quietly said. "That's exactly what he did."

I walked slowly down those steep steps of the Met that evening and wandered out alone into the herd heading down Fifth Avenue. It is where, back in the herd but alone, I have wandered—this kid called Miss'sippi who misses Henry—ever since.

One of the last parties Henry took me to was a New Year's Eve one at Howard Moss's apartment. Henry lived on 9th Street between Fifth and Sixth Avenues and Howard on 10th Street between Fifth and Sixth. Howard lived in a studio with a terrace in the back, but on New Year's Eve without the use of that terrace the place was as packed as a well-edited paragraph at *The New Yorker*, where Howard had been the poetry editor since 1948. I staked out a corner with choreographer Paul Taylor, who wasn't much of a conversationalist. In fact, I began to suspect he was an idiot savant whose only idiom was dance. When I began to bemoan the Moral Majority and Jerry Falwell to Paul he looked at me blankly and said he had no idea what I was talking about. I could not imagine a gay man not knowing who Falwell and his Moral Majority were. This was at the height of the hate they were fomenting against Paul and me and all the other gentlemen of a certain sort jostling about us, this smattering of smart homosexuals of cultural New York of whom one or two were even smartly dressed.

I've often wondered if that party was the night Henry handed me off to Howard, for the latter did land in that place in my life that Henry vacated. It all had the Shakespearean precision of a too-well-shaped narrative—even a stratagem—and it was certainly convenient, since he only had to walk around the block to execute the handoff. Henry knew I wanted to be a writer and Howard had entrée into the publishing world that Henry didn't have for all his lofty connections in the city. Indeed, the respect given to Howard and his opinion in the literary establishment of the time was best summed up by W. H. Auden's clerihew dedicated to him:

> Is Robert Lowell
> Better than Noel
> Coward,
> Howard?

Such a clerihew possessed the drollery that Howard himself possessed but that could be mistaken at times for a rather overly dear fussiness. But it was just such fussy dearness in others that Howard disdained. "There's nothing more dreary than pretense," he once whispered to me surveying the room at a boring function held at the apartment of some literary apparatchik he had taken me to. "Well, perhaps those drapes there are."

I became friendly with Edward Albee through Howard and he and

I began to talk about Moss, who died in 1987, when I was visiting Edward down in his loft in Tribeca one afternoon. "He was such a gentle, sweet man," said Edward. "What I also responded to in him—like you—was that he was quick to spot pretension and preposterousness. There's always a lot of that to be spotted in artistic circles. And you need someone like Howard—sweetly and gently since those were the stalwarts of his nature—to call it out."

I first met Edward at that New Year's Eve party at Howard's—he was one of the two smartly dressed guests—but he couldn't recall when he had first met Howard. "I just can't really remember—starting back during my formative years in New York City—when Howard wasn't around. I left home in 1948 when I was around twenty and moved straight to Greenwich Village. There was a ten-year period there between '48 and '58—like your own between '74 and '84—when I really learned everything and educated myself. We were all around each other, all of us who were to make it in the next generation, all the painters and poets and everybody. Nobody knew anybody and yet everybody knew everybody because none of us was famous at that point. We were all just at the cusp of doing stuff in that ten-year period.

"I had my own mentors back then, you know, a whole generation of them," said Edward. "You need all that. You have to have that. It's harder now. Everyone is so protected from everyone else these days. And it's too expensive now to be a struggling artist in this town. My second apartment here was on Henry Street on the Lower East Side. A sixth-floor walk-up. It was sixteen dollars a month. One of my later apartments was underneath Howard in that brownstone on 10th Street between Sixth and Fifth. That's when we really became close, when we were upstairs, downstairs neighbors.

"But back in the late 1940s and early 1950s there were only a few hangouts with their specific denizens. There was the Cedar Bar where all the painters would go and . . . hmm . . . lie down. I assume I must have first met Howard back then at one of those places. I don't remember when I actually met anybody, I've met so many people in my life. I just knew him forever. But it was probably in the early 1950s when our paths crossed. He was already at *The New Yorker*, so he was the impressive one. I was the impressed."

Howard continues to impress me with how he hovers about me in the most unexpected moments. Once when I was going to interview Michelle Williams for one of my Q and A's for The Daily Beast Web site I stopped in a used bookstore on Smith Street in Brooklyn a few blocks from the brownstone she and Heath Ledger shared before his death. Michelle had agreed to the interview because she had loved a cover story I had written on Heath for *Vanity Fair* even before she had met him herself. I had done the interview with Heath in Prague, where he was filming *A Knight's Tale*.

I knew Michelle loved poetry and found a first edition of Howard's *Selected Poems* at that shop on Smith to give her as a present. When I surprised her with it, I told her Howard had been a mentor of mine and she gasped, for Howard had written a poem that had helped her in her grief over Ledger's death. She had recently been trying to find it again and could not recall its title. She quickly scanned the table of contents and gasped again.

"Here it is," she said. " 'The Pruned Tree.' That's the title. This poem helped me so much after Heath died. So much."

"You know, Michelle, when I was in Prague doing that interview with Heath at one point we took a stroll across the Charles Bridge and I asked him if he wanted to smoke a joint," I told her. "I had sneaked one over in a rolled-up sock in my suitcase. He said yes. So we stopped and watched the moon rise over the Vitava River and took turns taking tokes. I got really stoned with him. At one point I thought that was one of the coolest things to have happened during one of my interviews. But because of the way Heath died that memory doesn't seem so cool anymore," I said, knowing by acknowledging it I was also acknowledging my own burgeoning use of drugs more menacing than marijuana.

"Thank you for telling me that," she quietly said, then just as quietly read aloud the words of Howard's poem:

"As a torn paper might seal up its side,
Or a streak of water stitch itself to silk
And disappear, my wound has been my healing,
And I am made more beautiful by losses.
See the flat water in the distance nodding
Approval, the light that fell in love with statues,
Seeing me alive, turns its motion toward me.
Shorn, I rejoice in what was taken from me.

"What can the moonlight do with my new shape
But trace and retrace its miracle of order?
I stand, waiting for the strange reaction
Of insects who knew me in my larger self,
Unkempt, in a naturalness I did not love.
Even the dog's voice rings with a new echo,
And all the little leaves I shed are singing,
Singing to the moon of shapely newness.

"Somewhere what I lost I hope is springing
To life again. The roofs, astonished by me,
Are taking new bearings in the night, the owl
Is crying for a further wisdom, the lilac
Putting forth its strongest scent to find me.
Butterflies, like sails in grooves, are winging
Out of the water to wash me, wash me.
Now, I am stirring like a seed in China."

When I visited Edward Albee down at his loft he and I had discussed
that very poem by Howard as one we both loved. "I was first attracted
to Howard because of his poetry," Edward said. "I admired his work so.
Howard was a brilliant, brilliant poet. Very much influenced, I'd say, by
Auden. And Elizabeth Bishop, who was a dear friend. But his poetry
was more than brilliant; it was moving. He was an elegist, I suppose,

except when he was not being one. All his poems are about Howard's perception of reality.

"Speaking of which—reality—I tried to persuade Howard not to buy that house of his in East Hampton where you'd often visit him," Edward continued. "It really didn't have anything to do with him. It was very modern. Too modern. It was a strange little house. It just didn't suit him. It wasn't proper for him. I kept showing him houses. Older houses. With all sorts of wonderful areas for books. Lots of little rooms hidden away. I thought he would have been happier in such a house. He did like to get away from the place and visit me in Montauk, as that awful dinner party you came to with him attests."

Edward was right. I'd often visit Howard at his home in the Springs section of East Hampton and we'd ride over to Montauk to have dinner at Edward's place. The dinner party Edward mentioned was for his mother, Frankie. He had invited Howard and me along with Joanna Steichen and Elaine Steinbeck, "two widows at their peak," as Howard described them on our drive over.

When we got to Edward's he was busy in the kitchen pureeing most of the food we were to eat, because of his mother's digestive problems. She was in the bathroom tending to such problems, I presumed, and, as Howard and Elaine and Joanna caught up with one another, Frankie emerged, all six feet of her, from the bathroom in her Halston Ultra-suede dress. She eyed me up and down. "You look like you're good with a zipper," she said, and turned around so I could zip up her Halston for her.

I then went into the kitchen to see if I could help Edward with the dinner. He was already mumbling to himself over by the blender. "Can you believe she is making me do this?" he asked, pointing to the pureed dishes he had prepared.

During the dinner everyone decided to pretend that nothing was pureed—at least no one mentioned it. Elaine Steinbeck, who still had the gruff charm of the stage manager about her—she was one of the first females to ever have such a job on Broadway (Howard had prepped me in the car about her) when she took the backstage reins of *Oklahoma!*

and then ran Paul Robeson's national tour of *Othello*—took it upon herself to keep the conversation going until the curtain could fall on this rarified bit of dinner theater.

A violent summer thunderstorm erupted by dinner's end and blew over a Henry Moore sculpture that was on the bluff outside the dining room's picture window. I volunteered to go outside to right it. As I stood it back up in the pouring rain I turned and saw Howard and Edward standing at the window with their backs to the women. Howard said something to Edward, something droll no doubt, something dear, and made him laugh. Edward then rejoined the women, but Howard stayed right there at the window. He stared at me where I had found my place that night there outside. He waved at me. I waved back. I am waving still.

"Did you know Henry Geldzahler?" I asked Edward that day down at his loft.

"Yes," he said, chuckling. "My most vivid memory of Henry is a look of utter terror on his face. For some reason, we decided to take a hot-air balloon ride together out in the Hamptons. As we rose higher and higher, Henry became more and more terrified. I remember laughing at his terror, which I shouldn't have done. He ended up sitting on the floor of the balloon's gondola. He held on to my leg. He would not look. One should always look."

"Did you look?" I asked.

"I looked."

My first mentor, a minister down in Mississippi, molested me. I was thirteen years old and he, in his sixties then, was preaching at a revival service in the Mississippi hamlet of Harperville, which had been the hometown of my grandparents. I had never felt the pull of an altar call before. Usually on a Sunday night by the end of a sermon I was still pouting about the guests I was missing on *The Ed Sullivan Show*. But his sermon that night seemed aimed directly at me. It was, I know now, a form of seduction as he saw me on the pew and upped his performance. Yet I, in my innocence, thought he was being divinely inspired as he threw down the typed pages of his sermon and proclaimed, "I feel moved to tell my own story tonight about how lost I was as a boy. And how the Lord found me in my loneliness."

I hung on his every word after that. At the close of his sermon, when the congregation began to sing, "Just as I am, without one plea, / But that thou blood was shed for me. And that thou bidst me come to thee. / Oh, lamb of God, I come, I come," I didn't hesitate. I walked down the aisle. I knelt at the altar and, sobbing, gave my life to Christ. The minister came to the altar and gathered me in his old arms and let me know I too had been found in my loneliness. "You are no longer lost," he whispered, his face so close to mine that I felt for the first time the scratch of a strange man's whiskers.

From that moment on, he began to mentor me. It is, in fact, the first time I had ever heard the word when he and my grandmother were talking and she was thanking him for all the time he was spending with me. He told her it was important for a parentless boy like me "to have a mentor in his life." But soon his mentoring gave way to the warped intimacy of molestation and that moment of my giving my life to Christ became so blurred with it that I could no longer tell them apart.

I have lived with that blur—a kind of second shadow—all my life. It is the shadow of my thirteen-year-old self that I see when I turn my head to watch it where it flickers by another nameless naked stranger's bed in the utter darkness so far from those Mississippi country nights when I would try to discern my parents in it. Such darkness I know now holds not the dead, but the deadened. Sex, in the moment of my molestation, became a violation of both my body and my spirit. Violation—not love, not intimacy—would be what I would come to seek sexually the rest of my life.

The only way to heal myself I decided was to mentor a young boy myself and prove to him—and to me—that it could be an act of purity even if sex no longer ever would be again for me. That is how, fourteen years ago, I came to meet Brandon Gonzalez through an organization called The Family Center. After an interview with the woman who ran its "buddy program" I was put through a weekend workshop with other volunteers and then an attempt was made to match me up with a child who would be compatible based on my interview and by observing me in the workshop.

After several weeks, however, I still was not matched up with a child. The woman told me not to lose heart, that she was trying to find just the right child for me. "It has to be someone bright and artistic," she said when I went in to talk to her again. Was this just more proof that I was supposed to be alone in life, that there wasn't even a needy child in all of New York City who could match my own neediness? "I want this to be a good experience for both of you," she said, reassuring me. "We're having a Christmas party tomorrow night up in Harlem. Many of our families will be there. Would you like to volunteer for that?"

I said yes and took a long walk home.

Three hours later I sat, naked, waiting for the whore to arrive. I knew even on that walk home that I was going to hire him and buy the cocaine he also sold me when he came over. He and it were the forms that violation had taken at that point in my life.

Cocaine came first. Then the whores. But once I met this particular one he was the only one I ever hired because he dealt coke as well. He was from Prague and claimed to be straight. I would straddle him and ease myself down on his uncircumcised cock and he would touch my nipples, which opened me wider, and call me a faggot, the word sounding like "figgit" in his accent. That night he brought not only coke with him for me to buy along with himself but also something he called crystal. I had never heard of it before.

He pulled out a pipe and a funny-looking lighter and started to explain how we could smoke it. He said this first time he would let me do it for free. But bringing such apparatuses into the act of taking drugs seemed like crossing a line to me and I asked if I could just snort it like the cocaine. He said I could but that it would burn. He made two lines on my glass tabletop and for the first time I did crystal meth. He was right. It was burning my nostrils, but it also seemed to be burning everything away, any sense of myself, all memory, any thought. All that was left was my racing pulse. I lay on my stomach on my bed. I raised my butt higher in the air in both surrender and defiance. Without asking, he stuck a fingerful of the crystal up my ass and the burning was intense until the wetness it also caused helped it to cease. He rammed himself into me, whispering "figgit figgit figgit" over and over. He hadn't shaved and his whiskers scraped my cheek. I thought of the minister and his whiskers and that altar and the first time I heard the word "mentor" and heard his whisper "you are no longer lost" and felt his old arms around me. I thought of the stubble on the ridge of my father's cheek I would always long to reach for when I was a child. I struggled to free myself, but the whore pushed me back down and fastened his hands around my neck. "Stop. Please," I begged. "No . . . no . . . please . . . no . . ." I thought of another Prague and Heath Ledger's face circled in the marijuana smoke we were inhaling together on the Charles Bridge. The whore choked me now. "Stop. No. You're hurting . . . it hurts . . . no . . . please. . . ." He choked me harder. I could barely breathe. Was I passing out? "Figgit,' he no longer whispered but growled the word until, when I shut my eyes, it and my pulse and his pounding all became one. "Forget it," I began to hear instead. "Forget it." And for the first time I did. I forgot it all. My dead parents. The race back home my brother could always win. Heath's stoned handsome face. Howard. Henry. Miss'sippi. A minister making me feel loved in order to molest me. That second shadow of my younger self had even deserted me. There was nothing left to discern in the utter darkness now descending upon me. A new memory—". . . forget it, forget it . . ."—was being formed. This was no longer—". . . figgit, figgit . . ."—the result of molestation in my life. This newest violation—". . . you fucking faggot piece of shit . . ."—had taken molestation's place.

I arrived at that church basement in Harlem for The Family Center's Christmas party the next night hungover and bleary-eyed, having had no sleep whatsoever because of the crystal and cocaine and violence the whore had doled out. I did not want to show up, but as long as I kept my commitment I convinced myself that I was okay. I was informed when I arrived there that I was assigned to the bead-stringing table, where a rowdy bunch of children were already making necklaces for their mothers and aunts and sisters. I pulled up the turtleneck I was wearing around my neck to hide the bruises left there from the night before and gingerly took my position on the stool at the table. There had been a bit of blood from inside me flowing down my leg when I finally showered after the whore left, telling me not to move until I heard the door shut behind him.

I tried to block out what had happened and pretended to enjoy being there as my head began to pound with the noise of the children surrounding me and the pain from the night before continued to throb inside me. Beside me I felt a flicker of a presence. I turned and saw a small six-year-old Puerto Rican boy from Brooklyn as he sidled up to me. "Hey, man, I'm Brandon," he said. "Whatcha doin'? Beads are stupid."

I explained the jewelry-making process to him while keeping an eye on the other children and tried not to focus too much on the dichotomy of the last two nights in my life. "You want to join us?" I asked.

"Are you crazy?" he answered with his own question. I wanted to say, Yes, I am, Brandon, yes, I am crazy, if you only knew what I had been doing twenty-four hours earlier. But the kid just stared into my bleary eyes as if he'd stared into the eyes of too many adults in his life with just my lost look. "I'm already bored at this party, but so what. I'm always bored," he said. "Come on. You're bored too, right?"

"I certainly am," I said, though I had to offer a slight smile at his blunt assessment of our situation. "So why don't you pull up a chair, Brandon. Let's find a way together not to be bored."

Brandon and I ended up talking for a long time that night. He even made a necklace or two for his sister and his aunt. I had found the child I would mentor. He would become a new kind of second shadow in my life.

Over the last fourteen years boredom has never been a part of the relationship that I have developed with Brandon. Empathy has been a part of it, as has anger at times. But a hard-earned love for each other is finally the basis of it all. In January of 2012 he graduated from high school, the first male in his family ever to do so.

In the fourteen years we've known each other, Brandon and I have gone to museums and movies, played basketball, and ridden miles and miles of bike trails. During the early years I ate more fast food than I'd ever eaten before until he learned his new favorite word: "brunch." Now he'd rather eat eggs Benedict than an Egg McMuffin.

Brandon's own story is his to tell. I can say it is quite a complicated one. At fourteen, when he was the age his mother was when she gave birth to him, I mentioned that to him—he really hadn't thought about it before—and it prompted our first grown-up conversation about forgiveness and understanding. The little boy with the tough-guy act I'd met so many Christmases ago in that basement of a Harlem church had matured into a young man who had begun to realize that toughness can be a shell that protects the tenderness inside.

Parade magazine at one point asked me to write a story about my mentoring of Brandon and I asked his permission while we were having dinner on our way to see Daniel Radcliffe in *Equus*. Brandon gave it to me and I began to interview him a bit that night. I was curious about what his favorite memory was of all the years we had been spending together. Would it be the time in my role as a celebrity interviewer I'd persuaded Mariah Carey to sing "Happy Birthday" to him on my tape recorder? Or when I introduced him to Marisa Tomei at my local flea market in Chelsea? How about the first time I took him on an airplane? The first time he beat me at bowling? His first horseback ride on Cape Cod, where he came to visit me for a week each summer at my cottage in Provincetown?

"I think it was the first time we played that board game Clue when I was a little kid and I suddenly had an accident in my pants," he said. "You didn't make fun of me. I had really bad diarrhea. And you took care of me." He paused, knowing he had surprised me with that answer. "I tell you things I don't tell nobody else," he said softly. "I'd have a lot more pain inside me if you hadn't been around."

I would have had a lot more pain inside of me too if Brandon hadn't been around. As we walked toward the theater that night where *Equus* was playing, I pointed out the place where we had seen *The Lion King* so many years before. It was the first Broadway show we had seen together, when he was six years old. He'd even held my hand that day, frightened of the matinee throng in Times Square. Now he's always careful to walk a few steps ahead of me with that sweetly thuggish swagger of a New York City teenager.

At the intermission of *The Lion King*, we had hurried to the bathroom and I had told him to meet me in the downstairs lobby when we each finished. But the place was so crowded I couldn't find him at first. I finally spotted him cowering over in a corner, his little face a fist of tears. I folded him in my arms and swept him back up the stairs toward our seats. "I will never abandon you," I promised as we made our way through the crowd.

It was then I realized it. I had searched my whole life to hear those exact five words ever since I was a child myself who had lost his parents. I had no idea that when I found them—when I finally heard them—I would be saying them to someone else.

During that first year I mentored Brandon, The Family Center arranged a camping trip for the boys and girls in its program and those of us who mentored them. We piled into busses and rode the couple of hours up into the Catskills to a site that contained a lodge and several rustic cabins.

The first day, it rained rather heavily and we ended up having to ad-lib games and other activities at the lodge. Toward the end of the long afternoon, Brandon and I were sitting next to a woman who was teaching her young charge how to paint her toenails and fingernails with the red polish she had pulled from her purse, the welcome heady fumes from the little opened bottle of polish cutting sharply through the lodge's musty smell. The slight dizziness I was feeling from the polish's fumes helped to wake me up from the afternoon's rainy stupor.

I found some paper and crayons and Brandon and I lay on the floor next to them as close as I could arrange for us to get without drawing attention to our proximity so I could continue to breathe in the nail polish. The paper and crayons—we'd have to draw something, I presumed—was just a ruse at that point, even for Brandon, it seemed, who pretended not to be looking at the reddening toenails of the little girl who was around his age.

"Do you know what a landscape is?" I heard myself ask him as I began to draw a couple of mountains on the piece of paper I had found.

He shrugged.

"It's a pretty picture of a mountain scene. I'm drawing a mountain scene—like right there outside the window," I said, pointing through the lodge's large picture window toward the two small mountain-like hills in the distance.

Brandon—as well as the little girl next to him—watched me continue to draw a facsimile of the two large hills out beyond the lodge. I took a blue crayon and formed, like an azure snake, the overflowing stream running through the bit of valley between them.

"May I borrow the nail polish?" I asked my fellow mentor, who looked thankful to be relieved of her toenail-painting duty. "We can use this red polish to paint some flowers. See?" I told the little girl, who was now fascinated by what was going on next to her. I asked if she wanted to paint a few flowers herself and, as I held the tiny bottle for her, she dipped the tinier brush into it, then began to dot the paper with a whole garden of red. I gave Brandon a crayon. "Want to draw some birds in the sky?" I asked him. "A sky is not a sky until there are birds in it."

"I don't know how to draw no birds," he said, shrugging yet again.

"Do you know how to make an M?" I asked him.

"Yeah, Kev. I ain't that stupid," he said.

"You're not stupid at all," I told him. "Just pretend you're making an M, but flatten it out and it will look like a bird flying in the sky." I took another crayon from the box and showed him how to do it. The mentor next to me had fished into her purse to find her phone and was busy perhaps typing Ms herself within the words she was texting to some unknown person. She giggled at the texted response back to her when her cell phone buzzed. The little girl, oblivious to her own mentor now, continued to dot the page with red flowers, her little wet fingernails imprinting their own bud-like images into the garden she was creating. Brandon edged closer to her and drew flattened Ms in the sky.

"What starts with an M?" I asked them.

"'Motorola,'" said the girl's mentor, snapping her cell phone shut and watching this most elemental of landscapes taking shape before us all.

"'Mama'?" asked the girl.

"That's right. 'Mama' starts with an M," I told her.

"'Mentor,'" said Brandon, filling the landscape's sky now with a flock of the flattened letters. "Your turn," he said. "What'chu think starts with a M, Kev?"

I looked away from the crayoned landscape and past my own reflection there in the picture window toward the landscape outside, the two small mountains blending with my face. "'Miss'ssippi,'" I said, remembering Henry, my own long-ago mentor, as well the heartbreaking landscape of that state where both my parents had been buried. "'Moss,'" I said, remembering Howard. "'Madonna.' 'Mount Kilimanjaro,'" I continued, the words spilling quietly from me. "'Me,'" I said, looking at myself reflected in the glass of the window, the only landscape lingering now in my line of vision. I turned back toward Brandon and the girl and her mentor and the room, rowdy with so many other boys and girls, so many other mentors, the mugginess mixing with the fumes from the nail polish still in my nostrils making it difficult to breathe. "'Methodist' starts with an M," I said, remembering when I was a boy and that first day I had attended such a church with my mother. "'Methodist,'" I said again, but heard only the word's first worrisome syllable.

"Look, Kev!" Brandon exclaimed. "Look!" The girl's mentor took the tiny nail polish brush from her, put it back into the bottle, and screwed back on its top.

Brandon touched my arm. "Kev, look!" he said again. He held up his drawing for me to see. "A landscape! It's a landscape! I made a landscape!"

I had made one too. And for the first time I was beginning to see it.

"Look!" Brandon kept at me. "Look! Look!"

I looked.

SIX

The Factory Worker

From *The Andy Warhol Diaries*
Entry dated Friday, October 31, 1986

Benjamin was supposed to pick me up but he never showed. I walked around. This was the day of the surprise birthday party Steven Greenberg was giving for Paige at Nell's. For days I'd just been shuffling papers for Paige's party trying to help Tama do a good guest list, and I couldn't get it together, and then Gael took over and did it all really fast. Worked all afternoon. I went home and then Paige picked me up, and as far as she knew we were just going to a blind date dinner at Nell's.

So we get to Nell's and Paige still doesn't suspect anything and then right at the last second, right outside the door Glenn O'Brien's wife Barbara was getting out of a cab and said, "Hi, Paige, we're here for your surprise party." We couldn't believe it, but Paige was distracted enough so it didn't really sink in and I think she actually was really shocked when she walked into the club and everybody shouted, "Surprise!"

Gael did a really good job of pulling it all together. And the party was so nice. I sat right where I did on the opening night— right by the front door—and I didn't move once. The party took over the whole street level floor, and then they let the public in at 10:00 but they sent them downstairs. And it's the new look in restaurants—going for the sort of phony rich look. Dark with stuffed furniture.

And let's see, Thomas Ammann was there and Tama and Nick Love from LA who's staying at Fred's. And Larissa was there. And Jay, and Wilfredo, and Gia, and Peter Koper. And the new kid who works for *Interview* who was at Paramount, Kevin Sessums.

After I gave up my dream of being an actor I got a job for five years at Paramount Pictures in the 1980s working as a highfalutin factotum in the marketing department for an executive vice president named Buffy Shutt. When that department was being moved out to Los Angeles I had to find another job. I had been writing short stories and plays during that time—Buffy was nice enough to pretend not to notice I was writing them at my desk outside her office—and since I had always been a lover of magazines I decided to try to find a job that could combine my writing with a job in some form of journalism. A friend of mine was giving up his position at Warhol's *Interview* magazine as the senior editor there so he could spend time at a Buddhist spiritual retreat in the Himalayan mountains and called to ask if I might be interested in taking over his job. I had no experience in the magazine business, but my past as an actor, my time in the movie business for those five years even as a factotum, and my ambitions to write for a living all combined to make me a good candidate for such a position. I should have questioned why I wanted to replace someone in a job that had sent him fleeing to a spiritual retreat in the Himalayas, one that would ultimately send me seeking my own form of spirituality years later. But questions back then were what I put to others, not to myself.

After I had several meetings with *Interview*'s editor, Gael Love, she offered me the position on a probationary basis because of my lack of experience. I did give her a few of my short stories to read, which I re-alize now must have seemed unnervingly innocent to her—yet, conversely, rather nervy of me as well—and I think those are the two reasons she gave me the six-week tryout. I don't think she ever even looked at the short stories after she'd laughed in my face when I handed them to her, which I came to realize wasn't rudeness on her part but a kind of cackle that erupted from her as a defense mechanism when she was caught off guard.

The stress of not being caught off guard myself in those early days at *Interview* was causing my first bouts of insomnia and making me sick with exhaustion. I'd walk back to the bathroom by Andy's little downstairs office at the old Con Ed plant in the West 30s that served as the Factory back then and close the door for a a pee-and-panic attack as I came to think of those frequent trips. One day I was in there for quite a while just staring at myself in the mirror. I looked awful. It was the first time I could remember ever having dark circles under my eyes. Nothing was worth making myself look that sick. "You're just a Factory worker," I whispered to the person in the mirror.

When I headed back to my office I saw that Andy was in his little downstairs lair. "Are you all right?" he asked me. It was the first time he had even acknowledged my presence in the office. I was sure he remembered me as the overaged urchin with whom Henry Geldzahler had gallivanted about town in the past when our paths had crossed, so I was perplexed by how he seemed to be ignoring me. Yet maybe that was reason enough for him to snub me at first, his perception of me as a gallivanter. There was a reason Andy referred to his studio and its offshoots as the Factory. He had a real blue-collar work ethic and expected those around him to have it too. But his wariness had only added to my stress. "I've noticed you go to that bathroom a lot," he said.

What was he intimating? That I was a drug addict? Did he have fantasies about my snorting coke off his toilet seat? "I'm not doing coke if that's what you mean," I came right out and challenged him. I couldn't tell if he looked shocked by what I had said or hurt that I had assumed he had been accusing me of taking drugs. But his usual enigmatic expression did flutter toward some sort of emotion. "Honestly, Andy, I've been stressing out about this new job. I just want to be good at it."

The confession—the friendly intimacy of it—seemed to shock him even more than challenging him about the cocaine. His face continued to flutter but could not find the emotion on which it wished to land. "Don't let Gael get to you. She can be a bit much. But she's so good at getting ads in the magazine," he said, summing up what he considered her editorial talent. "I have my other sources. They say you're doing a great job. Relax. I told Gael and Fred to go ahead and give you the job," he said, mentioning Fred Hughes, who served as the magazine's publisher as well as the business brains of Andy's art empire. "I didn't realize you were on probation," said Andy. "Welcome to the Factory."

Later that day Andy even stopped by my office to give me a welcome-to-the-Factory present. It was a photograph he had taken in Central Park of an olive-skinned, oily-haired boy opening his jacket to reveal a T-shirt with James Dean's face on it. On the bottom right-hand corner of the photograph Andy—or someone who worked for him—had embossed his name. I was touched by the gesture and told him I'd hang it on the wall of my office next to the poem I was at that moment cutting out of a book to frame and put above my typewriter in those precomputer days.

"What poem is that?" he asked, coming to stand over me and place the photo on my desk.

"It's by John Keats," I told him. "It's called 'On Fame.' I thought it was kind of appropriate for this place. "

"Oh, wow. We've never had anybody around here who reads John Keats," he said. "Would you read it to me?"

Andy Warhol stood by my desk and stared blankly off into space. He waited. I felt I had no choice but to do what he requested. I began to read:

"Fame, like a wayward girl, will still be coy
    To those who woo her with too slavish knees,
But makes surrender to some thoughtless boy,
    And dotes the more upon a heart at ease. . . ."

I read the rest of the poem and waited for Andy's reply as I stared down at the photograph he'd taken of the silk-screened face of James Dean on some banjee boy's dingy T-shirt. I touched the raised letters of his embossed name, lingering over that final *l* in "Warhol." "Wow," he finally said. "I haven't thought of myself as a thoughtless boy in a long time."

He turned to go but stopped in my doorway. His back was to me. He adjusted his wig. "Keats is buried in the non-Catholic cemetery in Rome," he said.

Andy Warhol and I had actually met several times before through Henry, who had championed his career at its beginning in the 1960s. Henry had even insisted to me that he was the one who introduced Andy to Fred Hughes and thus set in motion the making of his art empire.

Fred, ever dapper, loved to wear Anderson & Sheppard bespoke suits. His face was often flushed and the heat from it seemed to enhance the aroma of his eau de toilette, Penhaligon's Blenheim Bouquet, which he so liberally splashed on each morning, its notes of pine and black pepper competing with its top ones of lemon and lime and lavender. He favored French cuffs, his gold Swiss Mido wristwatch worn over one of them in the manner of Gianni Agnelli.

On Fred it all seemed, alas, only mannered, for he was the son of a Texas furniture salesman. Fred had, however, caught the eye of art collectors and philanthropists Jean and Dominique de Menil while he was an art history major at the University of St. Thomas, a small Catholic college located in the de Menils' Houston neighborhood. Still a freshman at the college, Fred was undaunted by the de Menils' wealth and taste and set out to enhance it, so much so that he became known as "The Dauphin" amongst their social set, which he quickly made his own.

Indeed, a de Menil daughter was the guest of honor back in 1967 at a party thrown by architect Philip Johnson at his glass house in New Canaan, Connecticut, at which Fred was a guest. Andy arrived that day with the Velvet Underground, who had been hired by Johnson to be the entertainment at the party. Henry was also a guest at the party that day, and that was when he had the curatorial matchmaking instincts to introduce Andy to Fred. "And then they walked off into a kind of empyrean," Henry told me.

The story itself didn't impress me that much the first time I heard it. Henry often held forth with such stories when we were together. I focused instead on the realm off into which Andy and Fred had walked—an empyrean—not knowing exactly what it meant but wondering if I would ever be able to tell a story myself someday that demanded a sentence with such a lovely word in it.

I've often thought about the two reigning Andys of the art world, Wyeth and Warhol, and how one became such a part of my brother's life and the other became such a part of mine, each in his way early champions of our careers. Two artists—two brothers—could not be more different. We formed a rather disquieting quartet—two polar opposite painters with Pennsylvania roots and polar opposite brothers from the backwoods of Mississippi.

By the time of my friendship with Henry Geldzahler, he and Andy had become polarized themselves. Maybe that was why Andy was giving me the cold shoulder at the beginning of my time at *Interview*— my closeness to Henry. Would too readily accepting me be a kind of forgiveness for Henry? They had once been daily telephone buddies, but when Henry fell in love with Christopher Scott and Chris moved in with him Andy "became jealous that there was another voice that answered the phone," Henry told me when we were discussing the falling-out. "Then when I curated the 1966 Venice Biennale and didn't include any Warhols he wouldn't have much to do with me after that. I miss him. But I guess I deserved it. I rejected his art. I had no art to reject in return. So he rejected me."

One of the first times I ever visited Henry at his place on 9th Street I noticed he had his portable television sitting on top of one of Warhol's Brillo boxes that had been exhibited at the Stable Gallery in 1964 when they were still close friends. "Give it a kick," Henry told me. I did as I was instructed and was astonished to discover Henry had put wheels on the bottom of the box and it coasted across the room toward his bed. "That's all it's finally good for," he told me, laughing, when I asked if he hadn't ruined the resale value of a piece of Warhol's art.

Maybe it was Henry's early influence on me, but I always considered Warhol and his world a bit tacky and was even a bit embarrassed to be working at the Factory. I knew, though, that others would find it glamorous. I was soon, however, caught up in that tacky glamour—as I came to call it—which had as its logical outcome all my years at *Vanity Fair*. Tackiness was more expertly tucked into the glamour at *Vanity Fair*, camouflaged, so highly styled it became a kind of knowing exaltation of it until the exaltation was itself nothing but a lark. The two were seamlessly blended there, their combination resulting in another logical outcome: the celebrity journalism that I not only practiced but also came to define for more than a decade.

And yet I never really considered myself a journalist. I considered myself a writer who could carry on a conversation and shape a narrative. I had lucked out. My only two jobs in the magazine world were at *Interview* and *Vanity Fair*. I never had to earn my stripes in the journalistic trenches. If I had considered myself a journalist I would have had a real inferiority complex, which I had to fight as it was—especially at *Vanity Fair*, where tackiness and glamour were sutured together by the high caliber and seriousness of much of the reporting and other writing within its pages. Don't get me wrong. I knew I was good at my job and my cover stories helped newsstand sales. But, as I once told my *Vanity Fair* colleague James Wolcott, "I'm the trailer park section here. I know my place."

Any time Tina Brown or Graydon Carter, the two editors I worked for at *Vanity Fair*, were criticized it was because of the celebrity angle of the magazine. All editors in chief want to be taken seriously by others in the insular journalism world of New York, and my stories served as the cudgel their critics could so easily use against them. When they looked at me what they couldn't help but see was a cudgel with a crew cut. I was that person in the mirror they too stared at after they'd close their own office bathroom doors and stare at their own darkly circled eyes when the stress got too much, having struck the bargain to edit *Vanity Fair* with its editorial recipe of celebrity, scandal, crime, and the many ways the wealthy won't let us forget they are in our midst. I had become to them the tacky reflection of their glamorously serious selves that they hated facing.

The person I was drawn to the most during my time as a Factory worker was the receptionist on "Andy's side," as we at the magazine labeled the part of the Factory reserved for Warhol's art empire. Each morning after I poured myself some coffee I'd stop by her desk to see what new item she was knitting. Her name was Brigid and her back was usually tight from all the incessant working of those knitting needles, so many mornings I'd even give her a massage.

"You don't feel any tumors?" she'd always whisper with the harried hope of a true but lovable hypochondriac.

After the massage I'd offer a bit of my morning cranberry muffin to her ever-present pug puppies, Fame and Fortune. The former was given to her by Andy; the latter was given its name as yet another way for her glibly to look upon her own. After a month of massages I discovered that Brigid was Brigid Berlin (or, for Warhol aficionados, Brigid Polk). Working at the Factory had still not turned me into a Warhol aficionado myself; therefore, Vincent Fremont, another person on the art side of the Factory who had been quite welcoming and friendly to me, had to explain exactly who she was. To me, she was just Brigid the receptionist, the person there who had been the nicest to me after my arrival.

She had once been known, explained Vincent—who began working there himself around 1969 and had risen to the VP of Andy Warhol Enterprises before later being named the executor of Andy's estate and exclusive sales agent of his works—as Brigid Polk because she'd poke herself with a needle full of amphetamines in the early Factory days. "Hard to believe looking at her now, huh," Vincent had said, smiling at my astonishment. He was right. I did have a hard time equating that old Brigid with the one I was getting to know and love. Over twenty years later, sitting with her knitting at the reception desk, she was now a sober version of herself. Even matronly. I loved to talk to her as she knitted. There was a Zen-like comfort I found watching her hands in a world of their own with those other kind of needles they now held. Needles, it seemed, had become the center of her sobriety just as they had once been the center of her addiction.

The daughter of Richard and Honey Berlin, Brigid grew up in New York at 834 Fifth Avenue. Her father worked for the Hearst Corporation for fifty-two years, the last twenty-three as the president and chief executive officer. Her mother was a social figure on the New York scene and was renowned for her extravagant parties. Brigid grew up around her parents' best friends—everyone from the Duke and Duchess of Windsor to the Richard Nixons and the Lyndon Johnsons.

"I attended a long list of boarding schools, but I didn't go to college," she told me one morning as I watched the needles. "I was sent off to finishing school, where they tried to finish me off."

Brigid's life changed in her early twenties when she met Andy Warhol, just as mine had when I was in my early thirties. Each of the succeeding Factories had been her second home, their inhabitants her extended family. In the early years, as a participant in such films as *Chelsea Girls* and *Ciao! Manhattan*, *Tub Girls*, *Four stars* (****), and *Imitation of Christ*, she was yet another bauble of a society girl Warhol could add to his collection. As the years passed, however, she became his confidante and best friend.

After Andy's death in 1987 I had moved up the masthead to executive editor at *Interview* and we put his picture on the cover of the February 1989 issue in order to celebrate the retrospective of his career that was opening that month at the Museum of Modern Art. I conducted an interview with my buddy Brigid, who gave me her own history of the Factory and Andy. The title of the piece was "Factory Days" and in it Brigid recalled the behind-the-scenes life of the world Warhol created for himself. I was shocked when I saw the layout and realized my name was the first to appear in the well of an issue devoted to the very conception of the Factory. And it was in that moment that I was embarrassed at ever having been embarrassed about working there. I cherish those memories now. I cherish too the memory of serving as an usher at Andy's funeral at St. Patrick's Cathedral. I cherish the tears I shed that day when I remembered how sweetly he said the words, "Welcome to the Factory," to me and had listened to me read him a poem by John Keats then, not knowing he'd soon be buried, told me where Keats had been buried in Rome. I cherish the following interview I did with Brigid after Andy's burial in which she makes so clear how much she missed him, how much we all did.

KEVIN SESSUMS TALKS TO BRIGID BERLIN

KEVIN SESSUMS: Do you remember the very first time you met Andy?
BRIGID BERLIN: I have two recollections about how I met Andy and I'm not sure which is the right one. Around 1961 or '62 I happened to know all the window-display decorators in New York. My future husband, to whom I was married for seven months, was the design director at Tailored Woman, which later became a part of Bergdorf's. Thursday night was window-dressing night in New York. I'd make plans to meet some of the decorators after they did their windows, which was around midnight or one in the morning. If I walked up either side of Fifth Avenue on a Thursday night, I knew everybody in the windows. Andy was then doing the windows for I. Miller Shoes.

I also had a house on Fire Island one summer. I had got a small inheritance from a friend of my father's. My father wanted to put some of it away for me—I was twenty-one at the time—but I demanded the entire thing. I had just married the guy from Tailored Woman, and we didn't really have any of our own money, so I took the inheritance and rented a house in Cherry Grove, which I called Brigid Dune. All I did was give parties. I gave luncheons for three-hundred people, sent out invitations on Tiffany cards with "No swimsuits allowed" engraved on the bottom, and ordered four hundred lobsters from Sayville. I was very, very grand. I'd hire private seaplanes to take me into New York to pick up my mail. On the return I'd ask the pilot to circle very low over my house so I could drop emerald cuff links and other kinds of jewelry into the pool so my husband could dive for them. And I think I met Ondine out at Cherry Grove at the Sea Shack. He thought I was one of the truly outrageously funny people. He might have been the first to take me to the Factory.

KS: Tell me a little about that first Factory. It was on East 47th Street.

BB: Yes. Between Second and First Avenues. On the corner of Second Avenue there was a Bickford's coffee shop—that's where all the food used to come from. Andy loved vanilla milk shakes and cheeseburgers. The Factory was like a big loft, but in those days we didn't call them lofts. It was one vast floor, which you got to by a freight elevator. It was always breaking down. There were three enormous windows that overlooked 47th Street. There were pillars holding up whatever pillars hold up. Billy Name started to live there and he was the one who painted it silver. When he started he just sprayed everything. Then we covered the ceiling with foil. Even the toilet was silver. There was no kitchen or anything—it was a broken-down kind of place. There was old furniture around. A ratty old couch.

Andy started doing his paintings—the flowers, the soup cans—up in front by the windows. He'd rope off the area with a string when he was working, and he'd always yell at me to get away from him when I was smoking my cigarettes because I could have blown up the place with all that flammable paint around.

KS: Did Andy demand quiet while he worked? Or did he like all the activity?

BB: Oh, there was always a racket going on. Billy Name loved the opera—*Madame Butterfly*, *Tosca*, always Maria Callas. It was like a show. I was there. Ondine. Rotten Rita. Billy was very tall and thin and elegant with his gold chains around his neck and a long cigarette holder.

KS: What was Andy's attraction to you?

BB: He was impressed by who my parents were. Especially my father and the whole idea of Hearst. He was intrigued if you were from a good family. We had such a good time. Such fun. We'd always go out from the Factory. We'd meet up late at night after Andy would get through working. We'd head for an ice-cream parlor around the corner called the Flick, or we'd go to Ondine's disco or the one that Richard Burton's wife owned. We used to go to the Village a lot. Andy was into wearing his black leather jacket and black chino pants.

KS: Do you remember him as sexy?

BB: Nooooooo! Are you kidding? I was never an Andy Warhol groupie. I really enjoyed Billy and Ondine and didn't give a hoot if Andy was along or not. A lot of these girls really had crushes on Andy—Edie, International Velvet, Ivy Nicholson. I just never did. I was never impressed with stardom or stars or who people were. I figured I knew them all already because of the way I grew up. I mean, I felt that Clark Gable and Spencer Tracy were the ultimate, and this was all just something different.

KS: How crazy was that first Factory? Were there drug parties? Orgies?

BB: Oh yeah. Everybody was taking speed. We were all on pills. But I never thought of it as "drugs." When I was sixteen my family doctor prescribed speed for me, but I didn't know what it was. It was just medicine to help me lose weight. I never smoked grass. I never did LSD. But I loved amphetamines.

KS: The films started at that first Factory.

BB: Yeah, but I didn't get involved until *Chelsea Girls*. That's when I took the name Brigid Polk, because I was poking amphetamines.

KS: Were you aware enough back then to know how decadent the whole scene at the Factory would seem to an outsider?

BB: No. Because I was "up there" all the time on speed I never even thought of the word "decadent." It was just the way we were living our lives. You know, Andy started taping in those days at the old Factory. That was before these little tape recorders, too. He had some big sort of contraption set up. He'd shove the microphone at me and tell me to go back and sit on the couch and talk. And I'd just do these monologues that would last for hours and hours, talking to nobody. I'd say, "Andy, can I get up now?" And he'd say, "Come on, there's another reel. Just go to the end of the reel."

KS: Would you do anything he told you to do?

BB: No. I just talked into that tape recorder because I thought it was fun. Plus I was flying. I was running around in these outfits I called my lavalavas. I had cropped hair. Elephant pants. I had the nerve back then to walk around completely topless to Bickford's down on Second Avenue to pick up the milk shakes. I mean no top on. This was right after Christina Paolozzi had gone topless in *Harper's Bazaar* in the sixties. That was the new thing, you know.

KS: What was the reason the original Factory moved down to Union Square?

BB: We were running out of room. Andy had to have more space to paint. The movies needed more room. Paul Morrissey got this idea that once we moved it should become more like a business. Like Hollywood. Like a movie studio. So they rented this place at 33 Union Square. It had a balcony. We mirrored the place. Made some makeshift desks with file cabinets. There was a reception desk with a phone as you walked in the door. There was this little room that Andy would disappear into. That's where Pat Hackett began to transcribe Andy's tapes. By then Andy was taking his tape recorder everywhere. In the back is where we showed the movies and kept the furniture that Fred Hughes had begun collecting in Paris. Billy was then sort of the Factory foreman. He also lived there—in a room no bigger than a closet. It was his darkroom and he also slept there. At night Andy wouldn't be there, so Billy would have me up there and Rotten Rita and Ondine. The opera would start blaring again. We would come there after a night at Max's Kansas City.

KS: Were you there at Union Square when Andy was shot?

BB: I was on my way to the Factory when it happened. It was a very, very hot day. I had just left my sister. I told the driver to take me on to 33 Union Square West, but I got to 23rd Street and changed my mind. I lived at the George Washington Hotel at that point and I went back and started to dye clothes. I dyed clothes every day in my bathtub. That's where I got the phone call. I ran to Cabrini Medical Center. It was a madhouse. Everybody was there . . . Viva, Ultra Violet . . . everybody was praying. There was this little chapel. Andy never let me up to see him in his hospital room because he thought I'd make him laugh and it would hurt where he'd been sewn up. Or that I might steal pills from the nurses' station. So I'd sit across the street at a friend's house—a cashier from Max's Kansas City—and just write him these long letters about how boring it was without him.

I was the first person he let photograph his scars after he got out. We went back to his little room at the Factory and he took off his shirt and I took off my top so he wouldn't be embarrassed. There I was, top-less, photographing Andy's chest full of scars. I was selling photographs of the scars because I was having my own shows then. But when all the scars were sold, I had to go back to Andy and tell him, "Look, I have to have twenty more pictures. You have to come back in the little room with me. They're selling like hotcakes. A hundred dollars apiece." He was really funny about that. He kept letting me do it. I never knew why. He wouldn't let anybody else.

KS: Did Andy become a different sort of person after the assassination attempt?

BB: No. I think the rest of us changed and became more cautious. We started having some security at the Factory. There were so many cra-zies around. They were just nuts.

KS: Did you ever see Andy without his wig?

BB: No. But when the Factory moved over to 860 Broadway the wig-maker used to make deliveries. He once had a store on 42nd Street but had gone out of business. He was still making Andy's wigs out at his home in Queens somewhere. His name was Mr. Bocchicchio. He'd deliver them in these great big green boxes. Andy would always come out with his check and take the boxes. Once he left one of the boxes in an office and I opened it up. I have pictures of me holding up one of those wigs. I always said if I did a book I'd have that picture on the cover and call it *The Lid Is Off*.

KS: Was Andy like a parent to you? A husband? A brother? A lesbian lover?

BB: I've always been a part of the Factory, but Andy and I also had a twenty-year telephone relationship. I mean, I got bored with going out with him all the time. But we'd have three-hour phone conversations. We'd tape each other. And that would confuse me—whose tape was the original? I always thought that it was sort of like a work of art—that there were two originals. I still have all those tapes. Fourteen hundred hours' worth. They cover 1968 through 1976. After I stopped taking speed and straightened myself out, I never thought of making another tape recording.

KS: Let's talk about the third Factory—the one at 860 Broadway.

BB: Well, we still needed more space. Andy had really become a pack-rat with his collecting and all. The first thing we did was put in a kitchen. It began to be a thing for people to stop by for lunch, although a lot of times we'd just order up box lunches from Brownies, the health food store downstairs, like we did at Union Square. Also, McDonald's was just getting to be big, and Andy would sit on the windowsill eating his hamburger. He'd sit there folding up the little tissue that the hamburger came in and save it. He just couldn't throw anything out. All of this began to go in the boxes—you know, the things we called his time capsules. At 860 Broadway this pack-rat part of Andy really got out of hand and drove me nuts. I figured out the only time I could clean the place and throw stuff out was early in the morning before he came in. But then he'd open up the garbage can, see what was in there, and pull out stuff to save—like empty coffee cans. We had so many cockroaches at 860. There was white powder everywhere because we were trying to get them under control, but we never did. One day I decided to clean out all the file drawers because the roaches had even gotten in there.

You know, just old paper clips and stuff like that. Well, Andy came in and got so angry. He started yelling at me, "I know you're an heiress, but who do you think you are, throwing perfectly good paper clips out!" He was really angry. He did have his quirks.

KS: Any others you can remember?

BB: Well, after he was shot he never opened a package. And especially he would never eat any food that was sent to him for Christmas. We would have to open the packages for him. I used to say to him, "That's a helluva thing—you won't open it because you think a bomb might explode, but you don't care if we get blown up!"

KS: How did he get along with your parents?

BB: Well, my mother never really forgave him for what he did to me in *Chelsea Girls*. She thought he was exploiting me. But in the end she began to come around. She was very sick and dying at the time Andy died. She died two weeks after he did. That was a rough month. About six or seven months before they both died I was coming out of the dentist's one morning at Fifty-seventh and Madison and ran into Andy. He asked me, "What are you doing up here? Why aren't you at the Factory working?" So I told him I'd just been to the dentist. Then he changed his tune and started showing concern for me. "It's such a pretty day," he said. "Why don't we go for a walk and buy your mother a present?" We walked across 57th and went into Chanel and he bought her a beautiful pair of earrings. You know, I buried her in those earrings. It's funny—since my mother's death I have not been able to picture her alone. But I don't picture her with my father. I always picture Andy and Mother sitting up there—I guess I do believe in heaven or something—looking down at me and gossiping. "See, she's fat," he'll say to her. Or she'll say, "See, she's bad. She's misbehaving. She's into a candy box today."

KS: You and Andy used to binge on chocolate together, didn't you. You both told me that once. And once you even let me binge with you. I felt so special—bingeing with Brigid and Andy.

BB: But Andy would spit it out. He'd chew and chew and chew—and then he'd spit it into a paper towel. A lot of times he'd give me a hundred dollars and say, "Go get the good stuff." That would mean, if we were here at this Factory on 33rd Street, to go over to B. Altman's candy department and get the best.

KS: Who first came up with the name "the Factory"?

BB: I never really thought that much about it. It was probably Billy Name. So much of it is a blur. It was like one big party.

KS: Was each Factory very different from the preceding one?

BB: Yes. But I think a lot of it had to do with maturity. Everything has evolved, of course, from that very beginning on 47th Street to where we are now on East Thirty-third. It has become more of a business over the years—but there still is that sense of family. I still think of it that way, except Andy isn't here. There's been a death in the family.

KS: Which was your favorite Factory?

BB: I grew to love all of them for different reasons. I mean, it would be a nightmare to go back to 47th Street now. I wouldn't dream of going back to Union Square. I just can't conceive of going back. It's the new generation of kids that is interested in the sixties. Come on, get with it! We're practically in the nineties now. I can't dwell on the sixties. I mean, I know I've been around longer than anybody who's left at the Factory. But I just don't have that kind of feeling about myself. It's been almost twenty-five years. But do you think I really know what's going on today? Nooooo. I've never been to M.K. Don't want to. I never even saw the Palladium. My stint ended with Studio 54. I just got sick and tired of being sick and tired.

KS: Did you always have a job at the Factory or did you just hang out?

BB: The job part sort of started at 860 Broadway. I never went every day to Union Square. I got involved when *Interview* started up. But I think *Interview* might have begun upstairs at Union Square originally. You know, Andy always said he started *Interview* for me. Because of Daddy. He wanted to have his own Hearst empire.

KS: Why do you think Andy always had to have people around him at the Factories?

BB: Because that was part of his art. He had to be stimulated by other people. He used to walk through here every day going, "What am I going to do, Brigid? I need some ideas. I can't think of any art to do. Everybody else is doing such great things. I'm doing awful stuff." And I'd say, "You gotta pay me for my ideas, Andy." Then it would be, "Brig, when is your mother going to have her portrait done by me?" And I'd say, "Andy, my mother would never have her portrait done by you. I don't want a portrait by you. I can't stand them. I wouldn't have one of your portraits hanging on my wall if you paid me a million dollars!" Maybe that's why we were so close, because I used to tell him the truth. I never liked his art! He used to offer his art to me for Christmas, and I told him I'd rather he get me a washing machine and dryer. And he did! Wasn't I a fool?

KS: Forget about the material things. What sort of emotional sustenance did Andy's friendship give you over the years?

BB: He just understood. If I was drinking and doing speed, he understood. If I was going to my A.A. meetings, as I do now, he understood. You know, he always wanted to write a book on me. All that taping he did of me all those years was the research he was doing for my life story. So, in a way, I'm really doing my book now for him. I don't know. What can you call something that you really, really love, that you have near you every single solitary day, but that you're not even aware of? Some people can be your best friends and you don't see them all the time, but I saw Andy practically every day for over twenty years. It's ironic—it's hard to describe because in reality there was no mystery in it. It was all so comfortable. If I didn't still come to the Factory every day I'd probably feel very lonely. I was just thinking this morning when I got to the Factory—I get here pretty early—how Andy used to call me around 8:30 A.M. knowing I was usually alone in the place. Sometimes I really do miss him. He'd call up—especially at 860 Broadway—and say, "Gee, Brig, what's new? Who's called?" And I'd say, "Nobody's called, Andy." And he'd say again, "What's new?" I'd say, "Nothing's new." "What's new?" "Nothing's new." "What's new?" "Nothing."

From *The Andy Warhol Diaries*
Entry dated Sunday, November 30, 1986

Stuart had a car and we went to Christie's and Stuart had to hide so they wouldn't see him—he still hasn't paid for the flute. They call him every day. Stuart regrets buying it because, I mean, what would he get for it if he tried to sell it?

And then we went over to the piers to the Antiques and Collectibles Exposition (ticket $15). And it's just the same stuff everywhere. Small and the same, no character. Nothing dramatic. That Modernism Show at the Armory last week was great though. But the guy wanted $5,000 for a World's Fair service for 8 or 12! I couldn't believe it. I was asking if I could buy the big spoons because I have a big service and I wore the big spoons out and he told me the price and I said maybe I could sell him my set.

Then we went down to the flea market. And we ran into one of the *Interview* editors, the new one, Kevin Sessums. He was alone.

SEVEN

The Dogged

I felt alone even in that year before both my parents died. "Leave him alone," was the admonition I most remember my mother saying over and over back in 1962 when she'd warn my father he was being too stern with me when I was doing my sissy best to please him and falling short. Appearing at a loss as he looked sadly back into her concerned eyes, he'd do just that. Relieved, I'd resort to my sissy ways and play with my little sister's first doll or dance about the house as the radio on the kitchen windowsill played Dee Dee Sharp's "Mashed Potato Time" or "The Stripper" conducted by David Rose or Little Eva's "The Loco-Motion" or Bobby Vinton's "Roses Are Red," the lyrics of which I'd sing along with my mother while she washed the dishes. When Chubby Checker's "The Twist" came on she'd stop her scrubbing and grab my hands in her warm, sudsy ones as we'd twist together on the linoleum floor, her blond hair bouncing to the beat. My father once found us like that and cut in. I pouted, thinking he was going to replace me as her dance partner, but instead he too grabbed my hands and twisted with me. My heart raced as I climbed atop his big coach's feet with my own little feet and rode them as he slid twisting on the linoleum floor toward my mother, whose hands were back in the dishwater. He growled like a dog and kissed her on her neck. He'd been telling her we were going to get a couple of dogs for weeks and took every opportunity to growl like one to remind her of it, since she didn't want to have to deal with two pets in addition to three young children. She giggled at his growling kiss and shooed him away with a handful of suds, some of the soft white bubbles falling atop my head like the snowflakes I still had yet to see in my Mississippi childhood. My father then dipped his own hands into the mounds of suds in the sink and surprised me by piling them on my head. I secretly imagined them looking like Shelley Fabares's pageboy hairdo as I began to lip-synch, hands on my hips, to her suddenly singing her 1962 hit "Johnny Angel," which came on after "The Twist" ended there on the window's radio. My father went to swipe the suds from my head in an effort to stop my impromptu performance, but I ducked without missing a faked syllable of Shelley's angelic voice I imagined coming from my mouth. My mother cut my father one of her concerned glares. "Leave him alone," she warned.

My favorite place to be alone was my parents' shared closet in that little house in Clinton, Mississippi. I'd sneak into the back of their closet and curl up amidst their shoes, my feet placed in a pair of my mother's high heels, my father's big Sunday brogues used as a pillow, the smell of his brushed-on cordovan shoe polish mixing with the remnants of my mother's perfume that clung to her dresses above me that I'd reach for, barely able to touch their hems with my six-year-old arms as I caused them to flutter in the breeze of my own making, a leafless landscape of longing. I loved lying there hidden in their combined smells and listening to their voices in their bedroom when they had no idea I was in there. Sometimes they'd make voiceless sounds atop their bed I could not decipher, but I knew I dare not move when such sounds were being made.

I was there in the closet when I heard their final discussion about my father wanting to buy those dogs he kept mentioning. He did not pitch it as wanting the family to have pets to play with but as a way of making some much-needed extra money for the family's expenses. He wanted to buy two Chihuahuas—a male and a female—and breed them in order to sell their puppies, another of his harebrained schemes, as my mother called it, and, as literal as I was little, I wondered if my brain too had hair on it like his, trying as hard as I could to find any way in which I could resemble him and please him more.

"Don't get smart with me, Nan," my father cautioned her in that surly coach's voice I'd often hear him use at basketball practice when, tagging along, I watched him get angry when his scrawny high school team wasn't scrimmaging well enough. "I'm gonna do this," he said. "It's a good investment. We need the extra money. I've thought this through. I know you don't want the extra work around here, so I've decided not to go all in with hunting dogs or hounds or anything of that size. I thought these little dogs would be the easiest for you to have around. I'm taking you into consideration in this. I am."

"Can't you go back to selling encyclopedias on the side?" she asked. "That sounds a lot more respectable than selling silly little dogs."

"Nan . . ."

"Go ahead. Do what you want. You always do," she said, sighing extravagantly in that way she had when she knew she'd lost yet another argument with my father, that lowest note her throat could make, no letters needed to make sense of it. It was close to the kind of sighs that could erupt from her more slowly, one right after the other, then rapidly in succession, when she and my father were making those other indecipherable noises atop their bed. Those sighs of hers, however, would ring out more triumphantly. They were more loosely formed—livelier— than her one dull, low sigh of defeat.

"But they can't live in my house. No way," my mother said. "No dogs in this house no matter what size they are. I'm putting my foot down about that. I'm not going to clean up after them. They have to stay out in the yard. No house pets. I have enough work to do around here. And they are all your responsibility. Yours, not mine."

One of my mother's dresses suddenly fell on top of me when I grabbed its hem instead of fluttering it in my excitement at the thought of our family having two small dogs, the dress's hanger clanging to the floor by my side.

"What in the world was that?" asked my mother.

My father opened the closet door. "Kevin?" he called my name, peering in to see the dress having fallen atop me and my feet still inside a pair of my mother's high heels. "This does it. Out!" he shouted. "Out of there! Right now! Out!"

"Howard!" said my mother. "Howard! Please! No, now. Leave him alone!"

"Not this time. See what leaving him alone does? He's in there trying on your clothes. Goddamn it. Get out here, boy."

I removed my feet from my mother's high heels and on my tiptoes tried to hang her dress back up. "Leave it!" my father yelled, and grabbed me by my shoulders and jerked me into the light of their bedroom. He grabbed the dress from me and threw it at my mother. I still had the smell of his cordovan brogues in my nostrils, which mixed with the stronger smell of liniment that lingered on him from his time in the locker room that morning. "What were you doing in there?" he wanted to know.

"Being alone," I said, telling him the truth.

"Oh, Kevin . . . ," said my mother.

"Don't 'oh, Kevin' him," said my father. "You pamper him enough as it is." He turned his attention back to me. I watched his anger redden his face, the ridges of each of his high, handsome cheekbones stubbled with a day's growth of his dark beard, which, when he was not angered by my presence, I'd dare to touch and run my fingers along the way I'd seen my mother absentmindedly do when they watched television together curled up entwined on the sofa, the feel of his stubble like the splinters on the wood outside he'd already bought and secretly hidden in the garage for the doghouse he planned to build if my mother gave her final approval. I'd found him stacking the wood behind an old tattered tarp the week before when he had told me not to tell my mother what he was up to. I had helped him lift a board out of the trunk of his car and cried out when a splinter of it lodged into my thumb. He hadn't even gone into the house to get the pair of tweezers my mother used to groom her eyebrows, the same pair she always used to pluck the stray splinters in the past that had lodged themselves into my fingers or feet. She was the splinter remover in our family, not my father. He looked stumped by my cries. The large splinter taunted us both where it stuck out of my little thumb. My father quickly stuck my throbbing thumb into his mouth and, in so doing, shocked me, despite the pain, into silence. The splinter was a big one and had not lodged too deeply, so he was able to dig it out with his teeth before licking my wound with his tongue—like a dog would lick me if we got one, I thought when I looked at where the splinter had been and where my father's spittle now soothed its sting. "Don't you dare tell your mama about this pile of wood yet," he made me promise, then wiped my tears away. "We're going to build a doghouse with it if she lets us. If not, then I'll be in the doghouse myself," he said—which my literal little mind was trying to picture, my tall, lanky father folded up to fit inside such a tiny structure.

I wished I had had a splinter for him to bite out of me in that moment he angrily pulled me from the closet. I wished there was something else he could tell me to keep a secret instead of being appalled by mine. "I've a good mind to whip you good, boy," he told me. "Walk back in that closet and get my big black belt."

"Howard. Don't. Please. Leave him alone," begged my mother.

"Damn it, Nan. You're the one who needs to leave us alone now. I'm gonna do this. Sometimes a son needs a daddy who'll whip him instead of a mama who won't."

Already crying, I handed my father his belt. "Touch your toes," he told me. I bent over and did as he said. My mother threw her dress on the closet floor and stormed off toward the kitchen. She turned on the radio as loud as it would go so she wouldn't hear my cries coming from the bedroom. The sound of "Green Onions" by Booker T. and the M.G.s filled the house. I continued to cry and imagined my mother dancing on the linoleum floor, so lucky to be the one all alone now. I stuck my thumb into my own mouth and longed to touch my father's stubbled cheek that felt like splinters. I raised my butt higher in the air in both surrender and defiance. I thought about the Chihuahuas coming our way.

After my father built the doghouse—but before the Chihuahuas arrived—it replaced my parents' closet as the place into which I loved to crawl and be alone. I had helped my father unroll the chicken wire he used to build a fence around the little house, as well as the latched gate. He had put an old pair of sweatpants of his inside for their bed and decided it would be best to make the doghouse three sided, leaving one side completely open, giving him easier access to the dogs if they, like I so often did, refused to come to him.

I was lying atop the sweatpants inside the enclosure when he finally brought the two dogs home. My little brother and sister were playing in the yard and came running to see them. Our father, holding a tiny dog in each arm, knelt in front of us all and introduced them to us. I had never seen him be so gentle in all the six years I had known him—not even when he held my almost-two-year-old little sister in those same sinewy arms of his and sweetly sang her songs that came on my mother's kitchen radio.

"This little brown one here with the snub nose is Chico," he told us. My little sister too quickly went to touch the brown creature and he snapped at her. She jumped back with alarm. My four-year-old little brother laughed at her. I stayed put, curled up on the sweatpants, taking it all in.

"Careful, now, Karole," my father told my sister. "Chihuahuas are nervous little dogs. You have to treat them with tenderness. Do you know what 'tenderness' means? It means you just touch them with one little finger maybe," he told her. He placed Chico, shivering from fright, on the sweatpants next to me. I wanted to show Chico I knew how he felt, so often had I shivered from fright myself in my father's presence. My father then took one of my sister's little fingers and petted Chico with it before reaching out to pet me on top of my head with his hand, the full force of all his fingers mussing my hair, as if I really were a dog lying there. "Kevinator, are you gonna help me take care of these critters?" he asked. "You're the oldest. You're gonna have to help me out here, boy."

I sat up, excited to be included in this endeavor of my father's and with one finger, as he had just instructed my little sister, I reached out to pet the tiny dog my father still held close to his chest. "This little black one here with the sharper face is Coco. Coco and Chico, this is Kevin, Kim, and Karole," he said, introducing his two new dogs to his three children.

"Well, they are cute," said my mother, who had come out of the house to take a look at them. She picked up Karole to take her back in the house and change her diaper. "I'll tend to this one. You teach the boys there how to pick up the mess these dogs are gonna be making in our yard. Dogs don't wear diapers the last time I checked," she said.

Kim didn't stay, though, and followed after my mother and sister. My father and I, watching them all disappear into the house, were left with our two new dogs. That is the way I began to think of them: Chico and Coco belonged to my father and me. They were ours. It would be the four of us against the three of them who had just walked away from us.

In the coming months I took it upon myself to feed the dogs each morning before first grade and hang out with them inside their pen every chance I'd get. Being alone with Chico and Coco was the newest way I'd found to be alone myself. I could now be alone, I was happy to discover, without really being alone. My father was amazed at how well I bonded with the two dogs and they with me. Often they would ignore him when I was around. I'd spend warm autumn afternoons after school curled up with them on those increasingly dirty sweatpants inside their makeshift doghouse. I was the one who took torn newspaper pages from *The Clarion-Ledger* or *Jackson Daily News*—never from the sports pages after my father had yelled at me once for tearing those out before he'd had the chance to read them—and picked up the dog droppings in the pen so they wouldn't smell up the yard. Chico, I discovered, liked to be petted on his back haunches and Coco under her chin. Chico liked the little red ball my father brought home one day for them both to play with, but Coco liked the rubber bone I'd helped him pick out as a toy for them. He even brought home a flattened basketball one day from the gym to enhance their bed, and Coco loved to curl up inside its concave center as I, pretending I was the kitchen radio, sang her to sleep with my own rendition of Ray Charles's "Hit the Road Jack," though she seemed to prefer Dion's "Runaround Sue."

As the weather got colder my father asked my mother if we could move Chico and Coco into the house, but she stood her ground and suggested putting an electric heater in the garage and moving the sweat-pants and concave basketball in there next to the car. My parents fought about such a plan and for the first time I took my father's side against my mother. She looked at me as if I were a traitor after all the times she had told my father to leave me alone in an attempt to protect me from his anger. I think the reason she had such trouble dealing with the presence of Chico and Coco in those first months they became a part of our family is that she saw how my love for them had slowly begun to switch my allegiance from her as my preferred parent to my father. She couldn't fathom it. But it wasn't something I fathomed. It was just something I felt. I had more love for those dainty dogs during their first months with us than I did for any family member. Maybe my empathy for them was the result of their physical exile just outside the boundaries of the house, for it corresponded so with the emotional exile I, a dainty creature as well, felt just outside the bonds of the family itself. I thought of myself in many ways as no longer a son or a brother but a third Chihuahua, cherished but apart. I knew I was Chico's protector. I was Coco's. And I knew by protecting them I felt protected for the first time myself.

When I was about to turn fifty years old I was once more alone and in need of protection. I was stumped as to what to give myself as a fiftieth birthday present. I had already lived in Paris for a time in my forties, so a trip to Europe seemed redundant at that point. I already had too many clothes. Too many pairs of shoes. My shelves were shrugging with books. I didn't have a driver's license, so even the extravagance of buying a sports car, which often men of fifty consider doing to make themselves feel younger, was not only too impulsive and expensive but also impractical. Perhaps I should just ignore the damn day, I thought.

Yet the day, damn it, was not ignoring me.

It loomed.

Abjectly lonely, I would walk around my Chelsea neighborhood in New York City and realize I was no longer being checked out by men of any age. I hadn't had a date in years and the only sex I was having was fueled by different forms of drugs and the fleeting hours-long flings one sets up when on such drugs while dredging up the semblance of company from Internet sites. I finally had to face this as my birthday approached: A fifty-year-old man finding sex online just wasn't dignified, dignity the one characteristic, if one wasn't indentured by it, which most endures.

All of these thoughts were on my mind in the month leading up to my milestone birthday when I happened by a pet store on 19th and Ninth and looked in the window. There inside was a dappled puppy that seemed to be delighted I had turned to look his way. A Chihuahua? I couldn't really tell. He had spots—brown ones atop his tiny white body—like my steer skin rug back on the floor of my studio on 21st Street. I stood looking at him and for the first time longed for Coco and Chico and how they could make me feel when I'd curl up with them—not less alone exactly, but alone together.

I went inside the pet store and stared down into the glass box in which the puppy was contained with a few other assorted pups—a piebald dachshund, a Yorkie, another Chihuahua or two. The spotted puppy tried to climb the glass walls up to me but to his frustration kept sliding back down onto the floor of his glass encasement that had shredded bits of newspaper on the bottom of it to cushion his fall.

"Can I help you?" asked the plump, willfully pleasant Asian woman emerging from the rear of the store. She had flung back a makeshift curtain to reveal the sheepdog she'd been grooming back there, its coat in the midst of being clipped by her, a clump of fur lying matted, motionless, on the floor like an indolent rodent.

"May I pick this little spotted puppy up?" I asked.

She nodded and flicked her clippers back on. Walking back behind the curtain, she flung it closed. The sheepdog barked. "Shut up!" I heard her voice too clearly tell it over the hum of the clippers. "Hold still."

"Hey there, Archie," I said to the puppy as I picked him up and he excitedly began to lick my face. Archie? Why had I instantly called the puppy that? The only Archie I could think of in that moment—other than the puppy itself—was Archie Manning, the quarterback from Ole Miss who went on to play for the New Orleans Saints, the favorite two football teams of my Mississippi youth. There was also the comic book Archie, but I had never read a comic book in my life. "Oh, Archie," I told the little dog. "Stop licking. Stop now." I lowered him to my chest and let him nuzzle me a bit like that before I put him back in his glass encasement with the other puppies. The Asian woman, her clippers still buzzing in her hand, came back out to the front of the store. She motioned toward the glass encasement with them. "You want him? He's fifteen hundred dollars. You can have him for thirteen hundred dollars. I can give you papers. He's a Chihuahua. I get 'em from a Mexican women in Michigan."

"Maybe," I said, and made my way toward the front door.

"That's the cutest one. You got good taste," she said, blowing at the vibrating clippers and sending bits of sheepdog fur flying toward me. "He may not be here if you come back. Many of the men just like you around here like that one," she said.

I smiled at her but left to walk home without purchasing a companion, it feeling in the moment too much like the times in the past when I'd purchased a human one.

Many of the men just like me?

Archie?

I continued to walk home. I began to plan which Internet sex sites I'd sign on to when I got there.

During the next couple of weeks running up to my birthday, I stopped by that pet store more and more to see the puppy I had for some reason instinctively called Archie. I stopped by so often he had even begun to respond when I called him that. "You have to buy him now. He knows he's Archie," said the Asian lady each time I'd go inside. "Just look at the way he looks at you. That's love."

That first moment I held Archie I felt a kind of emotional click I had not felt since the moment my father tentatively placed Chico by my side and I suddenly, at six years old, sensed that something had fallen into place. For six long years of my Mississippi childhood I had not felt comfortable in the world, yet that shivering little presence against my body there on my father's sweatpants conversely calmed me, gave me comfort, as I attempted to calm and to comfort him. As I trained Coco and Chico during my childhood, I trained myself. Together we all learned to traverse a world that could be treacherous for creatures like us who found ourselves in places we did not expect to be. I found a home by making one for Chico and for Coco. It was the first time I felt concerned for something other than my six-year-old self. With Chico and Coco by my side I felt more comfortable in the world. Their presence became my home.

The world had certainly grown more treacherous for me to traverse in my late forties as I got further and further away from the innocent comfort of that six-year-old I had been back in Mississippi. That was the click I felt when I picked up Archie: That six-year-old's innocence was awakened inside me that had not been completely curdled by an adulthood of glamour that had become methodical, a thudding presence, no longer thrilling but something that was simply there like weather—not even the threat of it but the dullness of endless cloudless days. I waited until the official date of my birthday, March 28, and strode back to 19th and Ninth to purchase the gift I had decided to buy for myself if Archie was still there. He was. I pulled out my credit card and took a breath when I signed my name under the little over fourteen hundred dollars he ended up costing me when the tax and food and new carrying case and a toy or two were added in. The next few weeks were taken up with toilet training as well as talking to him about everything in my life. That first night, I allowed him to sleep with me, and whenever we're together he has slept with me every night since. From that first night he curled up next to me I have never been in need of another sleeping pill. Archie ushers in my dreams.

———

A few months after Archie entered my life we were taking a walk when we ran into an old colleague of mine from *Interview* magazine. "You always loved feeding Brigid's pugs Fame and Fortune and hanging out with them," he said to me. "I always wondered when you'd get a dog of your own. What's this one's name?" he asked, bending down to give Archie a scratch behind his pointy ears.

"Archie," I said.

My friend straightened up and looked a little shocked but pleased. "No. Really?"

"Why are you looking so surprised?" I asked.

"Did you name him after Andy Warhol's Archie?"

"Andy had a dog named Archie?" I asked. Had I known that and just forgotten it? Then it dawned on me. Andy did once tell me how much he missed someone named Archie when he saw me feeding Fame and Fortune one morning, but I let it pass, thinking maybe it was an old boyfriend. When I asked Brigid about this person named Archie, Brigid laughed at my lack of knowledge about Factory lore and told me Archie was instead a dachshund. She told me how much Andy had loved him and how inseparable they had been. "God. Yes. Now I'm remembering. How could I have blocked that out?" I asked my old colleague. "I didn't consciously name him for Andy's dog, no, but maybe Andy's ghost was inspiring me. I called him that the first time I ever held him."

"Yeah, Jed Johnson, Andy's boyfriend back around 1973, suggested that they get a dog and Andy let Jed pick one out," my friend told me. "Jed chose a short-haired dark brown dachshund. Andy named him Archie. Took that damn dog everywhere. He was always in the studio with him or, when Jed couldn't go with him, he'd take Archie as his date to art openings. He'd even take him to restaurants and put him in his lap hidden under his napkin and feed him bits of food from his plate. Archie became a kind of alter ego for Andy and when he'd give press conferences—which he hated anyway—he'd take Archie along. When he didn't want to answer a question he'd direct it to Archie, who also refused to answer, though Archie would look back at the journalist with an expression at least a bit less blank than Andy's. Archie was finally a bit friendlier than Andy too. More outgoing. Jamie Wyeth even did a portrait of Andy and Archie. They were becoming more of a couple than Andy and Jed at one point. I think Jed was getting kind of jealous of Archie. So he suggested they get another dachshund. That's when they got Archie a playmate named Amos, but he wasn't as much of a socialite as Archie was. When Amos came into the fold, he and Archie stayed home a lot more and played with each other at Andy's town house. Archie and Amos were the forerunners to Fame and Fortune at the Factory."

Archie stood on the sidewalk and listened as intently as I did to the story. He wagged his tail each time my friend said the name "Archie" and put his paws on the calves of his legs. I said good-bye to my friend and walked Archie home, saying a silent thank-you to Andy Warhol for guiding me to 19th and Ninth that first day I ever picked up my own Archie and held him to me.

I put my own Amos into my own Archie's life about five years after that fiftieth birthday of mine. I had ducked in one rainy Thursday afternoon to take a tour of the replicated childhood home of Teddy Roosevelt on East 20th Street before stopping in a pet store on Eighth Avenue to buy Archie some food. When I entered the store I encountered a harried old Hispanic lady trying to quiet the stray dogs she had brought in to try to convince the store's customers to adopt or foster. Her presence there seemed to be a public relations ploy by the store's owners to quell any protests that they might encounter about being suspected of acquiring the array of for-sale puppies displayed in the back from puppy mills. All the little old lady's straggly dogs were yelping and barking in their stacked cages—about five or six of them—except for a tiny brown one that she held in her lap. I stopped to give him a little pet on his silent, shivering head. He looked up forlornly at me, his fur filthy and his body in need of nourishment. When our eyes met I knew I was in trouble. Not since Archie had first looked at me five years before had I felt such instant rapport. The woman sensed too that I was a goner. "I just got him this morning," she said. "Everybody in this neighborhood knows I come here on Thursdays even before the store opens so I can set up with my babies. Around six o'clock—when that rainstorm was really bad; I got caught in it myself—I heard a knock on the front door and a woman who was out in it walking her dog was waving at me. She was holding this precious little thing and trying to get my attention. I opened the door and she told me her dog—it was some kind of big Labrador mix—had gone chasing after this one. Told me he had almost broken his leash when he went after it. At first she thought it was a rat, but then she realized it was a little pooch—so skinny and scared and drenched to his bones. See how his bones show. Sticking out so. Poor little thing. He's starving. I've been trying to get some food in him. You want to hold him? Hold him. Go on. I give him to you."

"I'm not sure . . . ," I said, hesitating.

"Oh, go ahead," she said, handing him over to me to calm his shivering. I took him and whispered in his quivering ear, "It's gonna be all right. You're all right. You were saved this morning. You're safe."

"See? He likes you back. I already give him a name," the little old lady said. "I don't know why. I usually let people who save my babies give them names. But this one just looked like a Teddy to me. He's Teddy. It's like he told me so. Teddy."

I've always lived my life by signs and omens. Having just left Teddy Roosevelt's childhood home, where he had been a sickly creature himself, I knew I was about to play out a kind of narrative for myself. But first Archie would have to approve. After buying the dog food I had come for, I went home and walked Archie back to the store to meet Teddy. I was nervous he would not get along with Teddy, since Archie is fine with older dogs, but puppies make him peevish. To my surprise, he remained calm around Teddy and even took a few sniffs and licks at him. Archie didn't bark or growl or snip at him, so I took that as a good sign as well. "See. Already brothers," said the little old lady.

"I'm still not certain," I told her. "I did not wake up this morning thinking about adopting another dog. It's a lot of responsibility. I tell you what, I can't take Teddy just yet. I have things I have to do the next couple of days. Will you be here on Sunday?"

"No. I do this same thing at a different pet store on Broadway just above Houston Street," she said, giving me the store's name and exact address.

"Okay. I'll make a deal with you," I offered. "If you still have Teddy on Sunday, I'll foster him for a week and we'll see how it goes. This is Archie's decision more than mine."

"Okay. Fine. I see you Sunday."

Holding Teddy, I gave him one more little nuzzle before putting him down. He instantly peed on the store's floor. "He's been doing that. Poor thing's nervous, that's all," said the woman. "It's okay."

As we walked out, Archie looked back over his shoulder at the puddle Teddy had just left there and then up at me. Are you sure you want to put up with this? he seemed to be thinking.

The little old lady still had Teddy when I went down to the pet store on Broadway, so I brought him home to foster him for the week as I had promised. Archie didn't seem upset by the visitor, nor did he treat Teddy like an intruder. He neither barked nor growled. He never even gave Teddy a sniff. Archie just turned his perfect pink nose up in the air and ignored him—that is, until we went to bed that night and Teddy jumped up on the bed to sleep with us. Archie would not allow that. He was ready to attack Teddy for the first time, for Archie had been sleeping curled up next to me for five years and no interloper was going to take his place. Remembering the bed that Chico and Coco had first had, which was fashioned from a pair of my father's old sweatpants, I dug around in my closet and found an old pair of my own and put them on the floor next to the bed. Teddy curled up on them and slept through the night.

For the next couple of days Archie was fine with the company but continued to ignore him. I, however, was growing quite fond of the little dog who could not have been more different from Archie. Archie, who had been raised by me talking to him incessantly, had, I was convinced, developed an understanding of what I was telling him a lot of the time. I'd simply tell him what to do or mention something and he seemed instinctively to understand. At times, he even made sounds of frustration—not growls or barks—that seemed to be efforts to talk back to me. Teddy was an animal that had obviously been forced to survive by his instincts. He was stubborn but thankful to be in our household. Archie still wasn't allowing Teddy on the bed.

By Wednesday I had decided that I wanted him to be a part of our family, but I knew it was not my decision alone. "Okay, Arch," I said. "This is our decision to make. Not just mine. It's your world that I'm rocking with the addition of Teddy in it. His life hasn't been as nice as yours. We're going to have to have some patience with him at first. I would really like to adopt him, though. What do you say? I'm going to leave you alone with him for ninety minutes and then I'm going to come back home and you have to give me some kind of sign that it's okay with you that he be a part of our family. Okay?"

Archie cocked his head at me in the manner he cocked it when I knew he was listening and understood. I left them alone.

After ninety minutes I walked back into my apartment and, for the first time, found Teddy lying right in the middle of the bed and Archie lying on the floor at the foot of it. Archie looked up at me and almost seemed to shrug. If you want the little guy then it's all right with me, he seemed to be letting me know with his allowing Teddy up on the bed.

That night for the first time we all three slept together. Archie and Teddy curled up next to me and I spooned with them, an arm draped around each and holding a paw from each in my hand. Teddy even began to snore a bit. Archie snuck a look back at me. I thought of the first time I ever saw snow.

That winter Chico and Coco joined our family I fretted about their shivering out in their three-sided doghouse. As the winter settled in further, I also had nightmares about their freezing to death in the garage where my mother suggested they take up refuge as the temperature dropped.

As February rolled around, the forecast for the first time in my childhood predicted we'd have a snowstorm in Mississippi. My brother and sister became little lookouts at the living room window watching the sky for any sign of a snowflake. My mother stocked the pantry with cans of soup and extra loaves of bread and jars of peanut butter and jelly. My father brought home some long pairs of newly laundered athletic socks from the gym for us to use as scarves about our little necks, our mother shaking her head at his ingenuity but thankful too she'd not have to go into her grocery budget to buy us any extra clothing for the frigid weather that had already descended so oddly upon us.

I was the only one who didn't seem to be excited by the prospect of such unusual weather in our midst or the expectation of making our first family snowman or falling down on the newly whitened lawn to make something my mother called snow angels, pointing to a picture in her *Redbook* magazine that month of a mother and a child making them in the snow in some faraway enchanted place called Cape Cod when she was trying to take my mind off Chico and Coco outside. But I would not let up about them. I kept begging her to allow me to bring them inside so they wouldn't freeze to death outside. Finally, I began to cry uncontrollably when none of my arguments was working with her.

My father came to my rescue and picked me up. "What have you done to him?" he wanted to know. "Leave him alone," he told her.

"Oh, don't start with me," she said. "You two. You're ganging up on me. I know what you're doing."

"It's starting!" came my little brother's voice in the other room. "The snow! We see snow! Look! Mommy! Daddy! Look!"

My father put me down and I, drying my eyes, followed my mother and father to the window where my brother and sister were standing. We all stood there amazed as we watched the stormy swirl of flakes fall onto the frozen ground. I left them standing there in their amazement and, wrapping a long athletic sock around my neck, walked out in the storm to check on Chico and Coco in the garage. My father followed me. "They're going to be fine, Kevinator," he said, bending down to tighten the sock around my neck. "You can't stay out here without a coat on, though."

"They don't have coats," I told him.

"They have built-in coats. Their fur will keep them warm."

"But they're shaking, Daddy," I said, shaking now myself.

My mother joined us in the garage. Outside Kim and Karole were running around with their faces turned toward the falling snow and trying to catch it in their mouths. "Mama, please," I pleaded. "Can't we put them in the kitchen for just tonight until the snowstorm is over?"

"Nan . . . ," said my father.

"Oh, okay. You two win. But just this one night. And then we'll talk about it again tomorrow. Only in the kitchen, though. There's a box under the sink. Get that and put those nasty sweatpants in it and put them in that."

I picked up Chico, and my father, winking at me, took Coco. He put his other arm around my mother and gave her a kiss. She shrugged it off and scurried out into the yard to play in the snow with Kim and Karole. Once my father and I placed the dogs down into the box in the kitchen I ran back out into the garage to get the sweatpants and brought them back inside to cushion the bottom of the box. My father put a bowl of food and a bowl of water down inside it.

"Kevin!" my mother called. "Come play!"

I ignored her call and stayed inside the kitchen. I looked up past the silent radio on the windowsill and saw the snow swirling about outside.

"Howard!" called my mother. "It's fun. Come outside!"

My father gave my head a pat and did as he was told.

I sat silently with Chico and Coco. Free of my family, I listened to them frolic in the snow outside, merry, muffled, and free of me.

That night I realized how silent snow can make the world in which it falls. No cars passed by on the street outside my bedroom window. No one walked along the sidewalk. Sound itself seemed to have come to a standstill. It was so quiet I could not sleep worrying that either Chico or Coco, if they barked to complain about their strange new surroundings in the kitchen, would break the night's eerie silence and be exiled by my mother once more out to the frigid garage. I got out of bed and tiptoed into the kitchen to check on them. Coco was asleep, but Chico, the more fragile of the two (he would come to suffer, like the young Teddy Roosevelt, from asthma), was shivering in the box. The long athletic socks my brother and sister and I had used that day as scarves were on the kitchen counter. I retrieved them and stuffed them down around Chico in the box, which awakened Coco, who began to bark. I could not quiet her, and my groggy father came into the kitchen. He looked like he was prepared to bark himself at all three of us there on the floor, but then he softened. "Come on, Kevinator, let's get back to bed."

"Can I bring Coco and Chico with me?" I asked.

"Now, Kevin . . ."

"Please, Daddy. They're so cold. I can keep them warm."

Too sleepy to argue, he picked the dogs up and told me to come along. "Sshshshsh," he warned us, and led us back to my bed and began to tuck us in. He looked down at Chico and Coco so comfortably curled up next to me. He sighed. "Oh, hell, move over," he said, surprising me by climbing into my bed himself for the very first time. He lay behind me and pulled me up close to him beneath the covers, his head next to mine on the pillow, the rough stubble of his face no longer splinterlike but something more splendid that I had yet to have a name for. He wrapped an arm over me and then over Coco and Chico. I watched my father's big hand—could it really be the same hand that I had watched so often palm a basketball back in the gym where he coached his team or grab the black belt before it spanked me or even once slap my mother in my presence?—now gently hold one of Coco's paws and one of Chico's in its palm and then carefully, oh so carefully, enclose them there.

I looked up and saw, in the doorway, my mother taking in the tableau of her husband and her child in the bed with two curled-up Chihuahuas. She wore a woolen white robe. Her blond hair was mussed but magnificently lit by the snowy light that snaked across my bedroom floor and up one of her legs, snaring her whole lovely body before further whitening her face and finally forming a kind of halo that hugged those mussy curls. She moved a hand toward her hair and I knew in that moment she was real and not the apparition she seemed to be and, indeed, would become in two years once her cancer had killed her and carved this very image into my memory for the rest of my life, my mother's ghost-like presence suddenly spun from the first light I'd ever seen reflected from a snowfall, my first sight of any angel in any doorway.

My father let go of Chico's and Coco's paws and motioned for my mother to join us, but she did not take his cue. She turned instead to go back to their bedroom. Then, lifting her hand this time to her cheek, she kept it there. She hesitated. She pivoted back our way and I saw something flutter across her face—resignation? reality? love?—along with the light that seemed again to float silently about the room until it chose that cheek of hers on which to perch. She walked into the light toward us, wafting it about once more with the sway of her hips, and found a way to come between my father and me, slipping her body like a sliver of the snowy light itself into the bed. My father then laid his arm over both of us, my mother and me, his hand lying flat against the bed. I took a paw from Chico and one from Coco and placed them again into my father's open palm. He enclosed them, this time including my own hand in his gentle clench. My back was against my mother, whose back was against my father's. I moved closer to her, then she to him. I heard my father growl and kiss her on her neck. She sighed. She touched my arm. I finally fell asleep in a world that was no longer silent.

EIGHT

The Pilgrim

There are two kinds of people who work at the Factory," Brigid Berlin told me. "There are lifers like me and then there are those who walk through it to get to somewhere else," said Brigid. "Don't be a lifer like me. You keep walking. Promise me, Kevin. Keep walking."

I took her advice and kept walking straight through my Factory days to my days at *Vanity Fair*, to my freelance days as a writer, to now my days as a memoirist. But there was a time back in 2008 and 2009 when, finding myself in a corner, I could not find a way to walk out of it. I take that back. It was not a corner in which I found myself. It was, instead, more of a dead end, an emotional one.

That was when I got a phone call from my old friend Perry Moore. I had met Perry very soon after he had moved to New York from Virginia around 1995. We were at a Toys for Tots Christmas party full of gay preppies at the Ethical Cultural Center on the Upper West Side. Introduced by a mutual friend, we hit it off instantly. He told me he wanted to be a writer or get into some form of show business. At first I had a crush on him—so many people did when they first met him—but I soon fell into a kind of an older brother/younger brother mentorship relationship with him. I'd offer him advice, agree to read some of his writing, give him a shoulder to cry on when some much-anticipated date didn't pan out. I was working on a novel at that point and one of its main characters was named Hunter. Perry was so excited when he met a man who turned out to be the love of his life who had that same exact name. He couldn't wait to introduce Hunter to me. Perry and I believed in kismet of that kind; it's one of the things we shared: the love of narrative in one's own life.

Perry worked at *The Rosie O'Donnell Show* for a few years as a researcher. When my brother and his wife and children came to New York on a family trip, it was Perry who got us tickets to a taping of her show and escorted us backstage. After leaving Rosie's show he got a great job as the executive in charge of production at Walden Media, which was founded by the archly conservative billionaire Philip Anschutz. I expressed my dismay, at first, that Perry would be working for such a man—I was afraid of his being co-opted by the man's politics and the corporate culture that had sprouted around it—but Perry convinced me that he could do good working there, that his presence, as an out, proud gay man, would be an important one in the company.

That was a turning point in our relationship. I saw he was becoming the wiser and certainly more successful one even if I would remain the older one. Moreover, Perry and I—as southern boys at our core—couldn't shake the religious faith that had been inculcated into us by our upbringing and had to find ways to incorporate it into our lives as gay New Yorkers; it is one of the deepest aspects of our abiding friendship. I always looked at Perry as nicer than I. A better person. His presence in my life became a talisman of goodness. When I looked at him I always saw that lovely kind whippersnapper of a lad—so tall, so handsome—I'd met at that Toys for Tots Christmas party. He even made *People* magazine's list of 100 Sexiest Men one year.

Perry truly found a way to incorporate his deep religious faith into his fast-lane New York life when, in his role as an executive at Walden, he sought out the rights to the series of seven C. S. Lewis Narnia books, which are full of Christian allegories. He was instrumental in getting the first three films made—*The Lion, the Witch and the Wardrobe, Prince*

Caspian, and *The Voyage of the Dawn Treader*—and served as executive producer on all three.

Yet he still had dreams of writing his own novel. I was so proud of him when he published his first one, *Hero,* about a gay teenage superhero. In fact, we were both nominated for Lambda Literary Awards in 2007—he for Best Children's/Young Adult Novel and I for Best Men's Memoir/Biography for *Mississippi Sissy.* Perry wanted us both to fly out to Los Angeles where the awards ceremony was being held that year, but I talked him out of it. I told him there was no chance that we would win and if only one of us did then the other would feel a bit left out. We did participate in a reading of that year's nominees from the East Coast at New York's LGBT Community Center, however, and Perry surprised me when, before he read from his book, he singled me out for how important I had been in his life when he first moved to the city and how much it meant to him to be a part of a reading that night with me.

We ended up both winning the Lambda Literary Awards for our books that year. When I found out the next day about our winning, I telephoned him. He hadn't heard, so I was the one giving him the news. He started to cry and then I did too. We'd come a long way together from that Toys for Tots party.

In the year since that phone call about the Lambda Awards we had rekindled that friendship and spent a lot more time with each other on the phone and hanging out at our local Starbucks on 19th Street. It was good to get his phone call that day in 2008 when I was feeling so low about my life and the work on this book. "Do you think it's a creative crisis or a spiritual one?" Perry asked me. "Sometimes I can feel as if I'm depressed, but it's more of a spiritual malaise each time. Me? I head over to Grace Church for some prayer and solitude and meditation and partake in the Eucharist," he told me.

"I'm not sure, Perry, if the Eucharist is the solution," I told him, afraid to tell him that it might be the drugs I was partaking in that were causing the problem.

"Have you ever heard of the Camino?" he asked.

"I don't think so. There was a kind of combination car and pickup truck when I was a kid called an El Camino," I told him. "It was a Chevrolet."

Perry laughed. "No, Becky Thatcher," he said, calling me the name he called me when he was in a campier mood than usual and his other nickname for me, Tom Sawyer, wouldn't suffice.

"Okay, Huck," I said. "What the hell are you talking about?"

"You don't know? I love it when I know something you don't know," he said. "It's a spiritual pilgrimage across northern Spain. Shirley Mac-Laine wrote a book about walking it. I'll get you a copy. Want to meet at Starbucks later this week at our usual time? I'll bring it to you. There's another book in Germany that's a huge hit by someone whose name I can't pronounce—something like Kierkegaard but not Kierkegaard. I can't remember off the top of my head. I thought of buying the rights to Walden since the spiritual aspect fits into our family-oriented mission here, but I think it's finally a bit too irreverent. It hasn't been translated into English or published in America yet. And there's a Paulo Coelho book about his walking it too. I do think there's a film to be made somehow about the Camino. I've been trying to figure it out. I would love to walk it myself, but with all the back trouble I've been having and this chronic fucking pain from it I could never make it. It's also called the Way of Saint James. I warn you, though—it's very Catholic."

"Well, I bought a ticket to New Orleans for a change of scenery. That's about as Catholic as I can handle right now," I told him. A snowy February had given way to a bitterly cold lion-like first week of March that was just blowing in. After all my years in New York, the memory of the quiet beauty of that first snowy Mississippi night had given way to the reality of the beige slush of New York sidewalks. I had to escape the weather, if not myself. "I can see you at Starbucks, though. Bring Shirley's book. I'll read it. Thanks. Love you," I said.

"You too," he said.

After meeting Perry at Starbucks later that week, I came home and put the Shirley MacLaine book he brought me on my bookshelf. I didn't take it with me to New Orleans as he'd suggested. The next day I boarded Archie at his favorite kennel (this was before Teddy came into our lives) and headed for New Orleans to gather myself and try to figure out the funk I was in. I'd often head Archie-less in the past down to New Orleans to write and drug and drink and fuck and either feel something perverse and new that would move me forward, or, failing that, get so high and stoned I'd deplete all feeling and start anew.

Sitting at the Meauxbar Bistro on North Rampart the Saturday of March 8, 2008, I ordered a hamburger and a vodka and read *The New York Times.* In the past, this was the initial antidote I would self-prescribe for any semblance of depression or, at least, the aching loneliness that could creep into my life and settle into my chest like the low hum of an electrical current. Not even Archie's company—or Perry's—could cure it at that point. But sometimes a deliciously grilled patty of ground sirloin and a vodka on-the-rocks could. The Old Gray Lady smudged my greasy fingers as I slowly read each of her sections and calmed my mind with thoughts of the world's woebegone state and not my own.

That Saturday evening a profile in the *Times* by reporter Mark Landler caught my eye. Finishing my hamburger and ordering one more vodka before returning to my hotel room at The Soniat House on Chartres Street, I couldn't believe what I was seeing. Yet another moment of kismet was occurring in my life. The title of the *Times* story was "A Pilgrimage Tale (Not Chaucer's) Amuses and Inspires." The story, with a dateline of Dusseldorf, Germany, concerned a German comedian to named Hape Kerkeling and his pilgrimage on the Camino. The article was all about the book that Perry had mentioned in passing only a few days before. Mr. Kerkeling, I learned, had kept a journal during his trek across Spain to palliate his own palpable loneliness but had locked the journal away once he returned home. He didn't have any plans to write a book about his experiences until he discussed his pilgrimage on a talk show. A publisher then called him with a proposal. "The Camino really begins after you've finished it," he said in the article. "Life becomes more challenging."

Could life really become more challenging than it had been the last year or so? I wondered. But when I put down the newspaper I knew in that very moment that the trip to New Orleans was just the first part of the pilgrimage I had begun. That night I began to plan for my walk across the Camino. A year later I was in Spain retracing the steps of Kerkeling and countless others who have walked the Camino over the last two thousand years. Like Kerkeling, I kept a journal of my time there. Like Kerkeling, I put my notes from my journey away until right now.

4/29/09

Before falling asleep on my flight over to Barcelona I listened to my iPod trying to find the appropriate song to play as I set out on the Camino up the Pyrenees on the first day of my pilgrimage in a couple of days. I decided on "Human" by The Killers before settling in for the few hours of sleep I got before we landed here in Spain.

Took a nap once my room was ready for me, then took a five-hour warm-up walk to the Rambla and the Old City in Barcelona. At the Rambla I heard "Human" being played—was I imagining it?—and discovered that it was accompanying a street acrobatic/dance crew. I'll take that as an omen that I am doing the right thing by being here and embarking on this trek. Bought a postcard to send to Perry and thank him for putting this idea in my head.

I can't sleep.

I am jet-lagged.

I am worried about what awaits me on this pilgrimage.

What have I done?

What am I about to do?

4/30/09

There were nice friendly people on the train, but I was late getting to Pamplona and missed the bus to Roncesvalles. Shit. The next one is at 6:00 P.M. It is now 2:45 P.M. I have to sit in the bus station until then—my idea of hell as I set out on this trek that will supposedly get me closer to heaven. This is my first lesson of letting go. I am worried, though, about getting across the Spanish border into France to St.-Jean-Pied-de-Port, an unofficial starting point for pilgrims, too late to get my "passport," which gets stamped along the way to prove one has walked the Camino. I am also just worried about finding an empty bed at a hostel. I said my first prayer—not to get there in time but to stay calm and let God get me there when I am supposed to get there. The danger is competing with myself, to make this journey as quickly as I can.

One lesson: Slow down.

Another more earthly lesson: Bus stations are the same all over the world. I am looking around the station right now and seeing some scruffy young people. They look like they might be runaways. I just looked into their dirty faces and realized my face might look just that dirty and emaciated in a month after walking the Camino. One more prayer, one more lesson: God, don't let me be running away but toward.

I am now writing in my bed in St.-Jean-Pied-de-Port.

Back at the bus station in Pamplona, a black man from Toronto sat down next to me. His name was Basel and he told me his lovely accent was a Barbadian one. He too had come to Pamplona on the 9:20 A.M. train and was about to walk the Camino as well. He too had gotten lost.

"Why are you walking the Camino?" I asked him.

"My path in life seems to be changing, so I thought I'd walk this path to see if it could point me in the right direction," he said, reflecting my own reasons.

I asked, "Are you Catholic?"

He chuckled dismissively. "Far from it," he said. "Very far, in fact. I am an ordained Methodist minister."

"I was raised a Methodist as well," I told him, remembering that first day I had gone to the Methodist church with my mother back in Mississippi.

"But this is not a religious trek we are about to undertake," he told me. "It is a spiritual one. I came to terms with being a gay man two years ago and that has made me less religious yet more spiritual." He also told me he had a seventeen-year-old daughter and a fourteen-year-old son. I didn't ask if they knew he was gay.

We rode together on the bus to Roncesvalles and then in the taxi/van that was waiting for us pilgrims to take us across the border into France. That's the first time I've referred to myself as that—a pilgrim.

We were in the last taxi to arrive tonight and there were no more rooms for us at any of the hostels. So at a kind of welcoming center we had to be matched up with whatever bed-and-breakfast that could be found with an empty bed. We had met a hippie-like couple from California in the taxi ride over. At first I thought they were mother and son, but I figured out they were a couple when they began to make out in the taxi. They offered to get a room with the minister, but he declined, saying he would get one with me. The look of panic in my eyes—not only at that thought but also at not fully understanding anything the French intake person at the welcome center was saying—must have scared him off. Thank God. Funny. That's the first time I've thanked God on this spiritual trek as well.

So . . .

I have a room to myself my first night. Perfect for this solitary man who is about to walk deep into his own solitude.

5/1/09

I didn't finish writing last night because the proprietress of my bed-and-breakfast opened my door at 10:00 p.m. and said "Finis!" before abruptly switching off my light. This morning at breakfast I referred to her as "the sergeant" and everyone around the table smiled knowingly. There was a very handsome—pretty, actually—preppy young guy from Austria named Toby. German friends walking the path together who said their names are Peter and Elga. An Irish father and son. And a Canadian woman who said she was a newly divorced schoolteacher literally walking away from her marriage. That's why she was embarking on the Camino. Everyone seemed to be embarrassed by her acknowledging such a personal reason right off the bat to a breakfast table full of strangers, but I was oddly touched by her forthrightness. We exchanged a smile over the others' frowning discomfort.

Yesterday when I was getting my "passport" stamped in St.-Jean-Pied-de-Port—they call it one's credentials in France—the woman who was doing the intake kept saying, "Don't walk the difficult route over the Pyrenees, but walk the alternative one around the mountains and along the river." Someone standing next to me interpreted her warning to us, "It gets too cold up there, too strenuous, too much snow—two people died last month going over the mountain. Don't do it. Listen to an old woman like me."

When I got to the fork in the road to make the choice about how I was going to begin the Camino, I instinctively chose the harder route. I'd been taking my altitude sickness pills for two previous days in anticipation of a mountain climb. And I didn't come all this way to take an easier path. This is as much a physical test in my fifties as a spiritual one. In my forties I climbed Mount Kilimanjaro. What will my sixties bring? Will I even live that long?

The moment I put my foot on the Camino itself all fear left me. The anticipation of the walk I'd been having for months, along with the fear, left. I was now on the path. No turning back. Not yet at least. Only onward. I put the earphones of my iPod in and hit the "play" button and Brandon Flowers began to sing the first few lyrics of "Human." I sang softly along with him as I took those first few steps on the Camino. "Close your eyes. Clear your heart. Cut the cord," we sang.

I stopped singing and began to dance up into the Pyrenees. Yet the more I danced, then climbed, then trudged slower and slower and higher and higher up the windswept mountain the more I began to think I should have followed the Frenchwoman's advice and taken the river route. It was one of the hardest days I've ever experienced. When the guidebooks and Web sites about the Camino inform you that you will be crossing the Pyrenees they don't make it quite clear how steep the climb is. Up, up, up, up you keep going until you reach the snowcaps and the raw wind.

One of the things I told my friends and family before I embarked on this trip was how much I hate walking in the rain and that I hoped I wouldn't have too many days filled with it.

This first day it rained all day.

It even sleeted at the highest point of the walk. The mud at times through the forested parts of the slope was ankle deep. I was thankful for my boots. I even slipped and fell twice right on my butt, sliding down a bit of one slope in the snow and mud. Scared the shit out of me, but luckily nothing was sprained or broken.

Last night sleeping alone in my room at the quaint "sergeant-run" bed-and-breakfast has given way tonight to a hostel—an ancient monastery—with over one hundred people in its one dorm-sized room. I hope there is no symphony of snores surrounding me. It will be a real test to get some sleep, but since I haven't slept well in three nights and am thoroughly exhausted from the all-day climb, I hope to sleep through anything.

Two things I forgot to mention about the climb:

At one point the Irish father and son who were staying in my St.-Jean-Pied-de-Port bed-and-breakfast were ahead of me on the beginning of the Camino's path when, on my iPod Bernadette Peters began to sing "No One Is Alone" from *Into the Woods*. Yeah, I know: How gay is that—Bernadette Peters singing Sondheim in my ears as I walked the Camino from France back into Spain. But when she sang the lyric "Sometimes people leave you / Halfway through the wood" I realized watching the father and son walking up in front of me that one of the issues to deal with on this walk, this trek, this pilgrimage, is my own fatherlessness.

So two things in two days have spoken to me already as I begin the Camino—a minister named Basel's trying to rediscover his spirituality as a gay man and this father and son's reminding me so deeply of my own fatherlessness. What will day three bring?

———

Maybe the only thing more affected than listening to Sondheim on the Camino is reading John Keats along the way. I brought a selection of his letters and poems to dip into from time to time. These lines from a letter he wrote to Benjamin Bailey dated March 13, 1818, spoke to me after this first day: "You know my ideas about Religion," Keats wrote. "I do not think myself more in the right than other people, and that nothing in this world is proveable. I wish I could enter into all your feelings on the subject merely for one short 10 Minutes and give you a Page or two to your liking. I am sometimes so very sceptical as to think Poetry itself a mere Jack a lanthen to amuse whoever may chance to be struck with its brilliance. As Tradesmen say every thing is worth what it will fetch, so probably every mental pursuit takes its reality and worth from the ardour of the pursuer—being in itself a nothing—Ethereal things may at least be thus real, divided under three heads—Things real—things semireal—and no things. Things real—such as existences of Sun Moon & Stars and passages of Shakespeare. Things semireal such as Love, the Clouds and which require a greeting of the Spirit to make them wholly exist—and Nothings which are made Great and dignified by an ardent pursuit—which by the by stamps the burgundy mark on the bottles of our Minds, insomuch as they are able to 'consecrate whate'er they look upon.' I have written a Sonnet here of a somewhat collateral nature—so don't imagine it an a propos des bottes."

I then read, within the body of this letter, his first draft of "The Human Seasons." The first lines of that first draft spoke to me as well, since the natural beauty of the world about me is even more evident as I start this pilgrimage. At one point when the vast verdant vistas gave way to the snow clouds into which I was walking, I spotted a wild horse grazing in the mist before me. When I turned the corner on the mountain's ridge there was a whole herd of wild horses gathered there. They all raised their heads and looked at me. I stopped in awe. They were not awed but observed me nonetheless. I went to get my camera in my backpack, but before I could retrieve it they all galloped off into the trees down on the side of the mountain. It was in that moment, which galloped away just as suddenly as the herd of horses, that I realized that even though I was the one carrying the camera it was I who was being closely watched as this pilgrimage began—by nature, the universe, the eye of God.

Although the fog and clouds made seeing increasingly difficult, it also made the white birches towering along the path even more beautiful. As I struggled to walk on once I reached that peak of the Pyrenees, I concentrated on all the beauty before me. It was that beauty of the world that beckoned me onward more than any imminent spiritual marvels and it was then that I thought of these lines of Keats's first draft:

> Four Seasons fill the Measure of the year;
> Four Seasons are there in the mind of Man.
> He hath his lusty Spring when fancy clear
> Takes in all beauty with an easy span:
> He hath his Summer, when luxuriously
> He chews the honied cud of fair spring thoughts,
> Till, in his Soul dissolv'd they come to be
> Part of himself. . . .

I also concentrated, I have to admit, on the bit of beauty before me in the hostel moments ago when I saw it in the bed right next to me. The hostel is really an Augustine abbey built in 1130. There are about 120 bunks set up in there. And since the bunks are pushed together two by two you find yourself sleeping right next to someone. The someone I have found myself next to is, yes, thank God, a beautiful boy.

I snuck my camera out of my backpack to snap his picture surreptitiously while he too was writing in a journal and listening to his iPod. But since the ancient abbey was rather dark my camera's flash automatically went off. He hadn't galloped off like the herd of wild horses before I could snap the picture, but he did throw off his headphones. He then raised his head and glared my way much the way those horses had.

"Are you from America?" he asked, scowling.

"Yes. How did you know?" I answered.

"Americans never ask," he informed me.

I had to laugh at his perception. "May I take your picture?" I then asked.

He too laughed and posed for me.

"Where are you from?" I then asked him.

"I am from Switzerland," he told me.

"Basel?" I asked, remembering the first person I'd met on my pilgrimage back at the bus station in Pamplona.

"Yes. How did you know?"

"The Camino told me," is all I said.

The boy's name is Lucas and he has just finished serving in the Swiss army and is trying, like me, to figure out his life. We had a sweet half-hour conversation about the Camino and our respective stymied lives.

I am now at a bar next to the hostel having a much-needed Coca-Cola by a much-needed fire. Alternating between writing in this journal and reading my Keats. I made it over the Pyrenees today with just a cup of coffee and a piece of toast made by "the sergeant." I also had two swigs of water from the bottle in my backpack at one point. In a couple of hours I'll eat a big dinner and pray that these old legs hold up tomorrow.

One last thing. I said nothing all day on the path. At first I listened to music, but when I took my earphones out I realized that the silence was pleasing. As was my heartbeat in my ears. As was my heavy breathing. My own sounds within the eerie lack of sound on the Camino helped me stay in the moment.

When I heard the church bells of Roncesvalles pealing the hour I knew I was almost there. I looked up and there in a break in the trees I saw a glimpse of steeple looming before me. "Hallelujah," I softly said. It was a tired and disgruntled one but a "hallelujah" nonetheless. It was—this "Hallelujah"—the first word I was to speak on the Camino.

5/2/09

When I walked out of Roncesvalles this morning at daybreak, this was written on the first sign, on the side of road, before I turned and stepped back onto the Camino: "Santiago de Compostela 780."

It is a bit less than that distance to Santiago as I sit down now to write after having walked seven hours today.

Last night, after I wrote in this journal, I ran into the Irish father and son I wrote about before. They were sitting by the fire in the bar. The father is sixty-five. His name is Eugene. The son, Owen, is thirty-two. "Owen" is the Irish name for "Eugene." He is Eugene's oldest son and it's their first trip one-on-one without other family members. Eugene told me Owen carried both their backpacks over the Pyrenees when I told him that I had worried about his making it over when I saw them on the mountainside yesterday. Eugene says his hips are already giving him problems.

I told them that when I saw them yesterday walking together I realized one of the issues I was coming to terms with on my walk on the Camino was my fatherlessness. I told them my father had been killed in a car wreck when I was seven. "My father died when I was fifteen," said Eugene. "I was devastated."

"I couldn't imagine growing up without my father around," said Owen.

"That's why I didn't mind you carrying my backpack," said Eugene. "Because of all those years I pushed you in your pram."

After I talked to Eugene and Owen, an odd, rather disheveled man starting walking beside me on my way back to the hostel. He had a beard that was beaded with the cold mist. Long hair. He was wearing brown sackcloth clothing. A kind of tunic. Tattered. Frayed. I was, to tell the truth, a bit frightened by his presence. "I overheard your conversation with those two," he said to me as he fell in step by my side, although I had not noticed him in the bar. "Trust me you are not Fatherless," he said. "I mean Fatherless with a big *F* in front of it as big as this Camino," he told me, spreading his arms out wide and almost hitting me in the face. As I ducked I saw the shadow of his sudden motion there on the ground before me, his tunic seeming to untuck beneath his arms and flowing forth as if to lift him into flight. "And neither are you fatherless, that *f* now I say to you, as small as a child, as small as you once were. Are you feeling like a child on this walk you are beginning?" he asked. I was afraid to look at him. I have learned back in New York never to engage a crazy homeless person, never really look one of them in the eye, and this guy seemed a bit homeless and crazy to me. "I am here to tell you that both your Father and your father are here to guide you on your Camino," he now seemed to be whispering, his voice itself fluttering about me, his presence wafting to and fro like that now-swirling mist swept up in the damp and windy night through which I was making my way back to the hostel. The mist made the tiny pilgrim-centered village—there are only twenty-four year-round inhabitants who live there—even more numinous. The lone church that anchored the town was softly lit up the hill from us and encircled in a shroud of it.

I sped up, trying to lose such an odd and determined interloper who had eavesdropped on my earlier conversation, having decided he really must be Roncesvalles's lone homeless beggar who listened to and then preyed upon pilgrims. The faster I walked, the more he increased his pace. Was he out to rob me? I turned, chancing to get at a look at him, and realized he wasn't old and grizzled like I expected him to be but oddly sexy. Like Jim Morrison playing Jesus—or perhaps even the other way around. Was I, I wondered in that moment, becoming the crazy one? There was a monastery there. Was he a monk?

He touched my arm.

"Be safe, my son," he said, then slowed and seemed to be carefully following in the distance behind me, dropping back in the mist. Dissolving into it? I felt relieved that he had neither robbed me nor asked me for money, since I was on a strict budget during the month I have mapped out on this walk. I thought of the shower I longed to take before dinner back at the hostel, which calmed me. As I approached the door of the hostel I turned to see if the odd stranger was still following me, but thankfully he had vanished.

As I took my quick shower before the warm water could subside I kept going over the cryptic conversation I had with the strange bearded man in his tattered tunic. And then it dawned on me: I had not really felt his touch when he placed his hand on my arm. Had that been because the muscles in my arms and shoulders were already getting numb from carrying my backpack?

Once I dried off and got dressed for dinner, I stopped by the front desk of the hostel and asked the man who appeared to be in charge there if he had ever seen the man who had spoken to me wandering around Roncesvalles. "He kind of looks like Jim Morrison," I said. "Do you know who Jim Morrison is?" I asked.

"Yes, I know of this Jim Morrison. A man who is dead. He opens the Doors," he said in his accented English. He smiled. "Jim Morrison. That is the best description to me I have had in my ears."

"So you know who I'm talking about," I said. "Is it a local monk or a homeless person or something? He kind of freaked me out."

The man at the desk placed the cross around his neck in his hand and, looking concerned, clenched it as gently as my father had clenched my own hand along with Chico's paw and Coco's paw the night I had fallen asleep that first time I had known a world with snow in it. I haven't thought of that night in years and years. Odd that I would come up with that image. Was it the stranger and all his talk of fathers who had made me think of such an image for the first time since—well—that night it had happened? Was it the snow itself I walked through across the peaks of the Pyrenees? The man at the desk released the cross and uncreased his brow. "Did Jim Morrison . . ." He stopped and chuckled at the name, a kind of snort of amusement. "Did he say something important to you tonight that means something to you as you begin your pilgrimage on the Camino?" he asked.

"Yes, I guess he did. Sure," I said.

"In your own language?" the man asked.

"Yes."

He smiled once more. "Last week he spoke in Swahili to a woman from South Africa. Before that in German. Last summer: Swedish."

I was confused. "So he's an educated monk who toys with us

tourists—I mean pilgrims, sorry: pilgrims—who seem to need advice. Though we're all on this fucking pilgrimage—sorry, for my language, sorry—so I guess we all need some sort of advice or we wouldn't be doing it. Right?"

The man laughed, then decided laughter wasn't called for. *"Fantasma inquietante . . ."* He seemed to be whispering the words to himself, then looked up at me. "It is a haunting, I think you say in your English." He touched the cross again. "I think it is a blessing myself, not a haunting. You are a blessed one. Your Jim Morrison has only started appearing in the last year or so and only a few times. The people he speaks to are the only ones who peer him. Peer him? Ummm. . . . See. Sí? See him."

"A ghost?" I asked, laughing now myself but getting a little nervous remembering the Shirley MacLaine book about all her Camino experiences. Or was this one of Keats's no things? Was I consecrated by my having been seen by it? "Come on. You're pulling my leg," I said.

The man sat back in his chair with a quizzical look on his face, translating, no doubt, the literal meaning of such a phrase back into his Spanish. "You are joking with me," I explained. "A haunting? Go on. That's crazy."

The quizzical look on the man's face turned very serious. A calmness even covered his eyes with a sadness as he stared at my disbelief. "A ghost with wings," he said, each word spoken slowly and with great care, the tone my mother took when she first told me my father had been killed in a car wreck, her own eyes too eerily calm and sad when she too stared at my disbelief at what she was telling me. It is her voice I hear now, in fact, tonight here in the Spanish countryside so far away from the Mississippi countryside of my childhood as I record this Spanish man's words, record hers, and recall that moment yesterday as well as the one from my childhood so long ago. "Your father has flown off to heaven," said my mother that day, spreading her arms as wide as my own Jim Morrison spread his when his tunic longed to be winged as I watched his shadowy image unfold, my mother's arms—the shadow of which has defined my world ever since—folding instead about me and keeping me close to her, earthbound, protecting me from heaven and all it from then on held.

"Crazy, you think?" the man said in his heavily accented English. "Okay. I might be the crazy one. Or the crazy one: you. But I think you are, no, this: blessed. You are blessed to have been visited by the angel of Roncesvalles."

It was my turn now to crease my brow. We held each other's stare for a moment before I walked away from him. "Catholics," I muttered under my breath, and headed across the road to a restaurant to have some dinner. "Fucking Catholics."

Completely incredulous? Well . . . no . . . I can't say that I am. Especially having crossed that mountain and wondered what I had done it for. Was my reward yesterday a vision, a "waking dream"—to quote Keats again when he was contemplating a nightingale, another kind of creature with wings—for my making it up and over the Pyrenees and setting out on this spiritual pilgrimage? Is not one man's vision just another man's psychosis? Maybe instead of that Jim Morrison guy being the crazy one, it really is I. Maybe walking the Camino is about my coming to terms with that, and not my spirituality. This does seem to be seeping into C. S. Lewis fantastical territory. Maybe I should use this in a pitch meeting with Perry, since he's such a Lewis fanatic.

But let's face it. I have, after all, flown halfway around the world and traveled all day to get to the Pyrenees to wake up the next morning to walk this path all the way across Spain that people have walked for two thousand years in search of just such experiences. There is a kind of craziness in that alone. Some—the craziest of Catholics, no doubt, who equate physical suffering with a way to complete their souls in a way that I, a Protestant, cannot truly comprehend—have even walked it on their knees. Chaucer, upright, walked the path. Dante did it. Saint Francis of Assisi. Charlemagne. Ferdinand and Isabella. John Adams walked it in the eighteenth century when he was commissioned before his presidency to go to France to secure needed funds for the Revolutionary War. His ship began to take on water off the coast of Spain and he was forced to walk the Camino in the reverse direction toward Paris. He said in his autobiography that it had been a life-altering expedition.

And that is what I want: an altered life.

But do I have to achieve an altered state to get it?

Last month Hugh Jackman got it slightly wrong when he asked me if I had fucked the angel. An angel, it seems, its voice fluttering about me even now as I write this, is fucking with me.

My meal last night:

Potato soup.

French fries.

Delicious fresh trout caught from a nearby Urrobi river in Roncesvalles.

Wine.

My dinner mates were from France, Italy, and Denmark.

After dinner I talked some more to sweet Lucas, the Swiss kid—he's only twenty years old—before going to bed. But not much sleep came. I kept thinking about that Jim Morrison monk or the ghost or the goddamn angel or whoever it was who touched my arm without my feeling it and told me exactly what I needed to hear. Plus, there was a man who snored really loudly in the bunk next to Lucas and me. *That* was real. No doubt about that. In four nights now I've had about eight hours' sleep. I'm running on fumes. Maybe the "ghost with wings" was formed by such fumes. I guess "walking" is the right word. Not running on fumes—walking on them. Walking, it is dawning on me, will be my existence for the next month.

The hostel early this morning was awakened at 6:00 A.M. People applauded. I didn't. I gave the snorer next to me a dirty look and was on the road by 6:30. That's when I saw the road sign.

After all the rain this region has been having I had to walk through thick, awful—oftentimes ankle-deep—mud. There's a reason that "mud" is so close in sound to the French word "merde" I realized after walking through the thick, stinking stuff.

Outside one of the little villages I approached today my mood lightened when, as I stopped to take a drink of water from the bottle I keep in my backpack, a beautiful blond wild-haired boy came striding my way. At first, because of his beauty, I thought he might be a girl. But no: a boy. As he passed, I noticed he was palming some wooden Buddhist prayer beads. "Forward," seemed to be the mantra he was whispering to himself as he counted them in his hand. Just that: "forward." I quickly put my bottle again in my backpack and followed him, wanting to stop him to ask if I could take a photograph of his hand holding his beads, but he was already too far ahead of me on the path. His gait was almost a canter compared to mine. I thought I would probably never see him again as he disappeared in the distance. I could not get his hand and those beads—and his beauty—out of my mind's eye.

When I arrived in the village I sat on a bridge over a rushing river and saw him, the blond wild-haired boy, down below soaking his feet in the water. I waited until he and the equally beautiful young Asian man he was now with approached me on the bridge. I asked if they spoke English. The blond boy told me he was from California and his name was Daniel. He agreed to let me photograph his hand holding the beads. Japa mala, he called them. It is my favorite photograph so far on the Camino—a Buddhist image taken by a Protestant on a Catholic path.

As I walked on I carefully had to descend some steep steps since my knees are already killing me. "Are you okay?" I heard a voice behind me.

I turned and saw it was the young Asian man from the bridge a mile or so back. I told him I was fine and we began to walk together. "Are you Catholic?" I asked at one point, which has become my way of starting conversations on the Camino.

Unlike Basel, the Methodist minister, back at the bus station in Pamplona, he did not laugh dismissively at such a question. "Yes," he said. "I am a Catholic. Very." He paused. "I am a priest."

"You're my first priest on the Camino," I told him, and took his photograph to document it.

He told me that he was Korean and that he was thirty-two years old— the age my father was when he was killed in his car wreck. His Korean name is Hong, but his baptismal name is Raphael. He had a parish in San Diego but now has been assigned to a Korean Catholic church in Vancouver. He is walking the Camino before heading to Canada.

"Is your father proud of you for becoming a priest?" I asked him.

"My father died when I was seven," he told me, saying a sentence I have so often said in my own life.

"My father died when I was seven," I echoed him.

We walked along and talked for miles of our very different fatherless childhoods.

"Father Raphael, it's been really nice to meet you today," I finally said as we ran out of memories to share.

"Father," he said, repeating the word, shaking his head at such a thought, it seemed. I was twenty-one years older than he. Did the sound of such a word addressed to him by me strike him as odd in that moment as I was finding it? "Father," he softly said again, as if trying magically to find the meaning of some foreign word simply by pronouncing it. Then once more: "Father . . ."

I looked at the primitive landscape about us and remembered the one my own father had drawn so primitively for me. Three birds fluttered flat against the sky like the elongated Ms of that long-ago Sunday, an M now found at the beginning of "Morrison" and "monks" and "mala beads," not "Methodist" and "Mississippi." This Korean father and I found the same kind of silence that my first father and I could find ourselves enveloped in when I was a child and language too failed us. I marveled at the rough beauty of the world in which I now found myself and recalled that other rough beauty of Mount Kilimanjaro when I asked my friend how he had stayed alive and he had motioned toward it. "This," I said aloud now as he had so curtly said that one word in response atop Mount Kili.

"What?" asked Father Raphael.

"This," I said once more, and motioned at the world about us.

He smiled. "Yes, I know," he said, and I knew he did.

We fell back into our silence.

We moved steadily onward.

This.

This.

This.

5/3/09

I had my first dream in four nights.

I dreamed I was still at *Vanity Fair*, but I had on the type of ankle bracelet device that house arrest prisoners wear. A researcher brought me a portfolio of stories by someone who was obsessed by me and my writing, and handed it to me with concern on his face. I told him, "I don't give a shit what someone thinks of me. Take these away." He looked crestfallen.

I awoke—as I do several times a night—and dreamed next that I was scrubbing and scrubbing and scrubbing my apartment.

Whatever.

I began my walk this morning again at 6:30 but without my backpack. I hired a service to bring it to my next destination for me. It was my first Protestant decision. Catholics might believe that salvation comes from suffering. We Protestants believe it comes from acceptance.

I do know the decision saved my back and shoulders. Indeed, it made the walk even joyful for the first time once I was freed of the burden. I remembered I had the Mississippi Mass Choir on my iPod and this morning played it singing, "This morning when I rose / I didn't have no doubt!"

The fervor of the choir blasted in my ears. When they got to the part when they sing, "Hallelujah!" I shouted it at the top of my lungs, no longer disgruntled to be on the path. I was up on a ridge here in Basque country and began to dance about as if I really did have the Holy Ghost filling my body. Maybe I did. I came upon a group of girls who began to laugh at my dancing. I took off my earphones to say hello, but before I could one of them said to me in her blunt Germanic accent, "You are fully happy." No one had ever said such a thing to me before or had cause to. I don't know if I've ever been fully happy before that one moment or will be ever again. But I think I was fully happy in that moment, and if the Camino doesn't give me anything else it has given me that.

I walked on and came to Pamplona today on this sleepy Sunday afternoon. The streets and parks were mostly empty. I thought of how panicked I was to be lost last time and how calm I was today to be walking the empty streets. On the outskirts of the city I stopped at the nicest hostel so far where I am now outside at a table writing. My backpack was waiting for me here under the shade of a tree just where the service said they would leave it.

I just had a long lovely conversation with Toby, "the Austrian mountain goat," as I've come to think of him. He and Lucas have also become friends. Toby's sitting at the next table and writing in his own journal. He has passed me the last couple of days on our walk. I recognized him because he had stayed at the same bed-and-breakfast back in St.-Jean-Pied-de-Port and had even sat by me at breakfast when "the sergeant" fed us our bits of toast and tea. He asked me to walk with him tomorrow, but I don't think I can keep up with him.

My longest walk I have charted out is coming up in the morning—a Monday—my first full week on the Camino.

5/4/09

Today was fun. And moving.

Last night was just the opposite. It had to have been the worst meal I've ever had in my life. By the time the waitress got to us there wasn't

much food left in the restaurant's kitchen, we were told, and she offered us "hamburgers," which doesn't translate well in this part of the
world. I got a plate of cold, greasy french fries and a thin fried patty of
some indefinable meat. No bun. I asked, "Is there a skinned dead dog
in the back somewhere?" I know: rude. But last night I was a rude and
hungry American.

On the path I was longing for some chocolate and could have kicked
myself for not at least buying some Oreos from the vending machine
back at the hostel before setting out. All I could think of was eating
an Oreo for the first few miles of the Camino this morning. I turned a
corner and there was one on the ground. I couldn't believe it at first. I
thought I was hallucinating again. First an imagined angel who looked
like Jim Morrison and now a forlorn Oreo at my feet. I picked it up.
Yep: real. I plopped it right in my mouth and devoured it. It was still
crisp. Someone had obviously just dropped it. I laughed at how the
Camino really does provide what one needs.

When I arrived at the top of the first giant hill I saw a kid from Que-
bec I had met the night before who was complaining of having a broken toe already. He is always listening to rap music on his headphones
and had stopped to rest his toe and was bopping his head along with
the rap in his ears when I walked up. He saw my approach. "Ah! The
almond man!" he called, a nickname he had given me from the night
before because I was offering many of the other pilgrims some of my
almonds and raisins I had packed for the pilgrimage. He was munching on some Oreos.

"Did you drop one of those about a mile back?" I asked.

He shrugged. "Maybe."

"Well, you were part of my first answered prayer on the Camino," I
said. "All I could think about was not having gotten my own Oreos
from the vending machine this morning."

I watched him hobble off after wiping the chocolate crumbs from
his mouth and putting his headphones back on. "The almond man is
nuts!" he called back over his shoulder.

I stopped for a needed breakfast a few miles on and ran into a young girl named Doris from Stuttgart, whom I met last night at the hostel. We had coffee and pastries together and she told me she was walking the Camino to try to decide if she was going to break off her wedding engagement. We got to talking about what types of men we liked. "My type is that movie star who is named Hugh," she said.

"Hugh Jackman?" I asked.

"Yes," she said. "Hugh Jackman is an angel. I would fuck Hugh Jackman."

I actually did a spit take when she said that.

"What's wrong?" she asked, both of us laughing at her honesty.

I told her about meeting Hugh and what he had told me. We both shook our heads. "Does this mean I should get married or not?" she asked me.

"I think it just means we should keep walking and see what else the Camino has in store for us," I replied, stuffing the last of my croissant into my mouth and heading outside.

I stopped in Port de Rein and bought some fruit for the afternoon and some chocolate and a big piece of delicious ham. I also went into a pharmacy and bought some much-needed knee braces for the walk or I won't make it all the way across Spain. I haven't even been on the path for a week and my knees are now really killing me.

I stopped in one of the village's squares to eat a bit of the ham and attach the braces to my knees. Next to me was an elderly man and woman who also seemed to be walking the Camino and taking a break. Hunched and white-haired, their wrinkled cheeks ruddy with the morning's exertion, they were sharing a perfectly ripened tomato that the woman was cutting up with one of the blades of a Swiss Army knife. I was intrigued watching how careful she was to make sure the man— her husband, I presumed—got just the slightest bit more of the tomato than she was giving herself.

Our eyes met and we nodded and confirmed that we were all pilgrims on the path. "Are you guys Catholic?" I asked my usual question.

The couple smiled rather knowingly and shook their heads no.

"So you're Protestant," I guessed.

"Jewish," the old man mumbled, his mouth full of the tomato's lusciousness.

"And German," said the woman. "Don't forget German. German Jewish. From Frankfurt-am-Main."

The old man's smile widened, a bit of the tomato's juice sliding one of its seeds from the corner of his mouth and staying there in the white stubble of his chin where I stared at it. He brushed it away with an elegant sweep of his hand so quick and sure it convinced me he must have conducted a bit of Schumann at some point in his life. His brown eyes held mine. I turned my attention to the woman, who was offering me a piece of her portion of the tomato.

I declined it. "So why are you walking the Camino?" I asked.

"For our hearts," she said, shrugging, as I watched her pop that bit of tomato she had offered me into her mouth.

The man reached over and touched her hand, the one that wielded the knife. "For our one heart," he said, the sound of his own kindness—more fine-tuned than feeble—seeming to take him by surprise as it caught there in his grizzled throat.

It caught in my throat as well.

5/6/09

I fell into bed and had an odd dream about walking through one of these tackily ornate Catholic churches that dot the countryside on the Camino and are so filled with stabbed statuary profusely bleeding and a profusion of dark-haired rather harried angels painted along so many gold-leafed ceilings, not a blond one in the bunch. Blond ones seem only to come into my line of vision in Starbucks, I guess, or wild haired and holding Buddhist beads. I kept walking though the ornate cathedral and down a flight of stairs into a dank basement full of discarded statuary and dark-haired angels. I found my way out of the dankness into a clearing of trees yet couldn't get my bearings. I decided to turn

back into the cathedral and retrace my steps, but when I did the basement had been refigured into a well-lit gift shop filled with Buddhist
knickknacks. One particular one—was it Buddhist?—was glistening
and beckoning to me. I went to purchase some Japa mala beads and
woke up.

I couldn't fall back to sleep so decided to go down to breakfast. I sat
down at the table with only one other pilgrim, a Canadian named Colin who has become a friend of mine as well as of Toby and of Lucas.
Colin is a wiry little sixty-three-year-old Englishman who now lives in
Vancouver. He is walking the Camino after surviving open-heart sur-
gery only a year and a half ago. He and I haven't yet fallen into as easy
a friendship as I have with Lucas and Toby. In fact, I'd describe our relationship as a prickly one. He's married and plans to meet his wife halfway to Santiago so she can reach the cathedral with him. Maybe that's
the reason I find his incessant flirting with young women along the
Camino kind of distasteful. He certainly seems to find my being a gay
man so, especially my being so open about it. I will admit that my open-
ness about my being gay can seem to some to verge on aggression.

Colin and I groggily faced each other across the hostel's kitchen
table as I sipped my coffee and he his tea. To make conversation, I was
telling him about the wild dream I had had the night before.

"Maybe you wouldn't have such dreams if you stopped popping all
those pills you pop," he tersely told me.

"Those are my HIV meds," I blurted out in an attempt to deflect his
terseness. There was a shared intake of breath at the table, each of us
stopping just short of a gasp. What had I just done? Was this some sort
of confession on my part? Or was I just being, yes, aggressive and trying instead to start a confrontation? My eyes met Colin's for the brief-
est of moments and we each saw in the other an acceptance finally of
our own mortality—a shared humanity—this man with his stitched-
up heart and I with an immune system that could be described as mar-
ginal even as I rejected such a notion for myself.

It was in that instant of unlikely recognition that the reason for
my being on the Camino was revealed to me. It was no bolt to my

consciousness. No epiphany. Instead the reason seemed to come to rest there in that moment, flutter into place like the fluttering voice of the angel of Roncesvalles. Up until now, I have measured my whole life in the years before my HIV diagnosis and the years that have followed it. Nothing I have done, no matter how hard I've tried, has ever been able to erase that diagnosis as the demarcation that has defined me. But now there is another demarcation. This was the instant longing that I had experienced to be here in Spain on such a spiritual journey as I sat on that barstool back in New Orleans over a year ago now after Perry had first suggested it. It was a kind of cure that was incomprehensible to me before I began this pilgrimage. I will now measure my whole life in the years before the Camino and all the years that are still to come. The Camino has replaced HIV. Not in my body. My bloodstream. It has replaced it in some deeper stream I can't quite name. Some might call it my soul.

The walk today was long and arduous. Blazing hot. Not much shade. I walked over thirty kilometers and spent the morning walking with Toby. I told him too about my HIV status. He listened and lowered his eyes as I talked.

I went to a bar tonight with Lucas. I loved watching him relax as he drank a few beers and flirted with some young girls who were also walking the path. He has let his scant beard sprout about his face and I longed at one point to reach out and touch the ridge of his cheek—a bit pudgier than my father's long-ago more chiseled one—to see if his sparse whiskers felt as splintery as my father's once had. As he danced with one of the girls I sat in the corner by myself and remembered all those times I'd peek through the crack in my parents' bedroom closet when I'd hide in there all alone and watch them dance about the room, my father humming in my mother's ear before she'd reach up and run her fingers along those cheeks of his, then hold his face in her hands and kiss him. I wanted to watch Lucas kiss the girl with whom he was danc-ing, but he didn't. I wanted to kiss him myself. I knew I never would.

When he and I left I teased him about not being able to close the deal with the girl. We laughed and joked and lingered on the street a bit. He then said he and Toby had been talking about me. "We said one to the other one that though you are the one with the most pain we have met on the Camino, you are the one who makes everybody smile."

It was then that I reached up and touched the stubble on his cheek—it was more feathery than splintery—and said good night. I went inside my hotel but did not shut the door all the way. Through the crack, I watched him walking toward the hostel across the street. I imagined him turning around to smile at me.

5/7/09

Another long day on the path. When I arrived in Ventosa this eve-ning I saw Daniel—the California boy with the wild blond hair who was holding the Buddhist beads—emerging from the bathroom at the hostel where I've stopped for the night. He lingered and talked to me as I shaved my head. He's now tamed his own hair into a bunch of dread-locks and he has paired up with a lovely German girl who has a crew cut, so they are a very art-directed couple. Danny with his abundance of hair and she with her lack of it. Stunning really. Both gorgeous. She's now wearing his beads around her neck.

5/8/09

When I got back to the hostel last night after dinner with Lucas and a few others, I began reading the novel *The Weekend* by Peter Cam-eron in my bunk bed. I fell asleep after finishing a few chapters and woke up in the middle of the night to see Daniel and his new girlfriend in the lower bunk over to the right in front of me. They were naked and sitting cross-legged facing each other. They were staring into each other's eyes. The moonlight streamed in through the window and en-veloped them in a kind of velvety whiteness. They were ever so slightly rocking to and fro. They never stopped staring into each other's eyes even though I noticed she was masturbating him very slowly. I could tell he was uncircumcised, for each time she would stroke him the head of his cock would emerge from his ample foreskin and glisten a bit more in the moonlight. I waited to watch him ejaculate—I knew he was close—which he did in spurt after spurt, suddenly putting one of his new blond dreadlocks between his lips to bite down on it so as not to make any noise. He kept on ejaculating and it looked as if the moon-light itself had thickened and begun to streak the air about them. The girl lifted her hand, covered in what she had coaxed from him, and, taking the dreadlock from his mouth, smeared the concoction onto it and stuck it in her own mouth. She pulled him toward her with the sticky dreadlock lodged now between her teeth and kissed him. The dread dropped from their mouths.

Once they had dozed off in each other's arms I decided to just get up and sneak out of the hostel at 4:30 a.m. and begin walking. It was so dark out I had to make my way with the tiny light from my iPod to try to find the yellow arrows that mark the Camino. The arrows signal to us pilgrims which direction to go and which fork to take when the path confronts us with one.

It was deadly quiet at that time of the morning out in the country-side. Kind of scary. But I do love to start the walk each day before sun-rise and then watch the sky scare itself awake with light, scarlets and ambers and burnt oranges combining with yet another example of na-ture's orderly abandon that I've come to respect and admire these last few days on the path. The birds also awaken as the sky lightens, and I love walking in their early-morning songs. I've never really noticed how lovely the songs of birds are to wake to. I feel enveloped by them and their songs seem gently, knowingly, to urge me on.

Sometimes people leave rocks on the path in the shape of arrows to point the way for other pilgrims as well. Or, oftentimes, the rocks are left in the shape of hearts and crosses. I came upon one such formation today outside an ugly little city I quickly walked through to get up into the hills outside it. The large rocks I came upon were formed in the shape of a heart and inside, with pebbles, someone had spelled out this two days before: "MAMA 06-5-09." I stopped and stared at the configuration that had been formed with such obvious care and realized the Camino was once again speaking to me. Two days before had been my own mother's birthday and I had not thought about it since I had been so wrapped up in my own life and thoughts of my fatherlessness. But my motherlessness is just as big an issue to me and here was someone on the path who had honored his or her own mother, not knowing that in so doing my own was also honored.

I did the math. My mother was born in 1931. She died in November of 1964 after having turned thirty-three. Everyone said it was cancer, but I knew it had been a broken heart after she lost my father in that auto accident in August the year before after he had just turned thirty-two. My father was born only one day after my mother, on May 7, 1931. It was his birthday yesterday and I had not stopped to think about that either.

At that moment, for the first time, I knelt on the Camino. I then took some rocks and made a heart right next to the one that was already there. I took a handful of pebbles and spelled "DADDY" in it and beneath it "07-5-09" to mark his birthday yesterday. I did the math again in my head. My parents, if alive, if truly so, would have been seventy-eight today. I placed a hand inside each heart and silently asked them to keep guiding me on the Camino.

I then picked up a pebble from the M in "MAMA" and the D in "DADDY" and switched them one for the other. It was as if my parents were guiding my hands and in some way letting me know that they were still together somewhere, their souls combined in the way their bodies once could be when I, hidden with their smells in the closet, would hear their sighs mingling together atop their bed.

I stood to go and suddenly the wind on the Camino sighed just like them. I began to walk away, brushing tears from my eyes, but turned back toward the two hearts for one more look. I walked back and bent down and took the pebble I had taken from the M to put into the D and the one I had taken from the D to put into the M and put them in my pocket to carry with me the rest of the way on the Camino. I did not replace them but left the imperfection there on the path. Perhaps someone else—another orphan, a mother, or a father—will come along and see the slight but quite noticeable space left in "DADDY" and "MAMA" and place a pebble there themselves and, in so doing, think of their own stories. They will stay for a moment themselves. They will hear the wind sigh at them also as if to signal that the past is what passes through us all.

5/9/09

This was the day I let go of the "family" that I've formed on the path. Lucas and Toby have gone their own ways. I'll keep up with them by e-mail along the way in Internet cafés and when a hostel or a hotel has a computer to use. But I fear I am reverting to my loner mode and even isolating here on the Camino in the midst of all these other pilgrims. Does the Camino change you or do you become even more the person you've always been? I thought by staying in hostels along the way that I would find a way to cure my solitary life, but maybe I am here to learn to accept it.

I do know I have been walking to prove one important aspect of my life—that I can be drug free for at least a month, no pot, no meth, well, for five weeks in all if I count the days that bookend this pilgrimage. It hasn't been a problem so far.

5/10/09

I woke up this morning at 4:30 to start walking in the pouring rain up into the mountains. As I've written, I like being the only one on the path for an hour or so before the sun comes out. I thought it might rain all day, but it stopped early in the morning. Thank you, God. I do not find walking in the rain romantic in any way.

As I was walking up the path in the early-morning darkness I also became very frightened for the first time on the Camino. Really, truly, honestly scared. I thought I saw movement ahead of me in the darkness, flickering images moving about from the trees across the path in front of me and then hiding behind the trees on the other side of the path. I realized for the first time that the Camino so early in the morning when one is a lone pilgrim trudging along is a great place to get jumped and mugged if anyone wanted to do that to you. I—kind of smiling about this now that I'm safe in a hotel room after a hot bath—raised my walking sticks out in front of me as if they were swords in case I was actually jumped. I began to fantasize about how thieves back in earlier centuries must have hidden along the path if they had the same idea of attacking lonely pilgrims. I know: crazy. Right? It passed—such thoughts—but I did feel real physical visceral fear for a mile or so when I thought I saw movement ahead of me on the path.

By the time I reached the top of the mountain where there was a monument to San Juan de Ortega with the date "1936" along with a dove carved onto it—was this a monument to commemorate the Spanish Civil War?—I spotted an odd eerie light illuminating one spot in the otherwise completely dark sky. It was quite beautiful, but I couldn't decide what it was exactly. Heaven making itself known to me here utterly alone on the path? A UFO? I thought the theme to *Close Encounters of the Third Kind* was about to blare from the clouds when suddenly the clouds themselves parted and revealed the lowest-hanging and largest full moon I have ever seen in my life. It was as if it were moving toward me, daring me to touch it. I did, in fact, reach out toward it to see if I could feel its presence, then fell to my knees in prayer instead. It was one of those moments of sacredness that the Camino can offer you. I went into a kind of trance that was broken once again by the sound of one lone bird somewhere beckoning me back into its natural realm.

Reality quickly set in as the sun rose and I continued to walk. And walk. And walk. And walk. Nature is not always so sublime. One stretch of several awful miles was through a recently cleared forest, and the mud in places was so deep I had to find ways around it or walk almost calf deep into it. I worried about infections in my feet in the filth that was soaking through my boots.

I made it through the miles of muddy forest and later in the day—when I could barely move another step, the arches in my feet were aching so—I stopped at a dinky bar in a dinky village to down a dinky little bottle of Coca-Cola. Inside, I struck up a conversation with a cute Irish kid I had noticed back in Villafranca del Bierzo the night before. I told him about getting up and walking in the dark at 4:30 this morning and about how scared I'd been for a mile or so when I thought I saw movement and started thinking the ghosts of thieves or something were out to get me. The kid looked as white as a ghost himself when I told him that, for he showed me the passage in his guidebook that he had just been reading that said that in medieval times the part of the Camino we had walked up in those mountains outside Villafranca was where the highway robbers of the time would attack pilgrims. I'm not sure what exactly happened this morning in the darkness when I was seeing those flickering spectral images running back and forth on the path where the highway robbers once preyed on pilgrims and before the full moon convinced me to pray in another way, but I definitely walked through something ghostly to get to the top of the mountain and to witness—to feel—something sacred.

05/11/09

Yesterday I made it to the lovely city of Burgos, which reminded me a bit of Paris, and spent the night in a nice hotel room where I soaked in a deep bathtub. But I am now writing this in a gymnasium in the small village of Hornillos del Camino. The only shower in the place is reserved for the women.

The walk here today was a very long one without shade through miles and miles and miles of wheat fields in the high plains. I met a woman from Toronto along the way named Coral Jewell—love that name, so beautiful—who told me she was trying to catch up with her two friends from Toronto who went on ahead of her, a woman named Marge who owns a used-book store in Toronto named The Great Escape, and another woman named Judy. Marge is also walking with her sister from Melbourne, Australia, who is named Ginny. I met them all once Coral and I got to Hornillos. Judy is the blonde in the group—there's always one blonde. She even reminds me a bit of the young Joan Blondell. Ginny told me she is a hospital administrator back in her hometown of Melbourne, her keen wit as dry—and slightly dangerous—as the farthest reaches of her country's Outback. She and Marge were spending their first month together since their Aussie childhoods. Their short, cropped hair was an identical gunmetal gray. Their grins, infectious. I imagined them golf stars in the Presbyterian boarding school they reminisced about. Wash-'n'-wear females, I called them, which made them smile.

Coral and I walked into Hornillos together and she told me of the grief she is trying to walk herself out of. She was married for a while but came out as a lesbian two decades ago and her lover of seventeen years recently died of cancer. She was supposed to walk the Camino with Coral, but didn't live long enough to make the journey. We talked a lot about loss and I confided in Coral about my sister's recent breakup with her lesbian lover of seventeen years—it was like another kind of death, that of the relationship itself—and the lesser sort of grief that she was going through.

By the time Coral and I got into the village all the beds in the hostel were taken and there were no rooms in the one *albergue* in town, so we are having to sleep on cots set up in the local school's gymnasium. Not fun.

I am feeling very alone on this part of the path.

Very alone.

Am I going to make it all the way to Santiago?

Burgos was where "the angel" I met that day in Starbucks blew out his knee. I just remembered that. I just remembered his beauty. His kindness. I just remembered the vision of him in the door that day. I just remembered the vision of my mother in the doorway of my room the night it snowed before she decided to snuggle with my father and Chico and Coco and me.

"Have you fucked the angel?"

What did Hugh Jackman mean by that?

5/12/09

It was the worst day yet on the path. I wanted to give up and go home for the first time. My feet are raw and blistered. I've developed a painful rash around my ankles and it's begun to bleed through my socks. The braces for the first time didn't seem to help my knees. I felt hobbled. Horrible. But somehow I kept on walking until I got here today. How? I'm not quite sure.

Once I got here I was in a panic because the place where the service was supposed to deliver my backpack was closed and I had no idea where the backpack was—or even if it had arrived. I went all over the little hillside village trying to find an Internet café or a computer to find the number of the service, since I had left its number in the backpack. Plus—this was what was really freaking me out—my HIV meds are in it as well.

I finally found a hostel in town. The priest who ran it had a weathered face out of the fifteenth century. His scraggly beard reached down to his chest. Once someone translated into Spanish for him that I had lost my bag and didn't know where the service might have dropped it off he hopped on his bike and rode off, trying to find it himself, but came back empty-handed. While he was gone I went on the computer at the hostel and searched and searched until I found a number for the service. I contacted them and told them the name of the hotel where I had made a reservation. They told me to wait in the vestibule of the hotel—the hotel itself wasn't even open until the evening—so I took off my shoes and socks and stared at my bloody rash and blistered feet and tried to soothe them on the stone floor of the vestibule. I waited two hours sitting there for the bag to arrive.

At one point I decided to get in the lotus position and attempt to meditate. Anything to calm me down from the awful day and to take my mind off the pain in my feet and encircling my ankles. I put my hands on my knees, palms up, and began to think of the early mornings when the sun rises and all I can hear is the birds beginning their songs to one another as I eavesdrop on them. Phantom bird sounds began to fill my head and calm me as I closed my eyes and concentrated on my breath. My mind began to empty of its panic, its pain, and I tried to recall, as if in a trance, the first stanza of John Keats's "Ode to a Nightingale." But I couldn't. I could only come up with the first two lines, which pretty much summed up my mood:

> My heart aches, and a drowsy numbness pains
> My sense, as though of hemlock I had drunk,

Not being able to remember that first stanza, my mind flew to the last one and its first two lines that came easily to me, especially its first exclaimed word:

> Forlorn! the very word is like a bell
> To toll me back from thee to my sole self!

I then lost the words again until my mind alighted on the last lines of the poem:

> Was it a vision, or a waking dream?
> Fled is that music:—Do I wake or sleep?

which I kept repeating over and over, more slowly, then more slowly, each slowed-down syllable matched with each of my slowing breaths. "Are you okay?" I heard a woman's lovely Irish lilt ask. Do I wake or do I sleep? I thought once more as I was in that very moment imagining nightingales alighting on my outstretched palms. I opened my eyes and there before me stood a little auburn-haired ruddy-faced wisp of a woman as if a freckle had come to life. She looked down at my feet and appeared concerned.

"I'm okay," I told her. "Though I've had a rough day." I then explained to her about my backpack and how I was waiting for it to be delivered. She told me her name was Ethne and that she and her sister, Mary, had also booked a room at the hotel. I told Ethne it wasn't yet open, but the man at the restaurant down the street told me it opened in the evening. There was a sign on the lobby door that had been written in Spanish and English that informed whoever showed up to check in with him. She thanked me for the information. "And what's your name?" she asked.

"Oh, I'm sorry," I said. "It's Kevin."

She smiled. "Mind if I sit down next to you for a moment?" she asked, then sat. "You know, Saint Kevin is the local saint back in county Wicklow where my sister, Mary, and I live in Ireland," she told me.

"I never knew there was a Saint Kevin," I said.

"You're not Catholic, me boy?" she asked.

"No, Methodist," I told her.

She patted my hand that was still outstretched there palm up on my knee next to her as if I needed to be consoled for my Protestantism. "Are your feet okay? They look rough there, son," she said.

"I'm coping," I said.

"Like a saint," she said, smiling. And for the first time today I smiled too. "You know, 'tis said that Saint Kevin really didn't like women very much except, that is, for Mother Nature. In fact, he loved Mother Nature so much he'd take his baths in the ice-cold pond outside his monastery in our county back home. He'd stand in the pond and hold his hands out like yours are there on your knees—palms up like that—and all the birds would come land on them and serenade him. Some tell that even the nightingales would stay for his dawns to have the privilege of singing to him."

I took a deep breath. I tried not to—I took another deep breath—but I began to cry.

This little Irishwoman I had only met moments before reached out and held my hand. She gently rubbed it. "It's okay, me boy," she said. "Are you homesick? Are you in pain? None of us are saints these days, Kevin. None of us are anymore. Shshshhh. It's okay."

"I'm sorry," I said. "It's just that . . ." But I couldn't say anything more. I continued to cry as she rubbed my birdless hand.

5/13/09

Today I didn't trust the service to deliver my backpack after the panic of thinking I had lost it yesterday, so decided to trudge along with it on my back. I did, though, give the foam pad rolled up on it to the priest who had been so kind to try and track down the backpack yesterday. When the pack finally arrived where Ethne had left me in the vestibule, once my tears had ceased I carefully put my socks and boots back on my blistered feet and walked back to the hostel to give the priest the pad as a token of my thanks. His weathered eyes crinkled even more. He surprised me by giving me a hug. I asked someone standing by him what he was saying in Spanish and the woman told me that the priest had been praying for a pad just like the one I had given him, since the one he had been sleeping on for the last year had disappeared the week before and he had been sleeping on the floor in order to give all the beds to the pilgrims who came through his hostel.

I then ate alone last night but said a prayer of thanks before the meal for being part of an answered prayer for someone else.

This morning, as I strapped on my backpack and headed up the steep mountain outside the village, I put k.d. lang on my iPod and let her rendition of "Hallelujah" help me up the steepness of this part of the path. When I got to the top of the mountain the sun was still rising and it was truly a glorious sight. I felt a tap on my shoulder and it was Ethne, who was now with her sister, Mary. Ethne introduced us.

"Hello," I said, extending my hand.

"*Dia is Muire dhuit*," Mary said to me in Gaelic, and let out a robust laugh that seemed to shake the mountain beneath my feet as she pumped my hand in hers. "I'm the second most famous Mary!" she then exclaimed. The two women could not look more dissimilar. Ethne is but a slip of a woman. Rather serious in her demeanor. This second-most-famous Mary is quite burly. Ethne's perfectly pointed nose is . . . well . . . like I imagine a nightingale's beak might appear. Mary's is bulbous. Ethne was wearing her Irish green hiking attire today and she is so petite she looked like a lovely little sprig of ivy. Mary looks like Burl Ives in drag. What a pair. As instantly as I bonded with Ethne in the vestibule of the hotel, I adored her sister's Burl-y bonhomie.

"What are you listening to on that wee apparatus you've got attached to your ears, *me fae?*" Mary, munching on a bun of some sort, asked me.

"k.d. lang singing Leonard Cohen's 'Hallelujah,'" I told her.

"Got anything better on there?" she asked.

"Do you like gospel music?" I asked her.

"You mean from the American South?" she said, stuffing the rest of the bun in her mouth. "Oh yes. Very much. Yes."

I put the Mississippi Mass Choir on the iPod singing "When I Rose This Morning" and put one earpiece into Ethne's ear and the other into Mary's. Their eyes widened and they began to jig about. I grabbed their hands and we all three there on top of the mountain danced and laughed as the sun lit the sky and scurried the morning's clouds away. "*Go raibh maith agat*," said Mary when the gospel was over and she and Ethne handed me back the earpieces.

"Stop the Gaelic, girl," Ethne told her.

"That there may good at you," said Mary. "Thank you, Kevin. Did you know back in our county we have a Saint Kevin?"

"I already told the boy," said Ethne. "Now let him walk."

Mary laughed her Burl Ives laugh. "Walk along then. We'll see you later in the next couple of towns that be over."

I didn't see Mary and Ethne at first once I got here to this latest little town along the Camino. But I did meet another Irish lady as I was getting a coffee when I arrived at an outside café. She is much younger and hipper than Ethne and Mary and moved to Australia a few years ago. She was at the next table over. I asked if she had met Ethne and Mary along the Camino. "Oh, my word! Those two!" she said, and rolled her eyes. "They were what I moved to Australia to escape."

I also spotted two beautiful young boys in the distance—one tall and thin with long blond hair and the other shorter and darker. They each had on gym shorts with striped leggings underneath them. I wondered if the boys were friends or lovers. I couldn't tell. On my way to the hotel to check in I introduced myself—they were from New Zealand and were eating from a shared bag of lentils. They told me they were trying to save money since they were being sponsored to walk the Camino by donations and they were giving the money to charity. Sweet. I'd guess they're boyfriends but am not sure.

There were only two restaurants close by my hotel, and luckily I ran into Ethne and Mary outside the one where I was reading the posted menu. I asked them to dine with me. Both sisters are in their sixties. Ethne is a retired secretary and married. Mary—no surprise—has never married. She's a physical therapist. They told me they are from a family of thirteen children and a few months before they began their pilgrimage their favorite brother, Danny, died. He had "fallen alone in his house," said Mary. Not sure how that kills someone, but I didn't ask for details, since they are obviously so heartbroken about it. He was a bachelor and no one found him for a few days. They are walking the path in his memory. It was Ethne's turn to cry now and my turn to reach out and rub her hand a bit. Mary looked down at her menu until her sister's tears stopped.

"Tell me about your county back in Ireland where I'm a saint," I said, trying to steer the conversation away from Danny and their grief.

"We grew up in a place called Hollywood, Ireland. It's in county Wicklow. Only about a hundred of us villagers left there," said Mary.

"Do you ladies mind if I write about you if I ever do a book about my pilgrimage on the Camino?" I asked.

Mary: "Just don't write about the size of my arse."

"But I love seeing your 'arse' out in front of me on the Camino in the morn, Miss Mary," I said, trying to mimic her Irish lilt.

"Oh, now, Kevin, that's not very saint-like of you. Our Hollywood is known as Killinkeyvin," said Mary, laughing. "The Irish for it is 'Cillin Chaoimhin,' which means 'little cell of Kevin.'"

"I think the better translation is 'Kevin's little church,'" said Ethne.

Mary shrugged her burly shoulders.

"That's sort of what Hollywood means to me back in America too," I said. "It's always been—for better or worse—my church."

"Do tell now, me boy," said Mary.

"I'm just joking," I said. "I interview movie stars for a living, so this is all just part of the Camino speaking to me I guess," I told them. "I had no idea about any of this. You ladies are like Irish angels put in my path."

"We're no angels," said Ethne.

"Speak for yourself, Sister," said Mary.

"Well, I'm certainly no saint—far from it. Is there anything else I should know about the saint I'm named for?" I asked them.

"Well, like the Way of Saint James that we're all on right now," said Ethne, "there's a Saint Kevin's Way back home. Pilgrims walk that path as well—though it's only about thirty kilometers from Killinkeyvin— sorry, Hollywood—to Glendalough."

"It's a nice little hike compared to this backbreaker we're on here in Spain," said Mary. "It's a lovely, lovely way to see Wicklow Mountains National Park. Did Ethne tell you about Saint Kevin drowning the housekeeper in the lake where he liked to bathe?"

"That doesn't sound too saint like," I said.

"You must not be Catholic," said Mary, laughing.

"He's Protestant," whispered Ethne, not wanting anyone in the restaurant to overhear such a thing, and reached out to give my hand another sad little sympathetic pat.

"Our Kevin didn't like the women very much," said Mary, giving me a knowing look. It was Ethne's turn now to stare down uncomfortably at her menu. "There's even a song about Saint Kevin that begins . . ." She cleared her throat to sing the lyrics: "'In Glendalough there lived an auld saint, / Renowned for his learning and piety. / His manners were curious and quaint. / And he looked upon girls with disparity.'" She cocked an eyebrow my way. I said nothing. She continued. "So this housekeeper snuck, she did, into his room one night and attempted to 'polish his crockery,' as we say. Well, he was so upset he threw her in the lake and held her there till the bubbles of her breath stopped and the surface of the lake returned to its placid state. Some say he was keeping himself pure for God."

"Well, I'm far from pure and more sissy than saint," I said.

"Sissy?" asked Ethne.

"*Piteog*," said Mary. "That's how we say it in Ireland. *Piteog*, Sister. Pity, that," she said. "Though I have me thoughts about our own Saint Kevin back in Hollywood being called just that."

Ethne gave my hand another of her pats.

"You haven't drowned any housekeepers now, have you?" asked Mary, her shoulders not shrugging now but shaking with laughter.

Ethne, laughing too, rolled up her menu and gave her sister a smack.

I laughed along with them.

5/14/09

I made it to Carrión de los Condes—a lovely little town—today where I'm now writing this late at night in my room at this amazing hotel here, San Zoilo. The hotel was once a monastery. Truly beautiful. Ethne and Mary told me last night that they had also booked a room here to give themselves a break from hostel life. My room is beautifully decorated and looks out on the inner courtyard. The hotel is the oldest Romanesque building in Carrión de los Condes. It was built over the remains of a Roman camp and the first evidence of its existence dates back to the year 948. The abbey has kept the relics of Saint

Zoilo since 1047. In the Middle Ages it was one of the most important abbeys in Spain. It was also the seat of the court of the kings of Castile and León and served as a meeting place for several councils.

On the Camino today I met Ken—the shorter and darker of the legging-wearing lentil eaters. Adorable. He mentioned Jesus a couple of times. Par for the course when having a conversation with fellow pilgrims along the Camino. I really didn't think too much of it. He told me his friend Matt, the taller blond one, was up ahead and they were meeting up here in Carrión.

After I checked into the hotel—it's just outside of the village over a footbridge—I ran into Ethne and Mary walking over the bridge toward the place.

"What's the hotel like?" asked Ethne.

"It makes me feel like a monk," I said.

"And what does a monk feel like?" asked Mary.

"Sexually frustrated?" I asked.

"Now you're sounding like Saint Coemgen," said Mary, laughing. "You behave there, *me fae*. Behave. Bad boy. Bad!" she called back, laughing as they walked on to the hotel.

My feet have been aching from the boots I've been wearing on the walk. They are the same boots I wore to climb Mount Kilimanjaro and I wanted to wear them across the Camino. I'm discovering though that mountain-climbing boots are not the same as hiking shoes. So I stopped in town after seeing Mary and Ethne on the footbridge and bought a pair of shoes better suited to this pilgrimage I'm on. Hope they help my feet. I'll tie the boots to my backpack. I've been carrying it since I can't find a service on this last stretch of the Camino to haul it for me.

In the grassy square in front of the hostel in the middle of Carrión, I sat on a bench and watched Ken sleeping on the ground a few feet away. Matt came up and sat by me. Did he notice how I was mooning over his friend? He told me they're both losing weight because of living off the lentils. And they're even sharing them with other pilgrims on the path. I offered to take them to dinner tonight—which Matt accepted with alacrity. Was I being manipulated? I didn't mind. I'd love to sit across from two beautiful hippie boys tonight with New Zealand accents. Ken woke up and saw us and we told him of our plans. I then walked with them over to a group of young people who were sitting in front of the hostel and playing instruments and singing. Matt borrowed a guitar and sang—so beautifully—a song I'd never heard before. It's by a band called Live, he later told me. The song was titled "Overcome" and I felt a bit overcome listening to him singing it.

Dinner tonight with Matt and Ken turned a bit odd. First of all, they were so hungry they licked their plates. I was shocked when they lifted their plates to their faces and licked them clean. They also began to witness to me about Jesus and wanted to know if he were my Lord and Savior. Their fervor was moving to me and yet a bit freaky as well.

I decided to test their empathy and compassion by telling them I was not only gay but also HIV positive. I then told them I was on the Camino to wean myself from recreational drugs for at least a month and to get back in touch with my spirituality that I had allowed organized religion to steal from me because I am a gay man. I could tell it was their turn to become moved and yet a bit freaked out. It didn't stop them from ordering dessert.

After dinner as we were walking back down the street, Matt asked, "May we pray for you to ask God to heal you from your sickness?"

I wanted to ask if he meant my being gay or my being HIV positive, but I didn't. I simply said, "I am not sick." I looked him straight in the eye and said it once more: "I am not sick, Matt." I then said, "You can pray for me. I don't believe in telling someone what they can pray about."

"Let's go over here then," said Ken, pointing to a stone bench by the side of the street.

"Wait," I said. I stopped walking. They stopped. "You can pray for me anywhere," I told them. "I don't have to be there when you pray for me."

My heart began to race.

"But we have to lay our hands upon you for the prayer of healing to be effective," said Matt.

Now what? Was this their way of thanking me for dinner? Would I be rude if I turned down their offer to lay their hands upon me and pray? Then I thought: If you can't have someone lay their hands upon you and pray for you on the Camino, then where on earth can you have it done? I looked on it as a test of the Camino itself. These two young men were put in my path. I had been attracted to them physically initially and now the Camino was offering them to me as prayer partners instead. "Okay," I said, and gave them a shrug. I walked over to the stone bench. I sat between them. They each placed a hand on one of my shoulders and when they did—as if by reflex—my legs shot up in the air. I giggled. My feet plopped back down on the ground, my legs still spread. I began to slink down on the bench beneath their touch. Ken and Matt shut their eyes and earnestly prayed that whatever God considered my illness to be lifted from me. My giggle stopped. My eyes filled with tears. I was honestly moved by the way they phrased such a prayer, the way they left it up to God to decide what to lift from my body and my spirit. I was overcome.

When I got back to the San Zoilo after dinner I decided to take this journal down to the church that is located in the bowels of the monastery/hotel. I was the only one in there. I had to walk around a lot of construction, since they are doing some renovations—buttressing of columns, et cetera. Not changing things per se. I have to admit I've avoided most of the Catholic churches along the Camino since I find the aesthetic too ornate—even tacky—for my austere Protestant tastes. Give me one simple wooden cross to stare at above a simple altar—not all this pornographic violence that passes for religious idolatry, relics, statuary, et cetera. It reminds me of the tacky furniture one could often find in the old New York store Castro Convertibles. I've come to think of these churches as "Castro Convertible Cathedrals"—though I keep that to myself. Most of them are downright ugly—filled with guilt and gilt.

This evening, however, I thought I'd give it a try and sit in the ancient church here—it is thankfully much less "decorated" than others I've peeked in—and contemplate my trip so far. Meditate. See what moved me as I tried to decipher and sift through my experiences. Maybe do a bit of journal writing. I closed my eyes and drifted off—not to sleep exactly but to a fitful rest.

When I got up to leave—I decided to wait to write in the journal—I saw a door over by the side of the altar (my Catholic friends call it a sacristy, I think, not sure—sacresty?—something like that, not even sure how to spell it), so I thought I'd go have a look inside. When I entered I saw there on the wall the most bloody and bludgeoned Christ-on-the-Cross I have ever seen. His eyes were beaten to a plastered pulp and closed tight—as if the centurions had mugged him first before crucifying him. I kept thinking of Brad Pitt's face in *Fight Club*. Leave it to me—this Kevin who is not a saint—to make the connection to the Hollywood that is not in Ireland but back in California. The wound on Christ's rib cage was gaping and gushing blood. The crown of thorns was cutting into his head and dripping blood down on his face. His feet were gnarled in bloody pain beneath the spikes that had nailed them to the cross. His hair was not carved but real human hair that flowed down in front of his anguished face. I hated the awfulness of it all. But I made myself look up into the face. "Brad Pitt," I whispered.

And then—had the Brad Pitt whisper been a taunt and I was now going to be taught a lesson?—something occurred I cannot explain.

I don't think I will ever be able to explain it.

In fact, even as I'm about to write about it I am rolling my own eyes at what happened.

But it did happen.

It did.

I was not drunk.

I had not been smoking meth.

I had not been smoking pot.

I was tired, but my utter fatigue could not explain it.

Now that I'm sorting out what happened, the only thing I can come up with is there might have been a young priest working some sort of mechanism behind the wall where the cross was hanging for wary, overly discerning, austere Protestant pilgrims like me who wandered in alone and whose wariness took on a sarcastic edge. All I know is this: The eyes of the Christ figure began slowly to open and a white kind of light began to emerge from them. I don't know if it really happened. But it was true. It is true. I am telling the truth. The body itself seemed to lift a bit on the cross. The head lifted also slightly as if trying to get a better look at me. The hair moved a bit as the head cocked to one side to get a better look at me. I dropped this very journal and fell to my knees. I began to cry looking up into the white-eyed, shining face of Christ and all I could mumble over and over was, "Thank you thank you thank you thank you thank you thank you thank you. . . ." I am mumbling it again even as I write this. "Thank you thank you thank you thank you."

I then grabbed my journal there beneath that bloody bludgeoned Christ and quickly scurried out into the courtyard. It had all happened in a matter of seconds—maybe half a minute at the most. I turned the corner and ran into Ethne and Mary walking toward me. They saw the state I was in. It wasn't as if I were in the eye of a storm, but I were the eye itself. The experience was still whipping about me and yet a calm had overtaken me. "Something just happened in there. I can't explain it . . . ," I told them, my voice shaky but sure. "I don't know what just happened. The crucifix was doing crazy things and I started to cry and I didn't know what . . ." The calmness was suddenly skittering from me. I was about to hyperventilate. I felt a "Hallelujah" lodged in my throat, but I was able to suppress it. Is that what a vow of silence at its essence feels like? I wanted to drop to my knees again.

Ethne looked vexed herself now by my demeanor. But her burly sister attempted to calm me. "Shshshhhh . . . Kevin . . . shhshhshhsh," she whispered, and folded me in her big soft arms. "This," a woman named

Mary whispered in my ear as she held me to her breast, "is how a monk feels. Now you know, *me fae*. Now you know. Feel it."

John Keats to Percy Bysshe Shelley: "My imagination is a monastery and I am its monk."

5/15/09

On my walk this morning, Toby, surprising me, came up behind me and hit me on my butt. It was so good to see him. I've missed him and Lucas, who is several towns ahead of us now on the path. It's even Lucas's birthday today, Toby told me. Toby was with two beautiful German girls—Teresa and Aurelia—he'd met since last time I saw him. They have formed a little Austrian/German troika.

A stray dog came up and nuzzled me as I sat by the side of the road later. Made me miss Archie so much. I know my sister is taking good care of him, but I do miss cuddling with him under the covers when I go to sleep at night.

5/16/09

John Keats from October 27, 1818: "I feel assured I should write from the yearning and fondness I have for the Beautiful even if my night's labours should be burnt every morning and no eye shine upon them. But even now I am perhaps not speaking from myself but some character in whose soul I now live."

5/17/09

I ran into Mary and Ethne this morning as the sun was rising. They were taking a break in a field on the side of the Camino and eating a bit of fruit for energy. Mary said last night at dinner that she had pulled her back out a bit and I asked if she was okay. "I'll be fine," she said.

"Just be careful, *me cara*. If you see some handsome Brazilians, don't turn too quickly to get a second look. That's what happened to this old girl." Laughing, she went to retrieve another piece of fruit from her bag and when she did she also retrieved a funeral card with a picture on it. I had asked who it was and she said, "That be *mo dheartháir*. That's me Danny boy." He looks a lot like Mary. Same round, full cheeks. Same bulbous nose. No mistaking they are family.

"We stop every morning at sunrise before we really start our walk for the day," said Ethne. "And we sing for dear Danny. Would you like to join us this morning, Saint Kevin?"

"I'd be honored," I said.

With that, they softly began to sing "Danny Boy." Mary went to hit the high note but choked up. Ethne and I finished the song for her. We all had tears in our eyes. We sat in silence for a few moments. Their faces, already ruddy and redolent with sorrow, were reddened even more by the rising sun.

I don't like the ugly town where I've ended up for the night. I checked into an awful little hotel and feel as if I'm in a dive hotel around Times Square circa 1977. The walls are cardboard thin and I can hear a heterosexual couple fucking next door. Pilgrims? I am now leaning against the wall to listen to their moans as I write these very words. More moaning. My own bed creaks as I move closer to the wall to hear as much as I can in the next room. I want to masturbate to the sounds. I grab at my pubic hair and think of Kurt Cobain's when Courtney Love caught me sniffing a handful of it. I think of that Buddhist altar in her house. I think of my Buddhist dream. I think of those two old Jews who are walking the Camino for their "one heart." I think of Colin and his stitched-up one. I think of Keats and his poems and his letters. I think of a Banat Swabian émigré's ululating yell. I think of whores. I think of bridges from Prague. I think of Warhol's funeral at St. Patrick's Cathedral. I think of Christ on his Catholic cross who invaded my Protestant imagination and conjured my tears. I long for company of any kind right now. Any kind, I think, keeping time to the rhythm I can feel through the wall as I hear the thud of the man pounding his body into the woman. Any kind. I think of my father. Any kind. My mother. I hear the couple coming together in the next room. I can't. I can't come. I listen to their silence. I press my ear to the wall. I pretend my breathing is timed with theirs. I wonder what they look like. My own breath is all that I can hear now. I just took this pen and drew a tiny flattened M on the wall beside me. I wonder what the next person who rents this filthy room will make of it, that M. Will they think it an initial or the wings it is meant to be? Will they think it a bird? An angel? "Move over," I hear the man in the next room say. American. They must be pilgrims. "Move," he says again. I hear the woman moan and move. I hate being HIV positive. I hate it. I carefully point the pen (my Honey West ritual) beneath my lower lip, inking on a beauty mark as perfect as a period, the punctuation on a sentence my flesh still keeps trying to write.

5/18/09

I got up early from the horrible hotel today and had a leisurely four-hour walk into León, where I now am having lunch at a sidewalk café in this lovely city full of college students. There is a kind of pedestrian thoroughfare here in the middle of the place where all the kids seem to promenade and preen for one another. It's the first real city I've been in since Burgos.

Burly Irish Mary spotted me a few moments ago and strode over through all the preening kids. She told me that according to her guidebook the walk tomorrow is through some industrial sections and not a very pretty one. She then tried to convince me to take the bus with her to our next destination on the Camino. I told her since I had been checking into hotels along the way that I have to walk every inch of the Camino so I won't feel guilty about purposefully skipping so much of the hostel experience.

"Oh, now, you're being too rigid, Saint Kevin," said Mary before striding away. "Sometimes life is about being carried."

My grilled fish has arrived.

5/19/09

There was no hotel in the small village where I am now. But I was lucky to get the last bed in one of the hostels when I came hobbling into town. I am now at the computer terminal where I just checked my e-mails for any news from home. I did, sadly, get a shocking bit just now. An old friend, Rodger McFarlane, who was one of the founders of Gay Men's Health Crisis in New York, committed suicide. He also worked for Broadway Cares/Equity Fights AIDS and Bailey House and had moved to Colorado to work for gay multimillionaire Tim Gill in his philanthropic enterprises at the Gill Foundation. Rodger was a Southern sissy like me, but he grew up next door from Mississippi in Alabama. He was six feet seven inches tall and took up even more space than that in the world with his larger-than-life humor and social activism. He was a hero of mine. Rodger is the last person I would have thought would kill himself. He did it—this is so Rodger—in Truth or Consequences, New Mexico. I know, like Perry, Rodger had chronic back pain. Maybe that was the root of his despair. Maybe it was more physical pain than he could finally bear. I said a prayer for him. And for Perry.

Reading about Rodger just now made me stop writing and take a walk around the village to collect my thoughts. Calm down. I'm back in the computer room now sitting in a dirty old chair. On my walk I thought about the big, handsome German I met today. He was almost as tall as Rodger, come to think of it. Even kind of looked like him. His name was Kirk and he asked me if I had read the Kerkeling book about the Camino. I told him I had not, but neither my having not read it nor our language barrier deterred our conversation. He told me it was nice to meet strangers and talk and pass the time as he walked. He was from Berlin. The one subject, to my surprise, he was not keen on discussing was anything to do with spirituality. He was much more focused on the physical aspect of the walk. What moved him, he said, was walking in the footsteps of all those who have walked before us and connecting to the earth itself where they had once trod. "Ambled" is the English word he used. "Where they have before ambled." He seemed to be paraphrasing Jessica Lange and her own love of walking for the sake of walking. "Nothing really changes," he said. "That's what I keep thinking about as I walk this path that people have walked for two thousand years. What's new? Nothing's new. New? Nothing. Nichts. Nothing. Nothing." I tried to keep up with the long strides of this man named Kirk from Berlin as I thought of that needle-loving woman named Berlin from New York who told me the same thing when we talked about Andy Warhol after his death. "And he'd say again, 'What's new?'" said Brigid. "I'd say, 'Nothing's new.'" "Nothing's new," repeated the German, gesturing toward the horizon, the heavens, which we keep waiting to gesture back to us.

5/20/09

Each day here on the Camino I try to move on from moment to moment to moment. As the sun once again rose before me and once again the birds began their morning songs, I thought of another passage from my reading the other night of Keats's letters. It was in one he had written to his friend Benjamin Bailey on November 22, 1817, and it is how the Camino itself is schooling me. "Nothing startles me beyond the Moment," Keats wrote. "The setting sun will always put me to rights, or if a Sparrow comes before my window, I take part in its existence and pick about the gravel."

I got up early and was the first one out of the hostel this morning to pick about the gravel after having a wild dream in which I was trying to fall asleep in another hostel. A group of pilgrims arrived late in the dream and began to party in the courtyard. I woke myself talking in my sleep, which is something I never used to do. I think it's one of the side effects of my HIV medication. Lots of people who are on it have nightmares. I sometimes do as well. But usually my dreams just become more vivid and I've begun to talk aloud while having them. I always know it's happening because I have a hard time talking in the dream itself as I vocally begin to straddle the conscious and unconscious worlds. I first shouted, "God forgive you!" at the partying pilgrims; then when they wouldn't quiet down I shouted, "Fuck you!" That's when I woke myself. Those two admonitions pretty much sum up all of life, I guess—or, at least, mine so far. An overly friendly Swiss guy in the next bunk was staring at me when I startled myself awake. I guess I had woken him as well. "Which is it?" he whispered to me when I saw him staring at me in the moonlight. "Do you want God to forgive me or do you want to fuck me?" he asked. I ignored him. I went back to sleep.

Today I listened to Renée Fleming on my iPod sing Schubert lieder for the rest of my walk. I'm so surrounded by Germans on the Camino I thought I might as well go all in and listen to their music. I kept playing "Gretchen am Spinnrade" several times in a row. Though it was rather incongruous to be listening to a lied about Faust on such a spiritual trek, there was something about the hypnotic constancy of the "spinning wheel" piano accompaniment, which Schubert so brilliantly acknowledges in his musical interpretation of Goethe's words, that mirrors the hypnotic constancy that my walking day in and day out physically provides as it accompanies this spiritual quest. I haven't sold my soul, however. I've just misplaced it. After twenty days now on the Camino I am still trying to find it.

I kept thinking of Rodger's death all day.

And the name of that town where he chose to die.

I am writing this in my lovely hotel room in Astorga. The loveliest really of the trek so far. A boutique hotel called Casa de Tepa. It reminds me of Soniat House, where I stay in New Orleans and where I lay awake the night after I read about the Camino in *The New York Times* and decided to come here and attempt this spiritual journey I'm now on. I even invited Marge and Judy and Ginny and Coral over for gin and tonics earlier. The place even has an "honor" bar like Soniat House does. They practically swooned at how nice it is. Of course, it cost me fifty bucks to fete them with liquor, but it was worth it to share some time with them in comfort, especially after my long thirty-two-kilometer day.

Time for sleep. I had vodka, not gin. My eyes are about to close. Hope I'm not hungover tomorrow.

5/21/09

I woke up this morning after three weeks of walking and began to hate the Camino. I am *not* a Catholic. Why am I putting myself through this on such a Catholic pilgrimage? All day long I ruminated on how much I hate the Catholic Church. The pedophile scandal and the cover-up of all the molestation of girls and boys by priests. The vulgar and obscene wealth of the church. The pornographic idolatry of violence and suffering in its statuary. The misogynistic male hierarchy. And no, this is not just a hangover from last night.

The day was dusty and hot and the more I walked in its dusty heat the angrier I got. And the angrier I got the more I began to get a split-ting headache in the blinding sun from the gestureless sky. Was this part of my spiritual enlightenment—having to burn away some of this anger? Confront it. Is the anger really about Catholicism? Or were my ranting thoughts about Catholicism a way to exorcise some deeper an-ger in me?

I finally headed up into a lovely little mountain village at the end of the day. As I neared it I had to walk by a long fence by a field on which other pilgrims had stuck crosses made from sticks, broken bits of limbs, twigs. Hundreds and hundreds of crude crosses greeted me and my cruder anger. I succumbed, however, and made a cross myself and put it on the fence. The path by the fence was shaded and that calmed me as much as the sight of all those crosses after walking in that blazing sun all day.

As I entered the village there was chanting coming from an ancient little church. Were there really monks in there chanting, I wondered, or was it a tape? I went inside. The sanctuary itself was behind bars as if it were being jailed. The gate into it was locked. But the stone interior of the vestibule area was about twenty degrees cooler than the temperature outside. I sat on a stairwell in the back and listened to the chanting. I removed my boots and socks and put my feet on the stone floor. The coolness was just the comfort I was seeking. If it felt that good on my feet I wondered what it would feel like on my forehead, since my head was still aching. I knelt on the floor and put my face down on the stones. It was as if the whole day—the heat, my headache, my anger at the Catholic Church—had conspired to get me to that one moment: prostrate in a Catholic church accompanied by the chanting of unseen monks. God does have a sense of irony. All anger left me. All discomfort. I stayed facedown for several minutes. I decided since I was already down there I should pray. I asked for forgiveness for my anger. I asked to face the truth about myself or face the consequences.

5/22/09

Got up before sunrise to walk farther up into the mountains on this part of the Camino. Stopped off at a little hostel on the mountainside where I saw Toby and Teresa and Aurelia. They had stayed there the night before. I walked with them to the highest point of the Camino, where you place a rock at the foot of a gigantic wooden cross. Had my picture taken there. Sublime moment. But then I was brought quickly back to earth when I walked behind the outhouse structure there to pee, since there was a line and I saw that people had actually shit back there as well. Yet maybe that's what the cross is all about: the coming to terms with the most base of human conditions. Perhaps it comes down to that. The difference between man and God is that God doesn't have to take a shit.

The walk today up along the mountainside was the most beautiful yet. "The poetry of the earth is never dead," Keats wrote. But as I descended the mountains into Ponferrada—the last major town before I reach Santiago—my knees and feet began to kill me again. The pain was brutal.

But that is what is so sacred about the Camino. It is not just the spiritual aspect of it; it is also sacred in its brutality. It can break you down and make you call on reserves of strength you never knew you had. I have spoken about this aspect with some of my fellow pilgrims. It is hard to describe to others what we are going through, hard to put it down in words. For the rest of my life when I meet someone who has walked this arduous journey I will instantly feel a kinship with them. I will not only be aware of a kind of spiritual light in their eyes but also know that they will possess the shared knowledge in their bodies of how brutal the experience could be at times. Perhaps that's what it will be like to arrive in heaven—wherever, whatever, heaven is. We will look into the eyes of whoever it is who greets us and recognize that same spiritual light as well as share in the recognition of how brutal the human experience we just left behind can be. The brutality will live on as memory. The spiritual light will be what survives. Is that how I will feel about the Camino once I finish it? Will I finish it?

A man broke his leg today descending the mountain into Ponferrada. The other day another man died of a coronary right on the path in front of his wife. I told burly Mary about it and she said, "What a lovely way to die, don't you think? Right on the path where so many pilgrims for thousands of years have walked seeking spiritual enlightenment. That man's soul must have been so happy at that moment."

I had not thought of it in that way. I only thought how brutal it was for the wife to witness her husband's death.

I am getting quite tan from walking in the sun for the last three weeks. The creepy Swiss guy from a few nights back who was staring at me when I woke myself up by talking in my sleep passed me on the path as I was hobbling down the mountain to Ponferrada. "You're getting too dark," he said. "You look like a nigger."

I had imagined having lots of experiences on the Camino, but being called a "nigger" by a creep from Switzerland was not one of them. The n word knows no boundaries. Another form of brutality.

5/23/09

I am about to turn out the light and close my eyes and think of my Methodist mother. I long to see her standing in the doorway on that snowy night before she turned around and slid into bed with my father and Chico and Coco and me. But right now I'm staring out my window at the rain—not snow—that has begun to fall and thinking instead of her shadowy presence behind the shower curtain when she caught me staring at her.

I reach in my pocket and palm the two smooth black pebbles I took from the M in "MAMA" and the D in "DADDY" back on the Camino that I've been carrying with me ever since. I put them on the desk here next to this journal. They stare up at me as if fossilized pupils.

I hum "The Church's One Foundation," which I remember singing from the Cokesbury hymnal that first Methodist church service I attended with my mother. "The Church's One Foundation." I suddenly remember the words and am singing them as I write them here, "Is Jesus Christ her Lord; / She is his new creation, / By water and the word: / From heaven he came and sought her / To be his holy bride; / With his own blood he bought her, / And for her life he died."

I touch the staring pebbles.

The rain reminds me of its presence.

My mother's shadowy one moves about the room.

5/24/09

Only seven more days to go until I reach Santiago if everything goes well and my knees and feet hold up. No more blisters to speak of since I bought the new pair of hiking shoes. My heavy mountain-climbing boots tied onto the backpack have been weighing me down as they knock about behind me while I trudge along. I sat staring at the boots in the room at my inn this morning and decided to leave them there. It was very hard to let them go. They have been like talismans to me ever since I made the summit of Mount Kilimanjaro. But I did. I let them go.

5/25/09

I am now sitting in a ratty little hotel room in Samos with a bathroom down the hall from which I just hobbled after soaking in a tub for a bit. I walked forty-two kilometers today and my right ankle is now twice the size of my left one. I hope with just a week to go I haven't injured myself in such a way that I now won't make it all the way to Santiago. I was shocked when I took off my socks and shoes and saw the swelling. I have it propped up now as I write this and look out my window at the ancient fortress-like monastery here in Samos just across the street. Another pilgrim told me it is the oldest monastery in Spain.

I ate dinner by myself downstairs here tonight in the hotel's restaurant. It was hard to concentrate on the food with my ankle killing me so. I have never felt so tired. So alone. Staring at the Samos monastery across the way, I wonder how many monks through the ages suffered through such fatigue, such loneliness, such pain. Is this, finally, how a monk feels, Mary?

5/26/09

After the hard day I had yesterday I only walked fourteen kilometers today and checked into a hotel in Sarria. I am only one hundred kilmoters from Santiago now.

I just checked my e-mails and found one from my sister. I've been sending lots of e-mails to her and my brother as I've walked the path. I told her in my last one how I would have never guessed it would have been I out of the three of us who would have been the one to climb Mount Kilimanjaro or walk all the way across Spain on a spiritual pilgrimage. In the e-mail she sent me back she wrote: "The only reason we wouldn't have picked you to be the one to do this back then would have been because of those 'weak spells.'" That made me smile remembering how when we'd go out to play or shoot some hoops in our backyard after we ate a meal my blood sugar would become imbalanced and I'd get light-headed and kind of dizzy and complain, "I'm having a weak spell," and go inside and have either some juice or my favorite remedy, a glass of ice-cold water while I sucked on some peppermint candy. It all seems so long ago, those days when I was such a little Mississippi sissy complaining of my weakness instead of my ankles and feet and knees.

"Guess you've showed those 'spells' now!" my sister continued in her e-mail. "Reminds me of having fun growing up with my two brothers. I was telling a friend the other day about our bonding time growing up being over the kitchen sink. Washing and drying dishes and 'puttin' up.' I can feel it like it was yesterday and when I stop to conjure it all the only emotion that comes with it is laughter. So those must have been some fun times . . . laughter . . . how could we have come from the same address since you so often say how sad your own childhood was? I feel your life changing now though and you will never be the same. I hope you are not only finding some happiness there on the Camino but also real joy. Because joy is much deeper than happiness and not dependent on external conditions."

5/27/09

Such a lovely walk into Portomarín today on a long bridge over the Mino River. A pilgrim walking beside me pointed at the town sitting up on the hillside and told me it is hard to tell that it is only about forty years old. He then pointed down at the river rushing beneath the bridge and, reading from his guidebook, told me that the original village lies underwater beneath the Mino because when it was dammed by a reservoir upstream it flooded the place. The villagers dismantled many of the most ancient and sacred buildings submerged under the water and rebuilt them original stone by original stone up on the hillside. Still with his nose in his guidebook and not really seeing the beautiful hillside village before us, he said to be sure to check out the Romanesque church of San Pedro and the monumental church fortress of San Nicolás. Some of the old medieval palaces were placed in the main square of the new town, he continued, and the medieval bridge stayed underwater. All that remains of the medieval structure is the base and one of its arches at the entrance of the new bridge we were almost across by the time he finished his reading and little tutorial.

I am now at a bar on the banks of the Mino. I've come over to a table by myself to write a bit in my journal I brought here with me and stare at the river down below and think about how far I've come from the one named Mississippi back in America. In fact, I'd never even heard of the Mino before I arrived here today and the pilgrim with the guidebook told me of its history. I am staring down into the water and imagining the submerged village that I was told about. I think of the churches that were rebuilt stone by retrieved stone up here on the hillside. I think of my own life submerged in my memories that keep flooding back at me during my walk each day—my brother and sister and Chico and Coco and countless movie stars' mouths moving in conversation and crystal meth pipes and Howard Moss and Henry Geldzahler and my HIV status and the HIV-negative person I will never be again and Andy Warhol and Mount Kilimanjaro and so many cocks and so many asses of so many strangers and Harry Potter and Daniel Radcliffe and the sweet kid I've mentored and that sweet kid I once was myself who watched his father make flattened Ms fly and who held his mother's hand that first time he walked into a Methodist church and now writes of himself in the third person—and how he is (how I am) trying to rebuild my life stone by retrieved stone. I look down at the river and wonder about all that has been left submerged.

5/28/09

Last night I had a dream about Jim Morrison. He was swimming in the Mino and began to drown and I saved him. When I pulled him ashore he shook his head of long hair like a shaggy dog and the water from the Mino covered my own face. I turned to look at him and he had turned to stone—a kind of statue. I started to touch him. He shattered into many stones. I went to retrieve a few to rebuild him but woke up.

The dream had been so vivid that I stopped at the hotel's computer before having breakfast and looked up Jim Morrison and the Doors on Wikipedia to read about them. This is what I copied down, never having known it before: "The Doors were an American rock band formed in 1965. . . . The band took its name from the title of Aldous Huxley's book *The Doors of Perception*, which itself was a reference to a William Blake quotation . . . : 'If the doors of perception were cleansed every thing would appear to man as it is, infinite.'"

5/29/09

A bird shit on my head today.

After walking along a very rugged bit of the path, I decided to rest under a tree. Eat a pear. Read some Keats. I knew there was a reference to a "rugged path" in his poem "On Death":

> Can death be sleep, when life is but a dream,
> And scenes of bliss pass as a phantom by?

The transient pleasures as a vision seem,
And yet we think the greatest pain's to die.

How strange it is that man on earth should roam,
And lead a life of woe, but not forsake
His rugged path; nor dare he view alone
His future doom which is but to awake.

Then:
Plop.

I had an e-mail from my brother yesterday. In it he quoted the lyrics of a contemporary Christian song he likes by someone named Chris Rice. It's called "Prone to Wander." I searched for it on the Internet after I read the e-mail and listened to the music video of it.

My brother also wrote this: "Sounds like from your correspondence that this journey (if it doesn't actually kill you) has been full of mercy and might be bringing you back to life. I know it is one of those 'you'd have to be here to really understand what I'm talking about' things. But if anyone can communicate the experience in a palpable meaningful way after the fact and do so in the written word, it is probably you. You might be a sissy but you're a damn tough determined one. I'll give you that, brother. Come home in one piece. Love you."

5/30/09

I am now in the small village of Lavacolla, only nine kilometers from Santiago. When I set out in that tiny French village a month ago and crossed the Pyrenees I had planned to make it into Santiago on the thirty-first day. I think I will have accomplished it. But we shall see what tomorrow brings. Today was very, very taxing. I suddenly developed several painful blisters on my feet. It was as if God were telling me not to be so arrogant and reminding me who exactly the Boss is. It was as if I had to be taught one more painful lesson. I could barely walk by the time I made my way into Lavacolla a few hours ago. I am sitting in my room now in the Pazo Xan Xordo, a lovely stone guesthouse built in the seventeenth century. I just burned a needle with a match and pierced my blisters to drain them. If they don't heal and the bandages don't give me some comfort tomorrow then these very last few kilometers may just be the most trying of my whole pilgrimage, since I am so close to making it into Santiago.

When I got to the restaurant for dinner tonight there was a line of pilgrims waiting to be seated. I was asked if I would mind sitting with another single party and was escorted to a table with a handsome Australian woman who graciously allowed me to sit with her. We began to tell each other our Camino experiences and the conversation drifted to each of our lives back at our homes. She teaches nineteenth-century literature at a college and I told her of my much less scholastic endeavors as a writer who interviews celebrities but that I had written a memoir about my Mississippi childhood and was now working on its sequel. "This walk on the Camino is a way to break my writer's block about it," I told her. Though the nineteenth century was her literary interest—her field of study—she did know enough about the twentieth century and America to engage me in a discussion about Mississippi's Eudora Welty and William Faulkner.

I then told her that I had been reading lots of John Keats along the path. "I start my students out with Keats since his short life corresponded with the beginning of the nineteenth century," she said. "What was it that was inscribed on his tombstone in Rome in—dare we say it here on such a severely Catholic path?—the city's Protestant cemetery?" she whispered, leaning over her picked-at paprika-seasoned octopus. "'Here lies One whose name was writ in Water.'" She sipped at her Albariño wine. Her face was free of makeup though naturally rouged and dusted with freckles by her days in the sun along the Camino. I thought of

Ethne's vastly more freckled face and how much I miss her sister Mary and her. (I sang "Danny Boy" this morning for them as I set off and serenaded the Big Dipper, since no bird was ready to do it.) The creases about the literary professor's eyes were whiter than her cheeks. They didn't look like wrinkles exactly but more like crushed crinoline from her favorite century. They were eyes that had seemed to have read, squintingly, reams of nineteenth-century writers but had seldom cried. They were stern. Steady. I felt like one of her students as she stared at me over the restaurant's table. "I've learned to like octopus these last few days in Galicia," she said, as if the bits of the region's culinary delicacy she carefully placed into her mouth were the words of a postmodern poet surprisingly finding themselves in there. "Keats, huh? Hmmm," she said, swallowing the octopus. She rubbed her throat gently beneath the ribbon she wore as a kind of necklace. I noticed she bit her nails. She did not pluck her gray-tinged eyebrows and one touched her bangs as she arched it a bit and said again: "Keats." She ordered us a bottle of wine, requesting it be from the Rías Baixas region. "I've been reading Emily Dickinson myself the last few weeks on the Camino. Do you like her work? I love teaching her. Especially to my male students from, say, Coober Pedy or other far-flung towns in the bush. The lucky ones are civilized by her—or pretend to be to garner my good graces."

She buttered a piece of bread, its crust slightly crumbling on the tablecloth as if a few of her freckles had fallen from her face and landed there between us. "What's your favorite Emily Dickinson poem?" I asked her.

"This week?" she said with a mouthful of bread. She waited to swallow it. I watched the ribbon ripple atop her throat as she swallowed. She then recited this whole poem, her throat continuing to ripple as she intoned it:

> " 'Hope' is the thing with feathers—
> That perches in the soul—
> And sings the tune without the words—
> And never stops—at all—

"And sweetest—in the Gale—is heard—
And sore must be the storm—
That could abash the little Bird
That kept so many warm.

"I've heard it in the chillest land—
And on the strangest Sea—
Yet—never—in Extremity,
It asked a crumb—of Me."

she said, brushing her own few crumbs now from the table. She arched her brow again. This time, it disappeared beneath her bangs. "That's why I've been walking the Camino, I think. To find some hope again in my life. And you? It can't be just to break your writer's block. That sounds like an evasion to me. My guess is you've come to right yourself, not just write. Oh my. I do hate puns. Never more so than when I commit one. Am I being too pedagogic?"

"Not at all. Too charming perhaps," I told her.

She smiled. Her eyes crushed the crinoline-like lines that creased them.

"I'm trying to find some hope again in my life too," I admitted to her. "That's exactly what I'm trying to find: hope."

"Then I'd suggest more Dickinson and less Keats," she said. We sat in silence and sipped our wine. "So, lad, you interview movie stars for a living?" she finally asked. "How fascinating. Have you ever met Hugh Jackman?"

5/31/09

I just got up. It's 5:00 a.m. In a few hours I will finally be walking into Santiago. I can't believe I am actually going to do it. I have walked every centimeter of these eight hundred kilometers since setting out that morning from St.-Jean-Pied-de-Port. I knelt last night and said a prayer of thanks when I got back to my room here and asked for my painful blisters on the bottoms of my heels to be healed so the walk today will be a joyous one instead of one . . . well . . . lacking in joy. I think it worked. I put new bandages on my heels and I just walked around the room and I seem to be okay. I'll see in a few hours how I'm holding up.

More later.

The sunrise was glorious this morning. I put the Mississippi Mass Choir on my iPod and listened to them as I walked up the path into the mountainside.

I decided not to listen to any more music the rest of the way into Santiago, however, after the choir sang their rousing gospel number about not having any doubt when they also awoke this morning. I have instead let my thoughts wander back over the last month and all that I have experienced on this pilgrimage and all those I have met, including now myself.

A few miles back—I am just outside of Santiago; it's just over the hill there; I can almost touch it now; I can certainly feel it—I began to hum "Amazing Grace" over and over. I then heard myself softly begin to sing the words of the beloved old hymn. When I sang "that saved a wretch like me," sobs began to roll to the surface from somewhere deep inside me and I had to walk off the path and hide behind the tree where I am now sitting and bow my head in prayer. I certainly wasn't expecting such an eruption of emotion and tears. I got out this journal to try to calm myself. There are several birds above me singing and chirping and I am cherishing this moment—attempting to sit very still in it. I am no longer thinking back about the pilgrimage or what awaits me over that hill. I do think, however, of the woman from last night who dared me with her love of Dickinson and digested a delicacy, her throat in both instances rippling beneath that necklace-like ribbon bound about her neck. I am looking up at the birds. Will one shit on my head? Will I care? Had Dickinson looked up at such birds when composing her poem about hope? I feel something bird-like fluttering like a flattened M and perching in my soul. It is my father's feathered hand upon it. It is my Father's. The sensation is transcendently physical. True. Full of sin. Yet heaven-sent.

It is carnal.

It is spiritual.

Time to rise.

"Keep walking," said Brigid. "Walking for the sake of walking," said Jessica. "Tat Tvam Asi," Jackman said.

I look at the sky.

It gestures:

Onward.

NINE

The Addict

Y ou have to believe your first job is to be a powerful witness," Diane
Sawyer was telling me as I sat across from her in her office at ABC
in New York. It was January 2010 and she was just starting her new role
as the anchor of ABC *World News* and had agreed that her first cover
story for a magazine would be with me at *Parade* because we were friends.
"Well, we're more like heightened acquaintances," I had told her. "But
that's sweet of you to say."

Six months had passed since I had returned from the Camino and,
still high from the experience itself, I had stayed mostly drug-free as I
kept moving onward in my life past Santiago and through the summer
of 2009 in Provincetown, where I'd lived for four months in a converted
marine-gear storage house from the 1800s, and then, when autumn arrived, back at my apartment on West 21st Street in Manhattan. I had
began to smoke pot again and had done a bit of meth from time to time
when it was offered—but nothing major. There had been no binges since
my return. For that I was grateful. But the previous night—feeling as
lonely and bored as I had often felt before I ever set foot on that path
in Spain—I had received a phone call from the boy with whom I had
shared meth-infused sex the night before my lunch with Daniel Radcliffe, which, I came to realize, had been exactly one year ago that month.

At first I hadn't known who the caller could be, so I engaged him in conversation, trying to find a hint buried in it until it dawned on me who he was. I had been binge-free for so long that I decided in that moment that I deserved to be bad. I deserved a binge. It seemed as if it and the boy were being delivered to me. I looked on it as fate, almost God's will, which meant, as it was almost God's, there was room in there for it to be the Devil's.

I put the interview with Diane Sawyer out of my mind—I had been doing hours of research already for it—and told the kid to come over. He brought his pipe. I found the meth from an old drug dealer of mine who was glad to hear from me. The kid's bag of toys was again on my floor next to my bed. This time Archie had Teddy to keep him company as they both watched the sad antic display before them from their staked-out patch on my steer skin rug. Again the clock on the wall had finally informed me that it was 4:00 A.M. That morning, however, I only had six hours to get ready to be there at ABC and begin the interview. I was thinking of all of that—the binge, the boy, the bag of toys, both dogs—while Sawyer continued to tell me about being a witness.

"Are you sure you're feeling okay?" I heard her now asking me, having noticed, no doubt, not only how peaked I looked but also the odd reverie in my bloodshot eyes. I had—as I had done when I arrived at the Algonquin to have lunch with Radcliffe—lied to her about having been up all night with a stomach bug in case my appearance was puzzling. And yet I had still been able to find the nest in the conversation with her for the last hour or so—as I had with Radcliffe the year before—and I had gotten her to open up about the challenges of her new role at ABC, her marriage to Mike Nichols, and even her closeness to Richard Nixon when she worked for him at the White House and then returned to San Clemente with him after his resignation. I had gotten so much material from her that *Parade* would later run an extra Q and A from the interview on its Web site as an adjunct to the cover story. But being able to do my job while still under the influence—even if slightly—was not a blessing. It had become a curse.

"Yes, I'm fine," I lied again, and looked around the office so she couldn't focus on my bleary eyes. Sawyer's sixteen Emmys, haphazardly arranged around the shelves, were outnumbered by the myriad pictures of her family and friends. The furniture was surprisingly nondescript. There was nothing glamorous about the place or her at that early hour. Off-camera, in work mode, she had the bookish look of the Wellesley College student she once was who was unaware of her own astonishing beauty. She was wearing thick red-framed glasses and not a speck of makeup. A fleece top was slightly unzipped at her neck and her favorite pair of sweat socks, pilling around the ankles, was peeking from under her jeans. Her shoes were some sort of clog-like contraptions fashioned from soft fabric. Hanging on the door was an Ann Taylor suit Sawyer planned to wear that evening on the ABC *World News* telecast. "That's the other me," she had said, pointing at the clothes when I came in and falsely confessed about my stomach bug. I had offered to sit as far away from her as possible so she couldn't catch it, the real reason being I didn't want her to get too close a look at me.

I suddenly brought up my climb up Mount Kilimanjaro and my pilgrimage over the Pyrenees on the Camino not only to remind myself that I could be a disciplined person—my own "other me"—but also to use as a segue to talk about a news special Sawyer had done about the hardscrabble life in the Appalachian Mountains back in her home state of Kentucky. "I've always seen you as a kind of rarified woman living a rarified life," I told her, motioning toward all the photos and Emmys. This made her laugh, which seemed momentarily to ease her concern about me. The sound of such laughter—the fact that I had been able to elicit it so easily from her—eased, in turn, my own concern about myself. "When I saw that program you did on Appalachia, Diane, it dawned on me: She's a mountain gal. She's mountain stock."

"The music of those mountains and the enormous pride—and in some cases despair—of those people moves me," she said. "My ancestors were mountain folk. You're right. My mom did this great narrative in which she traced her childhood and even further back into her mother's and mother's mother's childhoods. She took pictures of the Cumberland Gap and the Appalachian Trail where they came across the mountains. She did it as a book for her grandchildren. It was such a beautiful story. And there is something about the exquisite poetry of the rugged life and what it took to get across those hills and survive that is still right there in the language of those mountains, in the DNA of it."

"You must still have it in your DNA to get through this first stressful month on your new job. You've been calling on your inner mountain woman," I told her, wishing I had some of it in my own DNA right about then to call upon to get me through the rest of the interview.

"You want to see pioneer stock! I'll show you pioneer stock!" she exclaimed.

I then brought up another of her special reports, this one about the foster-care system, using as its focus the Maryhurst School, which was also back in Kentucky, in her hometown of Louisville. "Was that a way of filling a maternal need—is that too part of your DNA—since you've never had children of your own?" I asked.

"I don't think of it that way," she said. "I just respond to a story. It's that feeling of response. There is a wonderful minister I used to go hear every Sunday who preached a sermon once that really spoke to me about where your great joy meets the world's great need. And I kept hearing the great need of these foster children who were moved sometimes to fourteen foster homes by the time they were ten years old. I loved getting their stories right and trying to get people to pay attention. So that's what it feels like to me. And every single one of them talks to you with such eloquence . . . they see their lives with unsparing clarity."

"It sounds as if you're describing what you have: the journalistic gene," I told her. "It's a survival mechanism for those foster kids as it just might be for you on some other level. I'm too lazy to be a real journalist myself. I think of myself more as a writer who works in journalism. But the same thing holds. I wasn't in foster care, but I was an orphan who was raised by my grandparents. I can only speak for myself. But that ability to separate myself from what it is I am seeing around me not only saved my life early on but has also later made me a writer. It's what still makes me one. Even right now. This moment."

"The story you are telling yourself about your life is so important," Sawyer said, leaning in and staring right at me. "As Leonard Cohen the songwriter says, can you stay the hero of your own story? That's the challenge, Kevin."

As I look back on that morning with Diane up at ABC News, all the major themes of my life were coming to nest in that conversation. They gave me a way to hold on to my place in it. "Are you especially aware of mentoring other women?" I asked.

"I hope so," she said. "I hope so," she repeated. "Now that I'm really two generations removed from the women and men coming up I think it is so important that with this new generation—especially in television journalism since we are forever racing down hallways to meet deadlines—that we the older generation be, whenever it's useful, the Global Positioning System for someone who may not be able to see that there is a shining path ahead of them."

"And also to impart some knowledge," I ventured.

Sawyer smiled. "My husband's favorite fact he ever found in that Harper's Index is that fourteen percent of high school kids thought Joan of Arc was Noah's wife."

It was my turn now to laugh, but I grimaced at how it made my head feel. I paused, allowing the throbbing to subside in my temples. "How does all your travel around the world covering breaking news stories affect your marriage to Mike?" I asked.

"He loves—God bless him—seeing the story with me in it," she said. "And he's excited to hear when I get home how it smelt 'n' felt. How hot it was. What it tasted like. So he loves seeing me stretched flat out."

"Not to put too Freudian a spin on it," I teased her, and thought of the boy from the night before and how he smelled and felt and tasted flat out on my own bed.

Again Sawyer's laughter filled the office; it erased my image of the boy. The laughter faded and she looked over at a photograph of Mike and her. "He said once—very early on in our marriage, because he used to go away for two or three months at a time to shoot a movie—after I wondered aloud if that were a wonderful thing for a marriage or a taxing thing for a marriage, he once said, 'It's both.' And that's true because you get to miss each other mightily and then everything becomes new and chosen again when you're back together. Talk about heightened."

"But more than acquaintances."

"Yes. Much more. Much."

"You are both in professions in which you have to be—or appear to be—invulnerable," I told her. This made her laugh yet again. "So is part of your love for each other finding someone with whom you can feel a private vulnerability?"

"Well, Kevin, I'll put it this way," she said, still chuckling. "It's wonderful to have a safe place to be a basket case. And Mike is a genius at helping you know who you are and helping you know what is real and what is not real in the world and keeping you aimed toward a North Star."

"Just as you'll always be a mountain gal in your deepest DNA, Mike will always be a refugee from Germany," I said. "Talk about a narrative—the two of you finding each other in the world is a pretty powerful one."

"And I love the fact that this son and grandson of blazing Jewish intellectuals ends up with this Methodist girl from the South," she said.

"Who can quote John Wesley to him," I kept it up.

"And sing all the hymns in the hymnal, including most of the second verses," she continued.

We both sighed at that. "I grew up with the Cokesbury hymnal," I told her, relaxing into thoughts of my first morning in a Methodist church, the one thought I could always circle back to as a kind of beginning in my life even as my childhood was about to come to an end with the deaths of my parents. Grief was the truest mountain in my own life, the truest part of my own DNA. But the memory of my first morning in a Mississippi Methodist church always had a way of comforting me, focusing me, making me feel connected to the world, no matter the condition I found myself in.

"I grew up with the Cokesbury hymnal too," Diane said. "I know that even now when I go to church and they don't sing the version of the hymn I learned growing up from the Cokesbury I find it personally offending. There is a church at Eighty-fifth and Park Avenue called Park Avenue Christian Church that you have to go check out. I was taking a walk one Sunday morning and wandered into it. There was a statement printed there on the wall that said that they believe in the divinity of difference. We believe in inclusion. And I thought to myself, Wait a minute—am I still on Park Avenue?"

How had Diane Sawyer and I gotten off the subject? Maybe I was still on the Camino after all. I was told by one pilgrim on the path that once I began walking it I would never leave it. "What books are you reading right now?" I asked as a kind of final question I always liked to ask anyone I'm interviewing. "Aren't you in a secret book club with Oprah?"

"Now?" asked Sawyer. It was the first time she had appeared a bit shocked by one of my questions. "Not now. No. There was a time a while ago she and I and a few others were making a point of sending each other things to read, but that trailed off after a few years because . . . well . . . we lead busy lives. I had never read any Trollope. . . ."

"Joanna or Anthony?" I asked.

She smiled at my literary preening—and at her own. "Anthony, my dear. So I just read *Can You Forgive Her?* which I liked," she said, mentioning the first of his six Palliser novels. "But I still like Edith Wharton better. If I'm going to go back there and read about that stuff, I'll stick to Wharton. I read Trollope on my Kindle on the way to Afghanistan this last time."

"I think you just summed yourself up in that sentence, Diane." Her laughter once more filled the office.

We said our good-byes. When I got to the door she called my name. "Be better," she said.

As I walked through New York City after that morning with Diane I recalled the first time years earlier we had sat talking together. It was back during my *Interview* days at the Factory. Shelley Wanger had taken over as editor in chief after Gael Love had been dismissed and Fred Hughes had asked me to run the magazine in the interim for a few months, even giving me a promotion to executive editor. Shelley was the daughter of film producer Walter Wanger and actress Joan Bennett and as a kind of rebellion perhaps against her Hollywood pedigree had become known for her intellectual heft in the literary salons of New York. She was certainly more literary than either Gael or I. Shelley had also married into East Coast aristocracy when she wed the grandson of W. Averell Harriman, David Mortimer. She was the perfect choice for the ever-aspirational Hughes. Plus, Shelley came with the stamp of approval of Diana Vreeland, who had suggested her as a candidate to Fred. Fred worshiped Diana Vreeland. He considered Vreeland, now that he had outgrown the de Menils in his debonair way, his own mentor. The walls in Fred's office were even an overly lacquered red, much like the walls of Vreeland's archly red apartment at 550 Park Avenue.

Shelley made her presence known at the Factory by instituting evenings of readings upstairs on the building's top floor from upcoming books by her favored authors and even from scripts by East Coast screenwriters. It was a way of mixing art-world glamour with mandarins of publishing and other media. At one such event—Carrie Fisher was reading from her first attempt at a screenplay adaptation of her novel *Postcards from the Edge* with Mike Nichols, who was slated to direct it—I found myself seated next to Diane Sawyer, who had only recently married Mike. During the reading Diane was having trouble keeping one of her earrings fastened to her left lobe. It kept dropping into her lap and became a kind of running joke between us.

The B. Altman department store was still open back then and located only a few blocks from the Factory in the West 30s. I'd often eat lunch there in the store's Charleston Gardens restaurant, which had the faux façade of an antebellum mansion right there on the store's top floor. The day after sitting by Diane at that literary/showbiz soiree I stopped off at the B. Altman jewelry counter after having yet another lunch at the Charleston Gardens and bought her a new pair of gold earrings. I sent them to her that afternoon with a note apologizing for my magnetic force field that kept pulling her earring from her ear and making it fall into her lap over and over. A few days later I got a thank-you note from her for her new pair of B. Altman earrings. But she closed the note by advising me to "never apologize for your magnetism." I had always cherished that piece of advice from Diane Sawyer over the years—even if it was a facetious one. So as I walked down into the subway that morning years later I was oddly challenged—even troubled—by her admonition to me as I left her office. She had not told me to "feel better" but to "be better." I hadn't exactly heard what she meant as I walked out of her office, but as the subway doors closed behind me and I took my seat I sensed what she was saying. Her journalistic gene had rightly sized up what she was seeing—someone in a state of distress. I needed to be reminded that there was still a shining path before me. For me to stay on it I had to be my own "other me," the better one. Yet was the better me the truer one?

When I got home, after giving Archie and Teddy a quick walk around the block, I sat on the bed and looked at the mess in the apartment from the night before. My sheets were still a landscape of lube stains and smudges and smells. There was a new burnt spot on my desk from the boy missing the wet paper towel he'd put there to cool the meth pipe and resting the pipe's freshly torched bulb atop the burled wood instead. I rubbed the blackened bit of desktop with my finger and looked down at the stack of old tattered *Interview* magazines by the desk. As I had felt during my walk from Diane Sawyer's office to the Lincoln Center subway station, I was again overcome by a wave of nostalgia for that time I was a Factory worker. What did it say about me that my two-year tenure working for Andy Warhol was the time in my New York life when I felt the most innocent? I picked up the old *Interview* from the top of the pile with Michael J. Fox on the cover—the one beneath it was my cover story on Sam Shepard—and leafed through it attempting to discern some of the innocence I had misplaced. "After that interview you left behind a piece of paper with some words on it," Fox told me that night at the *Vanity Fair* Oscar party all those years later, his words coming back to haunt me once again. "My dog Barnaby found it a few days later between the sofa cushions and I took it from him before he could chew it up," he'd said. "I've been wanting to tell you this for a long time. It was a litany for a word association game. Every word was sexual. 'Pussy.' 'Dick.' 'Cock.' 'Fuck'. . . ." Sam Shepard stared up at me from his own cover. "Everything is sexual to you," I heard Shepard say once more.

The Michael J. Fox issue I was holding was dated January 1988. I did the math—had it really been twenty-two years ago?—as I sat there in that latest January in my life. Fox was on the cover because he was about to open in the film version of Jay McInerney's 1984 novel, *Bright Lights, Big City*. A story fueled by Bolivian marching powder, not pipes packed with meth, it was about a young straight guy's anti-quest for love in downtown clubs instead of this old gay one's on Internet sites.

I sat staring at Fox's painted portrait on the cover. This was one of the issues of *Interview* I had been in charge of before Shelley Wanger took over as editor in chief. Inside of it was a short story by Charles Bukowski I had commissioned titled "Hollywood." I thought of that small town in Ireland where Mary and Ethne were from, the name that they swore to me meant "little cell of Kevin." There was a feature about David Hockney and his stage sets for a production at the Los Angeles Music Center of *Tristan und Isolde* and I thought of our crying together at Henry Geldzahler's memorial service at the Met when we told each other how he'd cut us out of the herd and how, when I left, I had found my way back into the midst of it, where I still, lost, remained. I flipped to the Fox story and skimmed the introduction before getting to my first sentence spoken to him in the Q and A. "I met Jay McInerney at a party at Norman Mailer's the other night . . . ," I began. I smiled at how easily even back then I could name-drop. "Jesus. What a New York sentence," Michael countered. I smiled too at his rejoinder but read it a bit differently that morning. Staring now at the burnt spot from a meth pipe left atop my desk, marveling at how less than an hour ago I had gotten through my latest interview those twenty-two years later, I felt as if I now were serving out the final days of my New York sentence.

I threw the Michael J. Fox issue back atop the pile and crawled atop my filthy sheet—turning over on my side in the fetal position. I shut my eyes. Archie and Teddy jumped up next to me and curled up against my chest. The musk of their fur filled my nostrils as I gently enclosed their tiny paws inside my palm. I moaned at my exhaustion and blotted out the memory of the last twenty-four hours by recalling how that Michael J. Fox issue had gotten me out to Hollywood long before I knew it too could be considered my cell.

Dawn Steel, then the president of Columbia Pictures, had known me during my highfalutin flunky years at Paramount before I got my job at *Interview*. She was then the president of production at Paramount and oversaw such hits as *Flashdance* and *Top Gun* and *Fatal Attraction*. She had read the Michael J. Fox *Interview* issue when it first came out and given me a call at my office. Dawn, who cut a fabulous corporate figure in her Giorgio Armani pantsuits, had once asked me why I was wasting my time at Paramount if I didn't want a career in the movie business. She had been dallying at my desk waiting for my boss, Buffy, to get off the phone and noticed that instead of doing the filing required of me in my job I was working on a series of short stories. "If you want to be a writer, write," Dawn told me. "But if you're a secretary you can't say, 'Fuck the filing.' Well, you can say it," she said, smoothing the lapels on her Armani. "But you've still got to do it."

There was a vulgar side to Dawn no Armani could disguise. She didn't deny it either but wove it into her public persona. What some found overly brusque I found rather bracing, even refreshing: her female ballsiness. I think she thought she needed such a demeanor in her office arsenal along with her tailored Armani suits in order to deflect the machismo of the male executives over whom she had risen and who resented her for it.

Maybe Dawn sensed I was the one male on the executive floor who was no threat to her, since I was sitting at a secretary's desk. Whatever the reason, she was always kind to me and, when she got me one-on-

one, took me quite seriously in a way those same men never did since they could not fathom why a male would be sitting at such a desk.

Dawn had moved on to head up Columbia Pictures when she was hired to replace former independent producer David Putnam, who wielded his British outsiderness in a punitive fashion in his disastrous foray into American corporate movie culture. After arriving at Columbia, she had quickly put down a macho chit, hiring Michael J. Fox and Sean Penn to star in an upcoming Brian De Palma movie, *Casualties of War*.

Dawn called me up to compliment me on my Fox story and, more important, for having followed her advice to pursue a writing career. "Fuck the filing now!" she exclaimed, laughing. She asked if *Interview* and I might be interested in cohosting a party for Fox and De Palma at her home in Los Angeles as an intimate little send-off for them as they left to make that film for her in the jungles of Thailand. I, of course, jumped at the chance—with Fred Hughes's approval once he made sure he would also be invited.

The party turned out to be my first real experience seeing Hollywood in its own close-up, which made it clear to me that glamour is but the bit in the bridle that buckles business to every social function there. That might sound cynical, but as I lay in bed curled up with Archie and Teddy that January morning in 2010 and recalled that party that Dawn and I threw back in 1988 I also realized how innocent we all really were—Dawn and Michael and Fred and I—as an unscripted De Palma digressed yet again when telling me the story of his upcoming film and Dawn rolled her eyes at me behind his back.

I introduced Dawn to Fred that night and the three of us, standing in the corner, later marveled at Michael J. Fox's grace as he moved about the party leaving behind him, in an echo of light, a bit of his stardom's glow to hover around those he had just talked to, displaying—no need for me to take that planned side trip to Griffith Park the next day— the real astronomy of Hollywood.

"He's so jaunty," Fred said admiringly. "And yet so cagey too—like Cagney playing George M. Cohan. You should do a remake, Dawn, and put that boy in it. Just look at the way he moves. . . . yes . . . jaunty," Fred said again, the word conjuring for but a moment—I couldn't help but notice it—an imponderable sadness in him even as he willed himself not to ponder it and just as quickly revived. "This is a jolly party, Dawn. Not exactly Hollywood in its heyday. But jolly, just jolly," he said. Dawn and I laughed at Fred's forced bonhomie, his backhanded compliment, and then both said at the same time as we all clinked our glasses, "Jolly, just jolly!' the three of us falling silent and watching Michael move so gracefully about, all of us, I assumed, dwelling on a future that would from that moment on be nothing but brilliant.

But it was not to be.

We were wrong.

All of us.

Dawn died, in 1997, from a brain tumor.

Fred died too, in 2001, after a long secret bout with multiple sclerosis that could no longer be kept secret, the last seven years of his life spent wordlessly in bed.

Michael was to discover his Parkinson's disease.

"And I'm a drug addict," I said aloud for the first time that morning as I lay, no longer wordlessly, in bed. I opened my eyes. "I'm a drug addict," I said again. I looked at Archie and Teddy still curled up beside me. They were the first ones to hear me say it. I cradled their paws more tenderly in my palm for telling them such a thing. And then I cried.

I wish I could say that the next day I went into rehab or found some other structural group equivalent. I didn't. Instead, though admitting I was an addict, I convinced myself that my addiction wasn't that bad. I only used meth for sex binges once a month—twice sometimes—and as long as I was only using it two or three days out of thirty I felt I was safe. The addiction was controllable. And as long as I only smoked it or snorted it and never administered it intravenously then I wasn't a serious addict. I had even thrown guys out of my apartment who arrived with a needle ready to administer it to themselves. I had been with people who were really bad and messy drug addicts. I knew what that looked like and I was not a bad and messy drug addict. I was still keeping my life together.

That all changed on July 4, 2010.

I was back in Provincetown that summer and had begun to get more heavily into using. The first of that July I had been awake already for a day or two smoking meth and fucking around with a few of my new drug buddies, so I was in no shape to go hang out at a Fourth of July party at the home of one of my oldest and closest friends. He had also had a son by a surrogate a couple of years before, and the thought of being around the innocence of his beautiful child in the condition I was in was too much for me to bear. Instead of trying to sober up, I decided to just keep bingeing and found a sex partner online who said he had plenty of meth. He invited me over. I put on my sunglasses and took an alternate route on my bike to his place so I wouldn't have to ride down the main street in town and chance running into people I knew. But as I approached the guy's address I realized he lived one street over from my friend's house where the party had begun. The back of the guy's apartment abutted the back of my friend's place. Should I chance being seen? Yes, I'd chance it, since I wanted more drugs. I wanted more sex. I parked my bike and quickly made my way into the guy's basement apartment without being found out—there was, luckily, an old wooden fence between the properties—but his place was so close to my friend's that I could hear the familiar voices of other friends at the party and my friend's son, laughing and playing, running around outside.

No turning back now, though. I was in the stranger's dingy, dark apartment. He quickly locked the door behind me. His curtains were already drawn. There were leather S and M accoutrements strewn about. We exchanged small talk as he saw me eyeing the bag of meth next to his computer on his desk. "Have you ever slammed?" he asked, using the blunt terminology that meth addicts employ for shooting up with a needle.

"No," I said.

"Want to try it?" he asked. "I can administer it. I'm good at it."

I shrugged. I don't know why I shrugged. I don't know why I was ready to acquiesce to a needle being put into my vein. I guess it was the natural unnatural progression of addiction, the chasing of a bigger, more intense and instant high. Maybe it was because I was already strung out from being up for two or three days. I am making no excuses for my decision. It didn't even feel like a decision. It felt instead like I was simply yielding to what I had become. It felt as if the fight were over. I was literally laying down my arms as I lay on the bed. I was ready. That was all. I was ready.

The stranger diluted the meth in the needle, carefully measuring it out.

He tied a strap around my biceps.

He touched my arm.

And when he touched it I felt everyone who had ever touched my arm touch it with him.

He touched my arm.

Again, he touched it.

"I'm trying to find the right vein," he explained. "There . . . here . . . this is a good one." His finger lingered atop me as if a blind man were reading braille and had found the word he'd been searching for in the coded raised script he'd read many times before. I was now no longer writing the text. I had instead become it, a text that I could not even comprehend. My heart raced. I didn't want to watch the injection, so I closed my eyes. I saw the two nurses standing over my mother so long ago and inserting that morphine drip into her arm. I finally felt the cold, sharp prick of the needle in my vein that I had wanted to feel that day I watched my mother drift away. I felt the push of it inside me. The stranger gently talked me through it. "I'm going to pull some of your blood back up into the needle," he whispered close to my ear where he bent over me. "There. Good. I got it. Now—breathe; that's it, breathe. I'm going to push it gently back in." I felt the warm rush of my own blood—mixed together with the meth—as it went back down into my body. He untied my biceps. He pressed a cotton ball with alcohol against me. "Hold this there," he told me. "And lift your arm above your head." I did as I was told as the world sprouted wings and flew away at warp speed. I held on. I felt its wings flapping against my face. This was as close to flight as I had ever come. "I'll be right back," the stranger said. "I'm going to go do mine in the bathroom. Are you okay?"

I moaned, a combination of exhilaration and fear. The sense of flight rose higher within me. I opened my eyes. I spotted a blindfold on the floor. I put it on. I lifted my hand in the darkness in front of my face and for the first time since I was a child—for the first time since I saw my mother do it—I traced the *Ben Casey* symbols in the air. "Man, woman, birth, death, infinity," I intoned in a tired whisper. I touched my nipples. I fingered myself. "Hurry," I heard myself begging. "Hurry. Please." I squirmed. The rush grew stronger and stronger. I struggled to stay atop the wings enveloping my body. The room spun. I splayed myself atop the bed. The bliss that settled over me was finally decipherable.

"Daddy!" I heard the innocent voice call next door. It brought me back to what I was doing for but an instant and I hated myself, but even self-hatred felt new in that moment.

"Daddy," I heard myself say when I was running around a yard in Mississippi.

Ready or not, here I come, I heard. This is what a valley is, I heard. Everywhere there was an exquisite incongruity. "My memories of her drift in and out." I had the sensation of leaving my own body by burrowing down to its deepest desire. "We shall not cease from exploration." Sometimes we get to cross the street. A lone labellum clinging to its own life. A bevy of bejeweled Arab women arguing about something. "What they call in Sanskrit my 'bhavana.'" Words were useless against it. Death, not a symbol, has many guises. A soprano. An alto. A hog caller. A stronger castle in the air. White-necked ravens. The scree through which one had to maneuver. "Kevin, honey, what are you doing?" She no longer walked her pet ocelot. I thought of the Vicious Circle. Radcliffe giggled. David Copperfield. "I know—right?" That freshly fallen pine straw carpeting our country yard. My arms— Twombly—became more frantic. My wrists were wrong. De Kooning. I caught a glimpse of her glistening body. There was a flash of nipple. "Do you know what a landscape is?" The bartender leaned in closer. "Lips?" "You're wounds of a feather." I wave back. I am waving still. A second shadow. To those who woo her with too-slavish knees. Penhaligon's Blenheim Bouquet. The tacky reflections of themselves. Ledger's face circled in marijuana smoke. The whore choked me now. "Figgit," he no longer whispered. His little face a fist of tears. "I will never abandon you." A de Menil daughter. Come on, there's another reel. Just go to the end of the reel. I was flying. My lavalavas. Dee Dee Sharp's "Mashed Potato Time." The smell of his cordovan brogues. "Being alone," I said, telling him the truth. A night that was no longer silent. Close your eyes. Clear your heart. Cut the cord. Things real. Things semi-real. No things. A wild horse grazing in the mist before me. "He opens the Doors." Chico's paw. Coco's. *"Fantasma inquietante."* A "waking dream." Japa mala. Father Raphael. "The almond man is nuts." He must have conducted a bit of Schumann at some point in his life. Some deeper stream I can't quite name. ". . . the one with the most pain we have met . . ." The girl lifts her hand, covered in what she had coaxed from him. "Piteog. *Piteog*, Sister." Piteog. The past is what passes through us all.

For the next seven months I became an intravenous drug user. I was bad at administering the meth myself and my left arm where I shot it had one long red track mark snaking down it that never disappeared. I bought a makeup stick and would draw a line along it to try to camouflage it. I began to wear only long-sleeve shirts. I thought I could never go any lower than sticking a needle in my arm. But I did. I became that stranger who stuck the needle in someone else's.

I never again, however, showed up for an interview after a night of debauchery. That was an odd detail about getting deeper into my drug use. As long as I didn't admit to myself I was an addict, I could be a bit messy and push the boundaries of acceptable behavior—both personal and professional. But once I realized I was in that deep I gave myself parameters professionally in order to keep up the ruse of reliability. I blocked out time in my calendar for use when I didn't have an inter-view scheduled. I was still only using once or twice a month. The dif-ference was in degree now. All was rationalization. But the race never stopped. I could never get off the track, that circular street where even now I could never catch up.

After seven months the use was no longer unpredictably thrilling. It had become just part of the routine of my life, which also included boarding Archie and Teddy at a local kennel when I knew I was going to shoot up. Teddy had begun to attack the drug dealer when he ar-rived and Archie would run frantically around the apartment the min-ute the tiny glassine bag of meth was produced. When I prepared a needle, an incomprehensible soul-rending siren-like cry he'd never made before would issue from somewhere deep within him. And if he was there when the sex began he would attempt to herd me away from the bed and make it all stop. Cutting me out of the herd had taken on a different meaning. More tragic. Truer. I hated Archie and Teddy see-ing me like that—and, more important, interrupting my addiction—so I just factored in the cost of the kennel with the drugs as the price of my use.

Another part of the routine was the recovery period of plying my-self with healthy food and juices and ounces and ounces of wheatgrass. That part of my early use remained the same and just got ramped up once needles became a part of the equation. The climbing back to nor-malcy was how I confirmed I was not only alive but also capable of liv-ing. I was still engaging in destructive behavior to prove I was indestructible. I was yet to see it as suicidal. There is a fine line. I was continuing to walk it.

On February 17, 2011, I had stayed up all night "slammin 'n' slummin,'" as I came to think of my sex life that entailed attaining the meth and then finding men online who were not disgusted by the sight of needles or my now-destroyed arm that no amount of makeup could disguise. The next day I was coming down and forcing food and juice and water in me when I went on the Internet to try to focus my jumbled, exhausted mind. I clicked on the *New York Post*'s Page Six gossip site. I don't know why. I had stopped reading Page Six unless it was linked from some other site. I had, for enlightened political reasons I convinced myself, broken myself of my daily *Post* habit. That was one addiction I had at least licked. But for some reason that morning my fingers were guided there.

I saw a picture of my old friend Perry pop up on my computer screen. I immediately felt guilty. What would he say if he knew what I had become? I also felt like such a failure, for I assumed the item was about his newest show business success or venture. He and his partner, Hunter, who worked at *Paper* magazine, were always making the gossip columns and party pages. They had even branched out into making films of their own, in addition to Perry's novel writing and producing the Narnia movies for Walden Media. I took a swig of water and prepared to be jealous.

My bleary eyes focused on the headline above his photo: "'Narnia' Producer Dies of OD."

I shook my head.

I read "'Narnia'" again. I read "Producer" again. I read "Dies" again. I read "of OD" again.

This could not be true. No: not true.

I felt the moment rewinding itself.

I read the headline a third time.

"'Narnia'"

"Producer"

"Dies"

"of"

"OD"

No amount of meth in no amount of needles had ever stopped my

heart, but that headline had. I could not breathe. I then suddenly began to hyperventilate. My heart seemed to jump-start itself. It wanted
to escape my chest.

Tears sprung from my eyes. Leapt to their own deaths from them.
When I think of the moment now I see it as animation. I become a
drawing of myself. It's the only way I can convey the unreality of it
all.

My tears, in the picture my memory conjures, are cartoonish.

They are giant drops drawn in the air, springing forth, falling.

Falling, falling.

Falling.

I did not exactly read these words through them but found them lined
up there before me through the blur of shock and panic of such cartoonish sorrow:

A Hollywood film producer and novelist was found dead of an
apparent drug overdose yesterday in his Greenwich Village apartment, police sources said.

Perry Moore, 39, was discovered at around 2 p.m. in his Houston Street pad, a doorman high-rise just off Sixth Avenue, the
sources added.

Moore was an executive producer of the blockbuster "Chroni-
cles of Narnia" trilogy and had penned a well-received fiction work
in 2007 about a gay teenage superhero.

I sat staring at Perry's face through my tears as I watched them being drawn in the air before me.

I sat there a long time. Or maybe it was only a second.

I stood.

I walked in circles around my apartment, trying to catch my breath.

I began to walk faster.

I fell to my knees.

I made a sound I had never made before, Archie's soul-rending siren-like cry suddenly issuing from somewhere deep within me. I could finally comprehend it. It was a howl of grief.

I don't remember much about Perry's funeral at Grace Church. I do recall the pews were packed. I do remember sobbing throughout the service. I do recall praying and in my prayer promising Perry I would get sober. I swore to him I would. Did I swear to God? I can't remember.

Neither Perry nor I had known about the other's drug use. Subsequent news stories reported that he had overdosed on Oxycontin. Could it have been prescribed for his chronic back pain? Of all the people in my life, Perry would have been the last person I would have suspected of being addicted to any drug. Would I have been the last person he would have suspected? I was having a hard time believing it had really been a drug overdose that killed him. Why could he not have confided in me? Why could I not have confided in him? If nothing else proved I was a drug addict—the needles, the depleting of my bank account, the continuing destructive behavior—that secrecy was the final proof. That shame. That unsharable shame.

I was able to keep my promise to Perry for a while but by the summer, when I was back for my four months in Provincetown, I gave in to temptation and again was buying needles at the local pharmacy and filling them with meth. This latest iteration of my addiction, however, was not about combining it with sex. Instead a new phase began: hallucinations. Or were they manifestations? I am not sure of the correct terminology, but I am sure of this: I loved them. Oh, how I loved them. So many people while on meth suffer from psychosis and paranoia. Not I. I reveled in the revelations that were being presented to me. It was all a kind of heightened narrative as far as I was concerned, as it will now become a heightened part of this one, so heightened that it might cause harrumphs of derision and even scorn from some. So be it. What I am about to relate is as much a part of my addiction—a bigger part really—as sticking needles in my arm, for I was convinced that the injected meth was opening a spiritual portal of some kind and I was being visited by the Angel of Light that I found written about in other reading I was doing that summer in the King James Bible. There—in Second Corinthians, eleventh chapter, fourteenth verse—it states: "And no marvel; for Satan himself is transformed into an angel of light." And yet I did marvel that Lucifer was letting me know of his presence and that it was becoming a spiritual experience as rich as any on the Camino. His minions of light were sweeping into my line of vision and would often transform themselves into different human aspects from all historical periods—old women, young boys, dashing men, female beauties—trying to figure out what appealed to me the most. They would astrally project themselves toward me and jerk about just outside my windows wondering, as I was wondering, who had conjured whom right before dawn approached—Lucifer's favored time, when darkness was at its glorious depth. A kind of seduction was taking place as they hovered into being in that haunting hour. The visions were more afraid to be entering my realm than I was of seeing them. That was what was so fascinating to me. Once I accepted them, it was I who tried to calm them once I realized they were the frightened ones. I felt such tenderness toward them and their fear. They seemed to be so perplexed by my lack of it. Were they truly demonic? Was their fright a ruse? I only know by my welcoming them they wavered. "You are revealing yourself to me for a reason," I told them once. "I am here to let you know that you are true. But don't expect me to obey you." And then I heard it, Lucifer's dulcet voice, the sound of light itself: "The key to joy is disobedience."

I had a real affection for my hallucinations. I even considered them holy in their way, for they were the flip side of the same experiences I had had on the Camino. They gave the mysticism back there a two-sided quality, rounded it out, even made more sense of it. Just as that bludgeoned Christ on the cross in that monastery had seemed to come to life and that bearded angel had milled about Roncesvalles like Jim Morrison, these newest visions may not have been real, but they, as I had told them, were true. They almost made me turn away from John

Keats and toward William Blake, but I remained steadfast. Loyal. Keats remained my "glorious luminary," as William Rossetti wrote of Blake. "I am certain of nothing but of the holiness of the heart's affections and the truth of imagination," Keats himself wrote, offering up his wise kindness once more to me when I was doubting what I had been seeing.

Had it really been one of them—these Angels of Light—in Roncesvalles whom I noticed that numinous night? Was it they who crept into the sacristy and emboldened the crucifix? Had God been taunting me with the Devil or was the Devil taunting me with God? If one believes in God and the transubstantiation of the Eucharist and the power of prayer and all the heightened spiritual light that the Camino can offer then one has to believe in the opposite side of that same exact light. God created the Devil so God could be God. One cannot exist without the other. Lucifer was God's greatest thought. And what are hallucinations if not God's thoughts placed before us? That is the conundrum that Lucifer can never overcome. Lucifer, once thought into being by God, is finally not thought at all. Only God could think a thought that is not thought. Lucifer is all sensation. But Lucifer is not evil. Lucifer is less. Ever so slightly, but forever: less. Which doesn't mean he is not magnificent. Think of the love that God must have had for him to bestow upon Lucifer the power of light. When that Christ on that cross that day in that monastery's sacristy opened those bludgeoned eyes and light shone forth from them and I fell to my knees bathed in it, it was not God's presence I was feeling. It was the magnificent love of Lucifer who had been allowed to latch on to it.

A monk's contemplation is the quiet, still center found in the midst of such a God/Lucifer continuum, which itself is found at the bloodshed heart of Christianity. Addiction is the blood that continues to be shed when that continuum is confronted with sensations alone and no contemplation is called upon. When I emerged from that experience in the sacristy that day on the Camino and Mary enfolded me in her burly arms, it was not a monk I was finally feeling like. She was wrong about that. I had emerged instead an addict.

When I returned to New York that autumn my addiction worsened. There were binges of sex again thrown into the mix. Humanity is, after all, the fleshy membrane that separates the light of God from Lucifer's illumined angels. But my hallucinations soon took on another even more dazzling aura. Another realm unexpectedly reared its godhead. Once the portal had been opened, other images of magnificent light began to manifest themselves. One night there was the image glisteningly carved into the darkness of a creature that was half man and half elephant. Its trunk came curling toward me as if beckoning me to its side. It was gargantuan—I counted four arms forming—and yet not monstrous at all. The arms reminded me of Daniel's dreadlocks back on the Camino that he had formed out of his wild blond hair. The glistening creature—I thought of Daniel's shaven girlfriend clenching a dreadlock in her teeth and pulling him toward her with it—was beatific as it continued to beckon and carve itself into the night. I knew enough to know it was some sort of Hindu or Buddhist god, but I didn't know the name for it. I then remembered my dream back at that hostel on the Camino when I returned to the church basement and it had been suddenly transformed into a Buddhist notions shop with tiny carved gods unknown to me lined along its myriad shelves. There had been one—only one—that glistened in that dream. It too had a trunk. It too had beckoned me with the trunk. What I was now seeing was a gigantic version of the god. The moment I remembered it from my earlier dream, it smiled, nodded—even seemed to giggle in delight—and retreated. Then row upon row of what appeared to be priests in turban-like headdresses of blindingly brilliant light projected themselves forward and hovered before me as if an assessment were taking place. I did not flinch from the visions. I felt fortified by them. I felt seen—as if I were their vision of light and they were trying to make sense of me. I smiled. I nodded. I too giggled in delight. I know all this sounds even more woo-woo than anything Shirley MacLaine has ever claimed, but like MacLaine, once one has experienced such visions all shame about acknowledging them vanishes. What I saw that night was the actualization of an eternal verity. Faith is not belief. Faith is the deification of doubt. Faith is surrendering to what you have never believed in before—what you never thought possible to believe in—so that impossibility can then believe in you. Faith makes you possible.

But, conversely, the drugs that were engendering such faith, such visions, were destroying me.

Addiction, I came to understand, is the proxy battle for the soul. I was in the midst of a pitched one, its violence veiled in beauty.

By the end of 2011 I had decided I had to have a plan of action to fulfill my promise to Perry that I would get sober. I was ruining my health and going broke. Hallucinations were neither feeding me nor paying my bills. In November, during a particularly messy binge, someone from whom I'd bought drugs and whom I convinced to stay behind and have sex with me even suggested I seek help. When a fat, tweaked-out naked meth dealer expresses concern for you, then you know you're in trouble. I looked at my calendar when he left that night and circled the date December 22. That was the day I decided I would walk into a fellowship at the LGBT Center in New York and begin my journey to sobriety.

There was no other choice left me. I had gone through my savings since I had begun using and knew that I was going to be unable to pay my rent much longer. I contacted my landlord and got out of my lease. I then e-mailed my brother and sister and told them the truth about my meth addiction and that I was using it intravenously. Two close friends talked to my brother, who told them they said, he would pay for me to go into rehab for three months down in Mississippi, since I didn't have the money to pay for it. I agreed to go. I did my intake interview over the phone. A bed was reserved for me, and my sister arrived to help me pack up my belongings, which I planned to store down in Mississippi while I was in the rehab facility. A plan of action was set in motion. I was scared to death. But I was ready.

And then everything went awry.

It was January 2012.

My sister had arrived to help me pack up all my belongings—my furniture, my extensive collection of art, my too-many clothes—for the move down south. I don't have a driver's license, so she was going to drive the U-Haul truck I had rented to Mississippi with Archie and Teddy and me riding shotgun. Where was I going to go after my stint in rehab down there? I had no idea. I could not get past one day at a time at that point. I still can't. I know now I never will.

When one is confronted with an intravenous drug user in one's family I am certain it dredges up lots of issues. Lots of fear. Lots of anger that has festered there for years and years. I could set out here in my narrative my own version of events that led to my brother deciding to decline to pay for my rehab. But I'm sure he'd have his own version that differs from mine. I will honor our relationship. What is important is the result of those events and the private e-mails that went back and forth between us. Two days before my sister and I had scheduled to pack up the U-Haul and depart, I suddenly did not have the money to go to rehab. I did not know where, in fact, I was going to go. Mississippi was now out of the question. After much prayer to every entity I had come to believe in I took a long walk in the freezing cold to collect my thoughts. I had only been sober for ten days after two years of heavy meth use. Did I even have thoughts to collect? I was attempting to release the resentment I instantly felt toward my brother for backing out at the last minute of his commitment to pay for my rehab and focus instead on it being a blessing in that it would make me own my journey to sobriety even more. Maybe he was seeing the bigger picture himself already and was doing what was best for me.

As I was trying to think all of that through, I heard a voice. God's? Lucifer's? That elephantine Hindu deity's? A Cape Cod drag queen's?

Whoever it was, it made instant sense to me. I had often heard back during my Provincetown summers when I asked what it was like to live there in the wintertime that "either you stay high all the time or you spend the time getting sober."

I came back to my apartment on 21st Street and told my sister we were turning the truck north and heading to Provincetown. I got online and found an eight-by-ten-foot room in a boardinghouse that would accept dogs that was available for a month. I would, however, have to share the bath down the hallway. My sister got on her computer and found a storage unit in New Bedford, Massachusetts, where we'd unload my stuff.

With two days to go, we now had a plan.

The next day I was even able to find an apartment beginning the second week of February until May 1. After unloading most of my stuff in New Bedford, my sister and I brought a few things along to Provincetown and stored them upstairs from my new place in an empty room in the landlord's apartment.

We then checked into the boardinghouse. She was going to spend the night with me and catch a flight early the next morning back to Mississippi. I was starving and knew that Archie and Teddy needed to be walked. The only place I could find open with food was a combination 7-Eleven-like store and gas station. I tied the dogs up outside and went in to find some potato chips and a ginger ale. When I was paying the cashier, a man came in with Archie on his leash. "Your dog got loose outside. I assume this is yours," he said, since I was the only one in the store. The cashier stared at me, waiting for me to take my change. She held it out with one hand and kept her place in the story she was reading in *Star* magazine with the index finger of the other.

"My dog?" I asked, panicked. "I have two dogs."

"There was only one out there, man. Sorry," he said.

I picked up Archie. The cashier shrugged at the man, who wanted a pack of Marlboro Lights. I rushed outside and stood in the freezing cold in the middle of the dimly lit gas station area screaming Teddy's name as if I were Shirley Booth bellowing for little Sheba. I had kept it together for the last several days under so much stress. But in that moment I fell to my knees with Archie in my arms and began to sob. Where was Teddy? Had I lost him on top of everything else? Had he been taken? Had he been run over and killed? "Teddy!" I called, and cried. "Teddy!"

The man who had found Archie got in his car and watched me from his window. He lit up a Marlboro. I watched the smoke fill his car as he cranked it. He pulled out of the parking lot while watching me the whole time and taking another long drag on his cigarette. He'd have a story to tell whomever greeted him when he got home, a home that was not an eight-by-ten-foot room in a boardinghouse where his tired sister waited.

I sat on the icy parking lot in front of the store and huddled with Archie. This is what my life had come to. This is what drugs had done to me. This is who I now was. I was tearfully tearing open a bag of potato chips and choking them down chip by chip while sitting on the freezing oil-stained concrete in a carless parking lot at a carless gas station at the end of the world at 12:17 A.M. in January. Where were my hallucinations now? Where was my hope? And still, if I had had a needle full of meth I would have stuck it in my arm right then and there. The certainty of that thought terrified me yet comforted me too because it was a form of clarity. I didn't like what I was seeing, but I was coming into focus. No Angels of Light hovered about in that moment. The night was not numinous but dimly lit by neon. My knees were aching on the concrete.

"Teddy!" I called when I spotted him suddenly running from around a hedge in the distance toward me. "Teddy!" For a moment that's all I needed to be thankful—Teddy running into my arms to join Archie. I fed them each a potato chip. My teeth chattered. The cashier came to the window and stared at us. She shook her head dismissively and went back to reading her *Star* magazine. I looked at the neon light above a gas pump. It flickered once. Then twice. A car passed by. I longed for angels of any sort. I longed for my old life back. I finished the bag of potato chips.

For the next four weeks Archie and Teddy and I lived together in a boardinghouse room just big enough for a bed and a chest of drawers. I waited my turn for the bathroom while the frowning female schizophrenic down the hall took her time in there not washing her hair. A David Bowie look-alike took even more time touching up his blond highlights. The twenty-something girl next door to me waxed her legs in there—and other regions no doubt—while her odd music selection included Shania Twain and the Thompson Twins, the latter's "Hold Me Now" and "Doctor Doctor" blaring into my room. It was like being in rehab after all.

I stayed to myself and stayed sober, luckily finding a fellowship of like-minded people in town. I was up each morning at 5:30 to have my Grape-Nuts and strawberries and blueberries with my 1 percent milk before catching a ride with the boardinghouse's manager who was also in the same fellowship that met each day at 7:00 A.M. at the local Methodist church. From that first day attending a Methodist church with my mother to attending that one in Provincetown had been quite a journey.

I soon had one month without meth.

The days continued to pile up one at a time after I moved out of the boardinghouse into my off-season apartment. It was lonely, but I had Archie and Teddy and tentatively made friends in the fellowship. I went out one night with a woman who had moved to town from New York as well. She had over twenty years sober and I was curious as to how she had managed it. We sat talking at one of the only three restaurants still open in Provincetown that time of year. I trusted her enough to let her know about all my hallucinations.

"The next day after that amazing night of seeing that glistening light-infused elephantine god I got on my elevator in my building and there was a family of Indians looking at me suspiciously. They even seemed a bit in awe," I told her. "I wondered if they had somehow seen what I had seen. I was on my way to the theater that night—without much sleep, I might add—down on Christopher Street at the Lucille Lortel. On the way there I was trying to figure out what exactly the godhead I'd seen was. I knew enough to know that it was one based on an Eastern religion, but I am a born-and-bred Protestant. All my religious belief is based on the conflict between God and the Devil," I told her. "On my walk down Seventh Avenue I turned to check out my reflection in a shop window to make sure I didn't look as worn-out as I was feeling and there in the window sat a golden statue of the exact half-elephant/half-man god I had seen the night before. At first I thought I was having another hallucination, but I realized, no, it was sitting there before me behind my reflected face. It even looked as if we were combined into one vision." The woman smiled. I thought she was going to say something. But she waited for me to continue. "I went into the shop and there was another even bigger, more golden elephant god posed next to the shopkeeper. I grabbed the statue's trunk and held on for dear life. 'What is this?' I asked the man. 'Is this bad or good if you are suddenly seeing this everywhere?' The man looked a little shocked by my desperate tone, but told me that such a thing was very good." The woman laughed. "'What's he called?' I asked the man. 'You've been put in my path to tell me what he is called. Who is he? Come on, tell me. Please.' The man placed his hand atop mine there on the golden elephant's trunk. 'Be calm,' he told me. 'It is good. It is a good thing. This is Ganesha,' he said. 'He has revealed himself to you in some way?' I told him that he had without telling him the details. I didn't want to freak him out any more than I already had. 'He—Lord Ganesha—is the Remover of Obstacles,' he told me. 'He is the God of New Beginnings. This is very good. Ganesha is good. Very, very good.'"

My new friend smiled again. She had finished her meal and placed her fork next to her empty plate. Behind her on the bar's TV screen the Boston Bruins were playing a hockey game. A fight broke out between two players behind her head, the arms flailing around her like the four arms of Ganesha himself.

"I then went to the theater and sat down in my seat," I continued. "While reading the program and waiting for the play to begin—it was *The Pride* with Ben Whishaw and Hugh Dancy, two of my favorite actors—I glanced over at the person sitting next to me who rolled up his sleeve and on his forearm there was a tattoo of Ganesha."

I shook my head, still feeling the wonder of that evening. I took a big bite of my pulled-pork sandwich. My new friend unwrapped her scarf from around her neck. She lifted her necklace and held it toward me in the table's candlelight. Its pendant was a golden Ganesha.

I gasped. Then—as Ganesha was beginning to teach me—I giggled with delight. My friend giggled with me. The hockey game commenced behind her head. The fight was over.

When I was ninety days sober I wanted to celebrate and get my first tattoo. I really didn't think I'd be able to stay completely sober for three whole months in the dead of winter in Provincetown without finding someone to use with and alleviate the abject loneliness that had begun to take hold of me. But I had. Did I want a Ganesha tattoo like I'd seen at the theater that night next to me? I went to bed on my eighty-ninth night of sobriety not knowing that something deeper than any tattoo would mark me, claim me, stir the deepest recesses of my soul where no drug could reach that had been kept safe there for just such a night.

I dreamed of the blond-haired angel from Starbucks so long ago who had walked the Camino and about whom I had confided to Hugh Jackman. The angel and I were in a mountainous region, but it was very different from Mount Kilimanjaro or the Pyrenees. I had no idea, in fact, where we were. There was a lake and the angel wanted me to swim in it with him. I don't like to swim. I almost drowned once on Cape Cod when I was touring in that summer stock production of *Equus* long ago and have never felt comfortable in the water since. But the blond-haired angel was insistent. He jumped in. I jumped in after him. We swam side by side, synchronizing our movements. As our heads emerged from the water and we stared at each other I managed to ask him where we were going. "There," is all he said, and swam onward.

"I'm going to that fallen tree over at the shore," I said, growing weary of the water.

"That's where there is," he said.

When I got to the tree I grabbed its trunk and, when I did, it turned into a wooden Ganesha. I looked up. I was at the foot of a glorious mountain. There was a pathway cut into it that encircled it, and robed priests and priestesses were walking silently along it up and down the mountain's side. I noticed then that the mountain was slowly beginning to rise above me in the mist and clouds that were enveloping it. At the top of the mountain—as if carved from the peak itself—was a beautiful dark-haired woman whose third eye in the middle of her forehead was staring more lovingly at me than any eye had ever done before. A crescent moon hovered next to her tangled web of hair forming a topknot that was the mountain's summit. When I met her third eye's gaze the heavens opened up and bright multicolored petals began to fall from the sky. I seldom remember my dreams in color, but these colors were so vivid I was almost blinded by them. The petals were falling everywhere, but none were touching me until one—only one—fell right in the middle of my chest. I folded my hands atop it and a sense of immense warmth—not fire, but something as fierce as fire—emanated from the spot where it had melded with my flesh. I awoke with a glorious intake of breath. It was the most blissful sensation I had ever felt. No drug had ever equaled it. Nor the cumulative effect of every ejaculation I'd ever had. No hallucination that had ever hovered into my line of vision could match it. It felt, in that moment, what it must feel like to heal. And I knew instantly that was what heaven is: the moment we finally heal. All our life is pointed toward that moment when we do not die but heal. The rest of my life will be spent returning to that instant that petal touched my body and where, next time, it will stay.

————

The important and vast difference between that dream and the earlier visions that I had encountered was that I was more sober than I'd ever been since I was fifteen and first began to smoke pot. I have been a pothead most of my life but knew that if I got sober I'd have to cut out marijuana as well as liquor even though liquor has never been a problem for me. I think I might have been drunk five times in my whole life. I only liked the occasional vodka when eating smoked salmon and listening to Nina Simone. But I had to make the choice to stop having even an occasional drink if I was to be completely sober. To be honest, I've always hated being around drunks. But being around them now in the fellowship I had chosen to join was sustaining me. I always thought that being cut out of the herd was my way to salvation, yet a herd was now saving my life.

My earlier visions had been illuminating and arrived to me through some drug-induced portal, but that dream that night had proved that I could be the portal myself if I remained sober. Yet I wasn't sure what it all meant. I only knew that not only was this true, but it was also real. That too was a difference between it and the hallucinations. Indeed, the world I had dreamed felt more real than my waking one. Reality and truth began to connect for me for the first time.

I tried to put the dream out of my mind for the rest of the day and go about my daily business but later decided to Google all that I could remember from it. I wrote it out all on one very long line, then hit the "return" button on my computer and an image came up of not only Ganesha but also exactly the woman who had formed the peak of the mountain that had risen above me. She was his mother, Parvati. I had never heard of her before. I never even knew he had a mother. This was the truest of revelations. He was leading me to her. And more deeply to himself.

I began to read about them, since I knew nothing of them. Nothing. My whole worldview up until that afternoon had been a Westernized one. There was a part of me that didn't want to read anything at all about them but to remain completely pure for their visitations. I was enjoying being the spiritual idiot savant. But I had to make some sense of what was going on—even if it was of the most primitive sort.

I looked up Ganesha on the computer after staring for a long time at all the images of his mother and him I kept pulling up that day that corresponded so startlingly with the dream from the night before. All I could really focus on was the mantra one offers up to him: "Om Gam Ganapataye Namaha." As suggested, I read it 108 times.

I then looked up his mother, Parvati, on Wikipedia. "Parvata is one of the Sanskrit words for 'mountain,'" I read. "'Parvati' translates to 'She of the mountains' and refers to Parvati being born the daughter of Himavat, lord of the mountains and the personification of the Himalayas."

Was Parvati—not forgiveness—what I left on the mountain? Is that what Ganesha had come to tell me? Had I last night left myself—my true self, my real self—there on the maternal mountain he had revealed to me? Or is the question not what one leaves on the mountain but what the mountain is.

I shook my head. I tried to grapple with all this but decided I needed to clear my mind—or muddle it—with diversions more earthly at that point and signed on to Towleroad.com to read about some gay pop culture or politics or gaze at some hot shirtless guys. Instead, the first posting there that popped up on my computer screen was not an earthly image at all but an otherworldly one sent back from Mars by NASA's Rover. NASA had sent it out because it looked as if someone in the tradition of Buddhist monk sand paintings had drawn the image of an elephant's head on the planet's red dusty surface.

I slammed my computer shut as fast as I could. I closed my eyes. I heard Hugh Jackman from our lunch a few years before. "I realized anew what a gift meditation is," he had told me. "I'd never thought of it that way. It is a practice of dying—what it's like to get rid of the ideas, the desires, the body even. There is a part of meditation that is a feeling of bodilessness."

Is not sobriety, at its essence, the freeing of oneself of the body's addictive needs and, hence, the body? Is not sobriety a form of meditation? Is not sobriety, when truly attained, a bodilessness? All my drug use and all the hallucinations it engendered—all the body's sensations—was the whole time a blessing from Shiva so I could then know what it was like continually to shed it all and to die and to die and to die and, thus, to heal and to heal and to heal. That—and not the battle between good and evil—was the new continuum in my life.

I came up with another idea for a tattoo. Ganesha would have to stay tucked into my subconscious where he felt comfortable for the time being. You'd think with my history with needles that getting a tattoo would have been an easy procedure to endure—maybe even a pleasurable one. But my use of needles involved one tiny prick and then the world would change. Getting a tattoo is much more painful than that and the world remains boringly the same as you lie there on the table.

I was nervous when I arrived at the parlor but was careful to write out exactly what I wanted the young artist to tattoo on my right forearm. I even Googled "Emily Dickinson" and pulled the quote up on the computer screen at the reception desk for him to look at:

HOPE IS THE THING WITH FEATHERS THAT PERCHES IN THE SOUL.

I then lay on the table and turned my head away from him and gritted my teeth as he made her words flesh. After about forty minutes he let me look at his cursive handiwork. I gave it a cursory satisfied glance, still a bit shocked I had actually gone through with getting tattooed since I had often sworn to friends that tattoos were too trendy for me ever to get one. I was much too old, I'd sarcastically scowl at such a thought, to attempt to be a hipster. But I decided that since my staying sober for three months was giving me a semblance of hope in my life I'd put some signage of it on my arm. It was also my birthday present to myself. I'd be fifty-six in a few days. Yep, my hipster days were over.

The young artist placed a bandage over his handiwork and told me

I could take it off that night. He also gave me a little tin of Tattoo Goo to rub onto the inscription.

Several hours later I did as I was told, but as I was rubbing the goo into my forearm I really focused on the quote for the first time that had been indelibly inked there:

HOPE IS THE THING WITH FEATHERS THAT PERCHES THE SOUL.

"What the fuck?" I said much too loudly. Archie hid under a chair at the tone of my voice. Teddy turned his head to me. "That kid fucked this up!" I shouted to them. I held up my arm toward them as if they could read. "Look at this! He left out the word 'IN'! Motherfucker!" Archie scooted more deeply under the chair. If Teddy could have shrugged he would have. Me? I stared in horror at the two lines inked into my flesh. One does not misquote Emily Dickinson when the whole point was to have an Emily Dickinson quote on one's body. I called the tattoo parlor and left an enraged message.

"What the fuck?" I said again, and lay on my bed. I tried to calm down.

I stared some more at the botched tattoo.

I closed my eyes.

I took deep breaths.

And then, as Ganesha's feathery giggles lifted and fell inside of me, I focused not on the error but on the absurdity of it. The word "FEATH-ERS" floated like a feather itself into my thoughts and alighted there. Ganesha's giggles grew at his own handiwork. Yes, that was the solution. I'd have the artist the next day ink a feather beneath the words "PERCHES" and "THE" with the calamus of the quill pointing between them as if the feather were falling from the crevice as I saw it falling at that very moment in my mind's eye from an angel's wing. I'd then have him perch the word "IN" atop the feather.

It worked.

And when it worked I realized that, like my tattoo, I am singular. I am imperfect. I am fixable.

Things continued to go well for my sobriety, though not my bank account. I was going broke. I had gotten a couple of interview assignments from The Daily Beast, which were tiding me over, but I did not have the money to rent a place for the summer and my lease at my off-season place was expiring on May 1. I called my old landlord at the summer place I'd rented for the last several summers in Provincetown and thought I had worked out a deal with her to pay a bit of the rent upfront, do the yard work for her instead of her hiring someone to do it, so I could have a decrease in my rent and then pay her the rest of the rent at the end of the summer. But then she called me and told me that she had rented the place out from under me and I had to have my things out of there in three days or she'd put it all out in the yard. In a month or so I'd have no place to live and no money with which to rent one. I trusted things were going to work out, but yet again I was feeling as I did back when my brother backed out of paying for my rehab. I would just have to trust that, like that occurrence, this problem would be a blessing in disguise and part of the universe's plan for my life. But this journey toward recovery was becoming exhausting.

A friend arrived in town to look at some work that was being done at his beach cottage and I told him of my predicament and he graciously and generously offered to pay for a rental on the wharf next door to where he also had a place he kept for guests. We agreed that I'd pay him back at the end of the summer after I found a way to earn some money. I was embarrassed to have to depend on his generosity, but I accepted it with much gratitude. Again: Somehow things were working out.

Then another blessing occurred. I got a call from the State Department asking if I would make the keynote address at the first LGBT human rights conference to be sponsored by the U.S. government on foreign soil. It was to be held in Tirana, Albania, in June and to focus on the Balkans and Eastern Europe. People there were fans of my earlier book, *Mississippi Sissy*, and were also aware of the political nature of my many Facebook postings—which sort of gave me pause. But I was flattered and for the first time I felt my life getting back on track with such an invitation. I even scheduled a few days in Rome on my way back home because I had never been there before and knew it would be as much of a pilgrimage as the Camino had been.

When I moved onto the wharf a whole new drama erupted because of condo rules about renters not being able to have dogs. Archie and Teddy were the only things I really had left in my life at that point—I barely had a career and was quickly running out of the little money I still had, and my sobriety was still tenuous. It was out of the question for me even to consider giving them up for the summer. I hated that I was causing my friend who had rented the place such tsuris. At one point, I thought I was going to have to move out and just get a tent and pitch it in the woods and eat out of cans and shit in a hole in the ground. It really was looking as if it were coming to that. But I still hadn't used meth. I was coming up on six months sober.

My friend thought he'd come up with a solution, however, by asking me to move into his apartment on the wharf, which he used as a place for guests, and move his stuff into the apartment next door to his, which I'd already moved into. If I was in his place, then maybe the condo board would overlook my being in someone else's unit with dogs. I would be more officially his guest. So I did what I was told even though I was behind on writing my speech for the State Department. That's how odd my life had become—I was flat broke, moving for the third time in three months, trying to stay sober, and getting ready to represent America by delivering a keynote address for the State Department in Albania.

I opened the door to the apartment on the wharf. The smell of marijuana almost knocked me down. I turned around and walked outside and said a prayer. As I've written, I've been a pothead myself as well since I was fifteen. And I missed it more than any other substance during my road to recovery. But I knew that if someone had smoked marijuana in the apartment, these might still be some there to tempt me. I had to go back inside the place and remove every vestige of it if I were to stay sober. I headed back inside and went through every drawer in the place, looking for every stash of pot and bit of paraphernalia. I looked through the bookshelves. I combed every corner for seeds and stems. I cleaned the place of every last bit of pot and put it in the place next door.

But in my search for it all, I did find a syringe still in its package. I have no idea how it got there or who left it. I stood holding the syringe in my hand. I felt the rush in my gut I would always get as I contemplated shooting up meth. I did not put the syringe with the paraphernalia next door. I stuck it back in the corner of the drawer and stuck the knowledge of it being hidden there in the back corner of my brain. It was the dumbest thing I'd done in six months.

And then I did something dumber.

I smoked meth with someone I met online.

I could say I did it out of loneliness. I could say I did it because I was tired of being a burden to my friends and family. I could say I did it because I was exhausted from being poverty stricken and being embarrassed to pay for my groceries with food stamps and, even though I had begun to volunteer at the soup kitchen in Provincetown, to be eating many of my lunches there myself. I could say I just wanted to escape what my life had become because of smoking meth in the first place. But all of those things are excuses.

I smoked meth when I had close to six months of sobriety because I am an addict.

I only smoked it for one night. It was not a binge. For those things I was grateful. And I knew that I would walk back into the fellowship I had joined within twenty-four hours of doing it. But I had to start counting my days of sobriety all over again. And I still had a speech to write for my trip to Albania for the State Department. The vast divide between the person with a meth pipe in his mouth and the man who was scheduled to have an inspiring speech in a little over two weeks bewildered me. Were the gods bemused by my bewilderment? I certainly was not. Yet I was not depressed by it either. I knew I was still on the path toward recovery. I had taken a slight detour. I had slipped a bit in its own scree. Like that night on Mount Kilimanjaro as I trudged toward another kind of summit: three steps forward, one step back.

I buckled down to write my keynote address.

Soon my sister arrived in Provincetown to take care of Archie and Teddy for ten days upon my departure for Albania and my pilgrimage to Rome.

I sat on the Spanish Steps rolling up my sleeves in the Roman heat. The speech in Albania had gone well and now I was on another kind of mission. I rubbed the tattoo on my right forearm and read the word "Hope" over and over as I listened to Haydn's last six sonatas being played by Glenn Gould on my iPod. I looked up at the window right above me at 26 Piazza di Spagna, John Keats's final address. Had he listened to some of these same sonatas by Haydn, his favorite composer, being played for him by his friend artist Joseph Severn on the pianoforte Severn had rented for them and put in their second-floor sitting room? Had listening to Haydn put some hope into Keats's own life or was he by then, suffering so from consumption, beyond hope? He had, after all, referred to his time there in the apartment above me as his "posthumous existence," a kind of existence I too had seemed to be experiencing for the last six months.

"Not only was Keats fond of music," Severn wrote after moving with him from England to Italy in November of 1820, "but he found that his pain and o'erfretted nerves were much soothed by it." It was blisteringly hot when I arrived in Italy in June of 2012 from Albania, but, as I sat on the Spanish Steps in the beating sun, the Haydn was soothing my own o'erfretted nerves, so excited was I to have finally made it there, a pilgrimage I had dreamed of making to this very spot ever since I first discovered John Keats and his work when I was in college back in Mississippi. Severn wrote that Keats had told him he loved Haydn "for there is no knowing what he will do next." That is also the reason I love Keats. When I first read his poems and letters during my college days I was never sure what line was coming next, where his thoughts were taking him and, thus, me along with him. I longed to have such a friend as Severn read me Keats's poems lovingly aloud as he had played Haydn so lovingly for Keats, so alone finally in his illness as I was feeling that day there in Rome in my addiction, having only eighteen consecutive days of sobriety once again since I had last used.

Above my sunburnt head, on the side of the building where the apartment was located, there was carved into the ochre walls a replica of the lute that Severn designed to be carved into his friend's gravestone where he was "buried in the non-Catholic cemetery," as Andy Warhol had told me that day he'd quoted Keats back to me. The lute was missing four of its eight strings to signify Keats's life cut short at the age of twenty-five on February 23, 1821. Severn lived on for another fifty-eight years after his friend's death but was buried next to him.

As I looked up at that carving I thought of Keats's quoting Milton in his letter on "The Vale of Soul-Making":

> How charming is divine Philosophy
> Not harsh and crabbed as dull fools suppose
> But musical as is Apollo's lute

Then, as Gould lutelessly leaned into Haydn's Sonata in E-Flat Major, I stood ready to enter the room where Keats had lived and died. I had always wondered when this day finally would occur and if, as usual, I would be alone when I experienced it. I had come to the conclusion sitting there on the Spanish Steps contemplating the life that had brought me to that place—more important to me than any cathedral or church along the Camino—that after a life of so much solitude it was only fitting that I would experience this place all by myself. "Though the most beautiful creature were waiting for me at the end of a journey or a walk," Keats's words, written in a letter to his brother George, circled in my head as I climbed the narrow stairwell of the house at Number 26. "Though the carpet were of silk, the curtains of the morning clouds; the chairs and sofa stuffed with cygnet's down; the food manna, the wine beyond claret, the window opening on Winander Mere, I should not feel—or rather my happiness would not be so fine, as my solitude is sublime."

I bought a ticket—the place is now known as the Keats Shelley House, with more than eight thousand books devoted to the Romantic literary period—and, walking through the library, entered his bedroom. After Keats's death from consumption all the contents of the room, as decreed by the Vatican, were burned. But the fireplace where Severn had cooked Keats's meals was still the same. The stone floor was the original. There was no one else there, so I lay on it. Its coolness reminded me of that stone floor back in the mountain village on the Camino that day I had been so angry at the Catholic Church and that Catholic path and needed such coolness at the end of such a challenging day. That day I had ended up with my face on the floor, prostrate in a Catholic church. But on this stone floor I lay looking upward. Prostration was not called for. I was not here seeking forgiveness. Neither was I here to fix blame. I was simply feeling blessed. Present. I felt more alive than I had felt in months. I looked up at the ceiling that was still the same one that had been there when Keats had lain in that same room feeling less alive by the day and pondered it through his own kind of pain. I said a prayer to the gods of poetry and to the poet himself who had lain there pondering.

I stood.

I walked over by the bed to look down into the hollow eyes of a replica of Keats's death mask encased on a table there. Upon his death there were casts made of his face, a foot, and a hand by Gheradi, who was Casanova's mask maker in Rome. Severn, grieving, used the mask to paint his famous portrait of his friend reading at Wentworth Place.

This was exactly what Keats had looked like, and I smiled knowing finally, yes, he really was my type. I stared down into the mask's vacant eyes. Why couldn't these be the eyes that came devilishly alive as I continued to stare longingly down into them and not those of that Spanish Christ on the cross back on the Camino that I had stared up into? Why couldn't light begin to shine on me from these? But standing there staring down into his face, I realized Keats had not been my spiritual guide all these years. There was no transmogrification needed to confirm his deity to me, for that was not what his role in my life had been. Keats's humanity had always been my beacon, not his soul. It was how he made the world a place where flesh rightly belonged. No wings were needed for flight when I read him. No feathery feelings filled my chest. He anchored me to this world where I so often felt but a visitor. That was the vision he offered me: to see the world more clearly unclouded by talk of heaven or the hovering before me of hallucinations.

I turned from Keats's face—freed anew by his long-ago presence in this world—and read Severn's letter describing his death. I then sat in a chair by the window overlooking the Spanish Steps and contemplated that view that Keats himself had sat staring at for those last two months he was confined to this very room. His eyes filled my head. His soul remained his own. Now, having made this pilgrimage so unlike the one that had spanned a month in Spain, mine could be.

Or could it?

There would be one more test.

One more battle.

The Sunday after I returned from Tirana and Rome I was sitting in the back pew of the Saint Mary of the Harbor Episcopal church in Provincetown. I often went there for Sunday services because the rector was, like me, from Mississippi and his soft Southern accent as he preached his heartfelt sermons comforted the lost little Southern sissy somewhere still inside me. I sat there that day right before the Eucharist was to take place remembering all that had transpired only days before in Albania and Italy. Someone tapped me on my shoulder, interrupting my reverie. It was one of the ushers who asked in a whisper if I would be a Bearer of Gifts up to the altar. I had never done it before. Was I worthy of such a task? I had not even been baptized in the Episcopal Church. I was still officially a Methodist. But I reasoned—if reason is needed in such a place where faith is the abiding principle—that if I was being asked then it was God's will that I do it whether I were a worthy Episcopalian or not.

I stared down at the altar but sank quickly back into my reverie, thinking of that day when I visited Keats's bedroom on that hot Roman afternoon and knelt at an altar of my own making. After a couple of hours I left the Keats Shelley House and started to walk over to the Trevi Fountain. But I turned back. I walked again up the narrow stairwell and told the young man who was selling the tickets that I had forgotten something and asked if it would be okay if I went back inside for a moment. He was nice enough to allow me. I let him assume I had left a book behind or my keys or some other item. When I walked back into Keats's small bedroom there was an old white-haired man sitting in the chair at the window where I had earlier sat gazing out at the view. We each waited the other out. He eyed me suspiciously as he sighed and got up from the chair to leave. I peeked through the door to make sure he was exiting the place, then turned and knelt in front of the marble fireplace. I said a prayer of thanks to whomever deemed to hear me in that moment for bringing me finally to that very spot and allowing me to be in the same room where Keats had lived his "posthumous existence" that continued each time I plucked a sentence or two from one of his letters or read a poem of his with just a bit more understanding. It was an existence that continued that morning at Saint Mary of the Harbor back in Provincetown even as I was given a silver box filled with the Communion wafers and walked down the aisle toward that more traditional altar to hand the box of wafers to the Episcopal priest. I looked out the church window at the sunshine on the bay—a deeper natural sacredness that Keats often credited more than Christ's.

When I got home from church that day where I was staying in my friend's place on the wharf I signed on to Facebook and had a message from a drug dealer I had not heard from in two summers, wondering how I had been and if I needed anything. Had my being made the whispered offer to be the Bearer of Gifts only half an hour earlier been a gauntlet thrown down? Was Lucifer rearing his head at such a gesture? My addiction was certainly whispering to me as I read the unexpected message.

I reasoned—as I had reasoned back at Saint Mary of the Harbor— that this too was somehow the will of the universe. I went into a trance. I sent a message back to the drug dealer and we made a plan to rendez-vous in a parking lot beneath a hotel for me to buy the bag of meth. I thought of that needle still hidden back in the corner of a drawer.

When I returned with the meth I diluted it in the syringe, which was much larger than the syringes I was accustomed to. But I still mea-sured the amount of meth to match the line where the "3" was labeled on it.

Archie began to race about the apartment. That cry he had not made in six months came howling from his little throat.

I ignored him.

I tied a belt around my biceps.

Archie cried some more.

I touched my arm.

"Archie! Hush!"

I touched my arm.

"Archie!"

I tried to find just the spot to stick the needle in one of my veins. I found it—there, right there—on the first prick. I pushed it in deeper. The blood rushed up into the giant syringe, turning the meth-infused water a scarlet as dark as the bloody bludgeoned eyes of that Spanish crucified Christ before they opened and bathed me in light. I was scared for but a second. Was I about to shoot too much meth into my body? I went ahead—all thinking stopped—and did it. The rush was instant. Staggeringly so. Phenomenal. Fierce. The flight was just as immediate. A thousand feathers flapped inside me. All those flattened Ms from one word only: "meth" "meth" "meth" "meth" "meth" "meth," turning into "me" "me" "me" "me" "me," until only Ms, the racing hum of millions of them, not thousands, filled my ears, my head, my body. I was bathed once more in light.

A few minutes later—fifteen, twenty?—the husband of my friend who was allowing me to stay in his apartment was knocking on the door. He held Archie in his arms. I hadn't realized I had left the door cracked open and Archie had run over to their cottage next door. He'd never done that before. Was he trying to save my life? Was he herding me back to it?

My friend's husband obviously knew I was high. I couldn't hide it. But he didn't say anything before he left. I lay on the bed trying to calm my heart. I had to have sex. But how? The sun on the bay was no longer sacred but seemed to curdle it, boiling it now in my vision. Would more of the hallucinations I knew were on the way be enough to satisfy me?

Archie crawled up under a chair and cried some more.

Teddy, confused, took it all in.

I told them both I was going to be okay.

But I wasn't. I wasn't okay.

I was drowning in the bath of light.

The sun shone brighter inside my body than outside on the bay.

Lucifer had come for me once again.

He had come.

This time he wasn't going to leave unless he took me with him.

The narrative of what took place inside my body over the next three days would take up as many pages as this whole book. I shot up once with that same needle after I tore up the apartment trying to find another one when I needed to feel even higher. I stayed up for almost four days. The hallucinations of Lucifer and all his minions of light became more and more pronounced, more and more magnificent.

But this time it became much deeper than that, for I had never visited him in his realm. He and his minions had only visited me in mine. This time he had come to take me to his home and, in so doing, force my earthly death to occur. He had through my addiction been seductively biding his time until he sensed I was ready to be taken. Addiction was the vehicle he used to arrive; it would now be the one he would use to take me away with him.

Call it an overdose.

Call it a near-death experience.

I only know it was the most blissful, most peaceful, most astonishing experience I've ever had in this life because it wasn't of this life.

The top of the apartment disappeared. The moon and stars became more beautiful and brighter because the sky became darker, inkier, more vast. The wharf unanchored from the beach. And slowly, ever so slowly, it, and I along with it, drifted out into the bay and then into . . . yes . . . another realm. I was aware of going through a scrim-like membrane of some kind. All was mist. The air changed. My breathing did also—or, more precisely, the lack of it. The sound of lapping water overcame me. We circled slowly in a vortex. Other vessels of light accompanied us. I was standing completely still. Lucifer's loving light-filled presence was behind me—hovering—guiding it all. Round and round we went. Round. And round. The lapping continued. I then felt my body hollow out—no lungs, no shit, no shame, was needed anymore. Then: no body. All that was left was feeling. And yet no nerve endings. Just ending, ending, endlessness. A sense of freedom. An utter lack of terror. "It's dying twice a day. I'd never thought of it that way. It is a practice of dying—what it's like to get rid of the ideas, the desires, the body even." And, yet, though circling, we were also moving forward. It's how completely still I had felt on the Camino as I walked on and on and on. There was an exquisite incongruity that kept gathering about me and

I was there at its dead center as I had been that night I stood so close to Love. Severn's letter about Keats's death I had read only days before floated into being. I felt each word. I became each word. "He is gone—he died with the most perfect ease—he seemed to go to sleep. On the 23rd, about 4, the approaches of death came on. 'Severn—I—lift me up—I am dying—I shall die easy—don't be frightened—be firm, and thank God it has come!'" At "God" the vessels of light closed in as if to attack. The sound of the lapping became louder with their approach. Lucifer's more powerful light waved them off. I felt him smile; his presence behind me wafted with it. I felt his own feelings meld with mine. Go on, we felt together. Had this been the way he'd come for Keats? Once more I wondrously became each word. "I lifted him up in my arms. The phlegm seemed boiling in his throat, and increased until 11, when he gradually sunk into death—so quiet—that I still thought he slept. I cannot say now—I am broken down from four nights' watching, and no sleep since, and my poor Keats gone. Three days since, the body was opened; the lungs were completely gone."

I felt that if we got to where we were going I would never make it back. And yet I did not panic. I conveyed to the Luciferian light that I knew it was an angel above all else. It was to its goodness I surrendered. And that was when a kind of confusion occurred, a disruption in the forward motion, that moment Lucifer and I became soul mates because I acknowledged he had one, felt it with all my being, which was all I was at that point. His light wasn't angry with me but greeted this knowledge I had of it with gratitude. And that is when we reversed course in the vortex, for it wasn't rejection the light was feeling. It was rejoicing in being understood. Had this been its mission all along? For me to see my addiction as evil but not myself as such, just as the role given by God to this Angel of Light was to be conceived by us on earth as evil even though it was not itself? We crossed back through the scrim. The mist gave way to the beach again where I lived. The wharf was reattached to its mooring. The ceiling alighted above me. I heard it latch into place as the sky itself did, its stars less bright, less numerous, less. My lungs, gasping, lunged with air.

And yet a veil of sadness—such sadness—instantly descended upon me. The light itself was saddened to be back in my realm, especially when he noticed the Bible there on my desk my mother had given to me the last Christmas she was alive. He silently commanded I remove it from his presence, but I refused. He actually cowered at my refusal at first. Was shocked by it. Then a great exalted anger girded him. I grinned at it. At him. I said aloud, "My goodness is a part of me. Deeply a part. I will not deny it. Especially in your presence. It is why you came for me. But your goodness is part of you. Deeply a part. You cannot deny it. It is why you brought me back." His anger dissipated. Disappeared. He hovered more closely to me. The smell of my flesh seemed to soothe him as his own slightly sulfuric scent did me. Indeed, the meth itself once inside one's body has a slightly pungent, sulfuric odor. Was that what he was smelling? Himself? Was that what I was smelling? Me?

We both knew that this final visit had taken a surprising turn for us both. We felt we were being melded for eternity when instead we were letting each other go. Before he left me he had one final gift to bestow upon me. A magnificent narrative began to play out in the immense storm clouds that erupted over Provincetown in which he allowed me to visualize the whole future I had given up with him and his minions in his realm that turned out to be not hell at all but a kind of alternate heaven. He entrusted me with these visions and I will never reveal them, but they were filled with ecstatic carnality and camaraderie. There was rapture to them. Regality as well as ribaldry. Lewdness. A soil-less soulful earthiness. There was a Greco-Roman manner to the dominion over which he ruled. There were chariots. Much was chiseled. Everyone felt chosen.

I went out on the wharf to take in the vast panoply of it all and allowed my friend next door in his cottage and my neighbors on the wharf and anybody who walked by on the beach below to witness the grief I began to feel at the loss of all this, even though I knew they could not see what I was seeing there displayed above me. I began to sob uncontrollably at my sense of loss.

That was what was so astounding about this last time I have, so far, used drugs—the shamelessness I had about it. The public display of it all. I had learned how to hide when I shot up meth. I knew how to lock a door and have sex with strangers I'd most likely never see again. But this was completely different. I have called it an exorcism when trying to explain it to incredulous friends as I've attempted to describe that abject grief I was feeling on the wharf that day when I stood at the end of it saying good-bye not only to the Angel of Light and his many minions but also to the addict I had become. Yet an exorcism implies evil was being disgorged and this was far from evil. This was generous. Transcendent. The addict in me had died the night before when I was being taken. That was Lucifer's truest lasting gift to me. He had absorbed back into himself that part of me that he had used to reveal himself to me and was letting me, reborn, live a little longer in my own realm. His mission was complete. I was saying good-bye that day not only to him but also to myself. Just as I had to grieve for my parents and for my HIV-negative life, I was grieving that day for the addict, no longer active, who was joining them. So alone out there on the wharf, I had found a way to preserve my own life. But, like my little brother so long ago taking aim, I had to kill something to do it.

This is what I've learned from my battle with addiction and its welcoming of the Angel of Light. Lucifer—as we so nominally label him—is not bad. There is, for certain, a playful vulgarity about him with which he likes to goad God. Lucifer can find enjoyment in being a bit mean as he toys with you. Takes pleasure in his power even as he's frustrated at not being the ultimate source of it. But there is also a grand streak of benevolence in him. I came to understand that he has no choice but to play the role God created for him to play. His existence is God's will. In that, Lucifer is God's servant. That is his faithfulness and not his fallenness.

I know now it wasn't the angel this whole time I'd been looking to fuck but the devil I'd been learning to love. For one can't completely love God until one loves the Devil too. Their divinity lies not in their division but in their duality, their abiding bond. I will be forever grateful that Lucifer too showed me such love at the end and enlightened me with it. He told me early on that the key to joy is disobedience. Through his patience with me—through his presence, through his teaching, through God's love manifested through him toward me—I came to disobey the dictates of my addiction.

I miss him.

I should have known there would be consequences from such a binge and such a display on the wharf. My friend who was allowing me to stay in his apartment there was more than concerned; he was deeply angry. He felt rightfully betrayed by me, his kindness taken for granted. His witnessing, which I allowed, much of my hallucinatory state must have scared him immeasurably. No. There was a measurement of it—he told me he was throwing me out and explained to me that he couldn't chance my dying in his apartment. I then tried to explain to him, in turn, I had nowhere to go. But he was adamant. He wanted me out. He told me to leave immediately and find a couch of some other friend to crash on. He insisted that I could not spend one more night in his place. "Just get out. I want you out tonight," he calmly stated. Any empathy he had had for me had been replaced with disappointment, even disdain. I had learned enough in my almost six months of sobriety not to step into his anger and reflect it back at him. I absorbed it instead. I was now a poverty-stricken, desperate meth addict. I was now homeless.

I begged him to let me stay that night. He relented. The next day mutual friends of ours lobbied him to give me at least a week to figure out where I could go. I will always be grateful that he showed a bit of pity on me once he calmed down and allowed me that. But he wanted all my stuff out of his apartment on the wharf and back in the one he had initially rented for me next door. So yet again I had to make a move.

He also was railing at me to check into rehab as soon as possible, as other friends were suggesting. But I had no money for that. I was down to a few hundred dollars in my bank account, even though, like the addict I was, I'd spent a hundred of it to buy the meth a few days before. I was even skipping meals to save money. No one seemed to understand what dire financial straits I was in as well as emotional ones. I even considered suicide for the first time in that following week. It scared me, since I'd never had such thoughts before. They weren't dramatic ones. Or even desperate ones. That was what was so scary about them. They were rational ones. It seemed a solution to my predicament. I was so tired of being such a burden to myself and others. But I was a survivor, I finally decided. I would figure out what I· had to do next. I wasn't dead. That was the whole point of the last few days. I had been brought back from the brink of death. Was I now going to kill myself? Was that Lucifer's endgame all along? No, I concluded. Death was the destination we all reached. It had not been mine yet. For that I was grateful. I was, yes, alive. I would stay that way.

As I was packing up my stuff for the move next door during the sunrise the next morning—I had been unable to sleep—I found a tiny Ganesha that the woman who had been wearing a pendant of one had given me for my birthday back in March. I held it in my palm and wondered why he had forsaken me for those four days. The rising sun bathed him in a crimson glow as I sat rubbing his tiny trunk and coming to the realization that he had not. He had simply stood back and allowed that last battle for my soul to occur so we could start together with a clean slate. That God–Lucifer continuum that my Western life had contained for fifty-six years was an obstacle that had to be removed before a new beginning could commence. That circle had to be completed, and once it had been, Ganesha and I could move beyond it to the even larger concentric one that contained it. "Thank you," I whispered, and heard, in that moment, the most innocent of giggles. Ganesha's? I looked at the sunrise over the bay and saw a father a few feet away beneath my window there on the beach with his tiny giggling son. The child was joyfully chasing a seagull whose wings lifted its escape against the reddening sky as if my own father had drawn them there. I knew for the first time as I sat there watching the two of them continue to play with each other right beneath my window that the great search in my life was over. I had been searching for the wrong thing all along. The father I had to discover was not my dead one or his replacement in some sexual sense. He was not a deity. The father I had to discover was the one within myself. And I did not have to give up being the son to find him. That was the final blessing of my addiction. It had delivered me to this destination of being both the father and the son. My sobriety was now my child. It was still in its infancy. I had to protect its innocence with all the loving ferocity that a father feels for his baby boy. I gently folded Ganesha in my palm. I sat and watched the father and son on the beach. I listened now not to the child's lone giggle but to their shared laughter rising, rising along with the rising wings of the seagull flapping like one magnificent flattened M against the rising sun.

Later that day I sent out e-mails to friends back in New York City telling them of my predicament. But I was now a woebegone addict—a kind of "boy who cried wolf." There was no help to be had that I could find from people I really knew. All that I was receiving was welcome concern and not-so-welcome sermons about going into rehab. I had come full circle from the December before when I was ready to do just that and had done my intake interview when my brother backed out of paying for it. I could not—nor would I—go back to him to ask for the money. I was no longer speaking to him at the suggestion of a person in the fellowship I'd joined to whom I turned for advice. My brother had seemed to make clear to me he didn't want to be a part of my recovery and I was honoring his wishes. I could have been incorrect about that. I only know how I felt.

Finally a person I barely knew back in New York to whom I'd shown some kindness when I once lived in Paris offered me a room in the loft he shared with his lover. The only caveat was that I could not have my dogs with me. Archie and Teddy were the only things I really had left in my life and now I was faced with not even having them any-more—at least for the time I was back in New York. I had no idea how long that would even be. I was assuming it would at least be for the rest of the summer. Three months perhaps. Archie had been in my life for six years. I had never been away from him for more than that month I walked the Camino. I had only been away from Teddy for a few days since he came into our lives.

But I knew I was going to have to do this. There was no other choice. Once I made the decision, I went on autopilot trying to find them a place to be fostered. That was my first priority. I could not focus on any-thing else until that was solved. It wasn't an emotional decision but a practical one. I had done this to myself and to them in the one second it took to stick a needle in my arm. I had to deal with the consequences. I could not find anyone in Provincetown or New York who would take them. I was becoming a bit desperate so put a posting up on Facebook saying I had to go back to New York for a brief period and was looking for someone who would agree to take my dogs for me until I could re-turn. I also posted the cutest photos I could find of them.

I quickly got a response from a man I didn't know named Jeff Lewis who lived outside Boston with his children and his husband. Lewis's ex-wife, he informed me, lived down the street. They already had four dogs. "We're dog people," he told me when I called him. "And I've got a built-in support system. They would love it here."

"What kind of dogs do you have?" I asked.

"Two Rottweilers and two bullmastiffs," he said.

I looked over at Archie and Teddy and feared for them in such com-pany. Yet what choice did I have? "Are they okay around small dogs?" I asked.

"Yes. Are yours okay around big ones?" he asked back.

"Only if they're not puppies," I said.

"One of the bullmastiffs is, but we can make this work," he told me.

I was so moved by this sweet man's generosity and kindness. "Why are you doing this for me?" I asked. "You are a stranger. I can't even find a friend to be this nice or take on such a responsibility for me."

"Well, you're not a stranger to me," he said. "I read your Facebook postings all the time and I loved your memoir, *Mississippi Sissy*. I feel as if I know you. You can trust us. We'll give them a good home. We love dogs here. We even show our Rottweilers. We're dog show people. Look, I want to do this. I just feel it's the right thing to do."

I then opened up to him as to exactly why I had to give up Archie and Teddy for a bit. I owed him that. "If this changes things, then I understand," I said after telling him the saga of my addiction and how I had used the last week.

"No. Of course not. Let me do this for you. I want to even more now."

I thanked him and we made plans for me to deliver Archie and Teddy to him on Sunday before I headed back to New York on Monday. I hung up the phone and lay on the floor holding them to my chest. I tried not to choke up. I would not cry. I would not. I had too much to do to plan for my trip back to New York.

I woke up Sunday morning and got Archie and Teddy ready for our trip to their new summer home. A friend of mine from the fellowship had borrowed a car from another friend from the fellowship to take me down there, since I don't drive. More kindness and generosity was being shown to me.

I'd been humming "Bridge over Troubled Water" for a couple of hours to calm my nerves at the prospect of giving up my boys and not seeing them for the next few months. I went on youtube.com and linked to Roberta Flack's version and listened to it a couple of times. I posted it on Facebook, then listened to it one more time before taking Archie and Teddy and their favorite sleeping pillow and their traveling cases and their favorite toy with me to the street to wait for my friend to pick us up in the borrowed car.

I didn't say much on the way there. Archie and Teddy seemed to sense something was up. When we arrived we were greeted warmly by Lewis, who was strapping and handsome, and his husband, Johnny, who was a bit older than he. Thinner. White haired. Their home was off a country lane and on several lovely landscaped acres. The huge backyard was fenced in so their dogs and now Archie and Teddy could romp about without being tempted to run away. We all sat on the flagstone patio and watched my boys check it all out.

"Where are your four dogs?" I inquired.

"We thought it best if we let them meet yours one at a time," said Lewis, who got up to retrieve the first Rottweiler. He was a handsome beast named Baron, who seemed friendly enough. But he also seemed to be looking hungrily at Archie and Teddy, as if they might be the first two courses of his Sunday brunch. I sensed—I hoped—he was only being protective of them finally. Archie and Teddy weren't so sure and both jumped up onto my lap to get away from Baron. "He's sweet," I reassured them.

Baron was put back into the house and a second Rottweiler was released who was even larger. His name was Rocky. He lunged playfully for Archie, who growled to keep him away from us all. Teddy began to shake. I looked over at my friend who had brought me there. She could see I was getting a bit worried and reached out to give Teddy a reassuring pet atop his shaking head.

I was becoming nervous about leaving them there, but what could I do? I had no choice. This was the plan I had put into effect. And these gentlemen had been so kind to offer to foster them, although Lewis's husband seemed not to have been fully informed of the situation. He kept eyeing me as if he had a few questions to put to me that were still unanswered.

Rocky was returned to his lair inside and the first bullmastiff— Rocket—was set free. He and Archie and Teddy, all barking at the same time, went bounding into the backyard. Archie, tiring of their play, came sprinting back up to the patio and jumped again up into my lap. Teddy, thinking he was as tall as his new friend, kept taking the bullmastiff's measure. Maybe this was going to work out after all.

Lewis led Rocket back inside and came back with the adorable bull-mastiff pup. Archie took an instant dislike to him, because he dislikes all dogs younger than he. Teddy just took it as another challenge and the two of them chased each other around the yard. "That's Jackson," said Lewis. "Rocket is his father. He sired him," Lewis said, speaking the language of the dog show aficionado.

As we all watched Jackson and Teddy run about in the backyard—Archie stayed in my lap, not liking what we all were watching—Johnny began his barrage of questions about who I was exactly and how his younger husband had allowed all this to transpire. Johnny seemed a bit suspicious of it all. Did he think I was some secret boyfriend? I explained to him about the Facebook posting about seeking someone to foster my dogs and that his husband had been so kind as to volunteer to keep them. Johnny looked over at Lewis as if he now had some questions for him. Before Johnny could start in on him, however, I turned the tables on him and began to ask him my own questions. I knew that Lewis was an executive with the Stop and Shop grocery chain. What did his husband do?

"I'm the comptroller for a charity that assists women and children who are victims of abuse or violence," he told me. "We provide social services for them and a range of emergency services. Shelter mostly. Many of them find themselves homeless."

"What's the name of it, the charity?" I asked.

Archie, jumping down from my lap, now surprised Johnny by jumping onto Johnny's lap. Teddy, back up on the patio now with his new buddy Jackson, sniffed at his ankles. "Bridge Over Troubled Waters," he said.

I gasped and started to laugh and explained about the Roberta Flack video from earlier that day. "Ask Jeff to sign on to Facebook. He reads my postings. He can prove to you I'm telling the truth," I said.

"Is there any reason I should think you wouldn't be?" asked his husband.

I knew if I waited much longer to leave it was going to get harder and harder to do so. But first I took Archie and Teddy down to the lower part of the backyard and tried to make them understand that I was leaving them there but I would be back for them as soon as I could.

I told them I loved them with all my heart. I felt like that little boy back in Mississippi confiding in Chico and Coco all those years ago. "I am so sorry I have done this to us all," I told Archie and Teddy, blinking back my tears. "Daddy is so sorry," I said, kissing them all over their little heads and using the term I used for myself when we were out of earshot of the rest of the world. Archie rolled over on his back for me to scratch his stomach. Teddy pawed at my face and licked it. He put his face next to mine, which was his insistent way of telling me to kiss him on his cheek. I breathed in their distinctive smells as deeply as I could. Teddy's was a bit muskier. Archie's sweatier, sweeter. "I'm so sorry," I kept telling them. "I'm so sorry. Daddy's so sorry."

I then walked with them back up toward the patio where my friend and I said our good-byes to Lewis and his husband. We all started for the house and the front door. Archie and Teddy followed excitedly after me, thinking they were leaving with me. When I got to the glass door, I bent down to hug them and kiss them one more time. They tried to get through the opened door with me, but Lewis picked them up. Archie began to bark. Teddy cried. They both scratched frantically at the glass trying to get through it to me. I turned to look at them one more time and their little faces were full of confusion. They kept scratching. Barking. Crying.

"Go. Please. Get out of here," I told my friend when we got into the car. My throat was tightening. My heart was racing. As we drove down the drive I couldn't hold it in any longer. I began to sob. "This is killing me," I told my friend, and buried my face in my hands. "It's killing me."

She reached out and touched my shoulder. "This is what surrender feels like," she said.

When I got back to my place on the wharf for my final night in Provincetown I packed up a bit more stuff, having already mailed some boxes of summer clothes and shoes to myself at the loft where I'd been offered a place to stay. The woman who owned the apartment on the wharf that my friend had rented before he threw me out gave me permission to leave the rest of my stuff—art and a few pieces of furniture—there even as she acquiesced to his wish that I move out.

My phone rang. It was the person who had offered me the room in his loft. He told me that his lover had decided that it wasn't going to work and that he had to rescind the offer at the last minute. He deeply regretted having to make the call, but they had to back out. I was in shock at first. I was leaving at 10:00 A.M on the first ferry out of Provincetown to head to Boston to catch the train to New York. My friend had told me I could not stay a moment longer. I had no choice. I had to leave even though I now had nowhere to go. Oddly, I was in such shock that I was truly about to be homeless heading to New York in a matter of hours that I couldn't even feel panic. I was numb. I sat out on the wharf contemplating the last two weeks. I had gone from delivering the keynote address at a human rights conference in Albania at the behest of the State Department and standing before all those brave young LGBT activists as a symbol of some sort of strength and rectitude, to being on my knees in gratitude in Rome in John Keats's bedroom, a place I had longed to visit all my life, to, in a matter of hours, being a homeless person in New York City. Would I be in a men's shelter at that same time tomorrow, all because I had stuck a needle in my arm a few days before?

I found the will to finish packing. And even fell asleep that night for six or seven hours. I prepared some breakfast the next morning before catching the ferry and sent out an e-mail as a last resort, trying to find a place to stay. I couldn't believe I was heading to New York in a matter of minutes with no idea where I was going once I stepped off the train at Penn Station. I sent one e-mail to an old friend, Michael Smith, who lived around the corner from my old apartment in New York. He had owned the Depression Modern furniture store on Sullivan Street in Soho for years and had a new store called Adelaide on Greenwich Street in the West Village. When I did have money and even a loft of my own down in Tribeca I bought lots of furniture from him. We had become friendly over the years and bonded over our shared aesthetics. I knew he had a huge apartment and just might have space for me for a while. It was worth a try.

There was, however, one blessing on that otherwise bleak morning. A few days before, I had stopped off at an old boyfriend's place in Provincetown to see if he and his husband could take Archie and Teddy in, but they had just adopted a cat and couldn't do it. I had sat out on my friend's beautiful screened veranda and told him the saga of my addiction. When we had met thirty years ago when he was a hip young East Village boy with multiple piercings in his ears and a winged tattoo across the magnificent expanse of his broad shoulders he had confided to me that he had been trying to kick a drug habit. I had stood by him way back then even with that knowledge. And he confided that he and his husband had also had a bit of a problem with drugs themselves at one point. "But our fellowship is each other," he'd said when I asked him if he had joined the one I was in, since I'd never seen them there. "Do you need any money?" he asked.

The question embarrassed me, but I, indeed, did and admitted it to him. That morning after breakfast he stopped by and gave me a check for one thousand dollars as a loan to tide me over during the summer, since I had confessed I was down to my last two hundred dollars after buying my ferry and train tickets. We hugged and he wished me luck and told me to call him any time I needed to talk. In that moment I felt the instant love I felt for him the first time I ever saw him and his pierced ears parading around the East Village when I thought he was the most beautiful creature I'd ever seen. As he walked away from me down the wharf I had the same feeling. Yet how far we both had come. Now I was the one battling needles and neediness.

I went inside to check that the apartment was clean enough and put my bags out on the wharf to take the walk down to the dock to catch the ferry. I already missed Archie and Teddy terribly. I restacked some books on the floor and stopped when I saw my late friend Perry Moore's novel *Hero* there on top. I knelt and placed my hand atop it as if it were a Bible on which I was taking an oath. "If you can hear me, Perry, I need you, buddy," I said aloud. "I need your help in this. Please. Help me. If you are there somewhere in some parallel universe, if your spirit is here this morning, I swear to you I will stay sober this time. I swear I will to honor your memory. To honor our friendship. Can your hear me, Huck? I swear. I swear. But help me, man. Help me."

I made it to the ferry just in time. I found a seat and concentrated on the horizon as that old boyfriend of mine who had just lent me the money had taught me to do to ward off seasickness when I accompanied him to the Caribbean a couple of times to visit his mother and father, old hippies who lived on a gaff-rigged schooner down there. To calm myself I thought of other trips I'd made in my life as I was embarking now on this one. I'd remembered to pack my journal from the Camino in my backpack so I could work on this book while I was in New York and I took it out to read that last page I'd written in it.

5/31/09

. . . I am writing this sitting in the square outside the cathedral here in Santiago. I sat at this very spot earlier today when I walked into it. I was having a hard time believing that I had made it all the way across Spain and had walked over seven hundred kilometers to get here. I sat as far away from the cathedral as possible with my back to the wall of this building all the way across the square where I'm sitting now and stared up at the cathedral's spiraling magnificence and said a prayer of thanks before walking over to go inside for the pilgrims' mass.

As I was sitting on a pew earlier Toby and Aurelia and Teresa grabbed me from behind to give me a hug. They had arrived the day before and had been coming in for every mass ever since, they said, to see if they could find me.

"There's someone outside looking for you," Toby whispered. "Did Lucas e-mail you about a man who he told to be greeting you when you arrived? That man is out there now. Lucas wanted for him to be the surprise for you when you walked up the stairs to the cathedral. You should go thank him. He has a note for you."

Yes, Lucas had e-mailed me about some man, but I had decided I wasn't going to spend my time looking for him after thirty-one days walking on the path. I needed this pew. I'd earned it. "Toby," I said. "I'm tired. Could you tell the man to come see me sitting here instead? I don't want to lose my spot on this pew. I'll save you a place here with Aurelia and Teresa and me."

Toby laughed and shook his head at me. Aurelia and Teresa knowingly smiled at me as they sat down. "Still so . . . mmm . . . *hartnäckig?*" Toby said, turning to Aurelia.

Aurelia: "Stubborn."

Toby: "Yes, still so stubborn, Kevin, even after your many days on the Camino. Have you not learned a new patience?" He patted me on my shoulder. "I will go get this man who Lucas said would be there for you."

I thanked Toby and turned to watch the preparation for the Botafumeiro to be swept from side to side in one of the most renowned rituals of the mass that is held here for the pilgrims. The thing was as big as a Buick. They have been doing this for centuries, because in ancient times, I was told one day on the Camino, the pilgrims arrived having not bathed or showered and the smell of them was overpowering. Several young priests were preparing the elaborate pulley system that was rigged up at the front of the cathedral that took even more of them to pull in unison to get it to swing back and forth. The ornate thing looked like it weighed close to a ton.

Suddenly I felt a pair of hands on my shoulders. I turned around and the man whom Lucas had told me would be meeting me was Lucas himself. So that was the surprise he and Toby had been planning for stubborn me. I jumped up to give Lucas a hug and now felt guilty I had not gone out there myself, but if one had to feel guilty what better place than a Catholic cathedral? I couldn't believe I had begun my Camino lying in a bunk next to this boy—now a young man after his own month on the path—and was about to end it with his sitting next to me at this mass. Toby and Lucas and Aurelia and Teresa and I all lined up sitting in a row down the pew. Lucas reached for my hand and slipped the note in it that he had written for me upon my arrival. It read:

Lass Los
Der Eine kommt, der Andere geht
Schau nicht zurück, geh dein' Weg!

This means:

One comes, another goes
Don't look back, go your way!

I turned to him. I folded the note gently in my palm. "Thank you, sweet Lucas," I whispered. "Thank you."

The mass was beginning. The young priests were taking their places at the pulley. The pipe organ moaned into being from somewhere in the cathedral. "Those are lines from a song by a singer named Dennis Lisk," Lucas whispered to me as I marveled at the beauty of the cathedral all around us, at all the grimy pilgrims crowding the pews, at my friends seated down the pew from me. The moaning of the organ grew louder, as it became its truer self and filled the place with the amazing music it was created to make. Lucas leaned closer to me. His whisper competed with the music. "Do you know what *lass los* means?" he asked. I shook my head no. The music now thundered. The incense was being hoisted. It hung above our heads and, burning, swung in its vast encasement to and fro, its perfumed pungency released in puffs and adding even more clouds to the celestial scenes painted on the ceiling. "It means 'let go,'" said Lucas. "'Let go.'"

I closed the journal.

"Let go," I now whispered to myself.

I looked again toward the horizon, the low gathering clouds seeming to rise from it like puffs of perfumed incense in a Galician cathedral.

I peered past them up at the sky.

It gestured:

Onward.

———

I checked into a cheap hotel on 23rd Street when I got to New York and went to a meeting of my fellowship. I went to bed that first night back in the city still not knowing where I was going to live. I had enough money in my shrinking budget for one more night in a hotel and then I'd have to find a bed in a men's shelter, which I had resolved I would do if all else failed.

Luckily, the next day my friend Michael called to tell me it would be okay to stay in his extra bedroom as long as I needed. He was my last option, but sometimes it only takes the outstretched hand of one person, one friend, to save a life. With that one gesture, Michael saved mine. I will be forever in his debt. His kindness might have kept me from killing myself that final night in that hotel room. I wasn't even that sad or upset. As I've said, it just seemed like a rational decision. It was the solution to a problem. I'd had a nice life. A long run. A semblance of a career in the magazine world. My first book had been a *New York Times* bestseller. I'd even had one or two boyfriends I could say I truly loved and still do and will for as long as I do live. But maybe it was time, I reasoned, to call it quits for good. And then again I once more thought of that Angel of Light who gave me his reprieve and allowed me to live. There had to be a reason for that. Maybe it was even to give me time to finish this book. I know some readers, if you've made it past those passages, are rolling your eyes at my bringing him up yet again. I don't care if you believe any of that or not. But believe this: My belief in him and his benevolence toward me and his giving me a second chance at life kept me alive long enough that day in that cheap hotel room to get that phone call from Michael.

I was asked by Michael if I could spend one more night at the hotel on 23rd Street, because he was away at an antique show in Massachusetts. I could swing that if my credit card wasn't rejected, since I had had to stop paying all my bills in order to eat during the last month. That's how broke I now was. I had bought a sandwich at the barbecue place next door to the hotel and saved half of it to eat that night for supper. I wolfed it down, then went online to find another meeting that night of the fellowship I had joined to get sober.

Once I moved into Michael's I went to up to three meetings a day of the fellowship—that is, when I wasn't working in Michael's store. Not only was he allowing me to stay with him rent-free, but he had also given me a job one day a week as a "shopgirl" so I could make a hundred bucks to live off during the week. By the end of three months of sobriety I had gone to close to 270 meetings. If I couldn't find a way to afford rehab or an outpatient program, I would just triple up on the fellowships I'd found. I was more serious about my recovery than ever.

I even called up Brandon, the kid I had mentored for years, and asked him to see me one morning. I had disappeared from his life in the last year and I wanted to explain to him why. I felt guilty that after telling him when he was a child that I would never abandon him I had done just that in many ways. It was another promise broken because of my addiction. I met him at the Starbucks where I had first seen the "angel" while I was reading Shirley MacLaine's book about the Camino. I told Brandon about my meth addiction that day. He sat and listened as I talked for thirty or forty minutes and told him the whole saga, all the ups and downs, as many of my secrets as I thought he could take. I owed him that. We'd been through so much together over the last dozen years. In many ways he knew me better than anybody.

Brandon was now eighteen and attending Borough of Manhattan Community College. In fact, we were meeting before he had to head downtown to his statistics class. I was so proud of him. He was the first male in his family to have ever graduated from high school, much less attended college. I had watched him grow up from a six-year-old and I now sat watching the young man he'd become absorbing all I had told him. I saw in his eyes a glimpse of the fright I'd first seen in them when I met him when he was still such a child. "I would never have known it, Kev. That you were in that kind of trouble," he finally said. His voice was very quiet. There was none of the thuggish bluster that he could summon now that he was an urban teenager. "I did once see some pot in one of your drawers in Provincetown when I was visiting, so I knew you smoked that, but I never knew you were doing the hard drugs. You were still always there for me." He paused. He gently touched my arm, not knowing that underneath my sleeve was the place, still red and scarred, where I'd last shot up. "Are you going to be okay?"

"Yeah, Brandon. I think I am going to be," I told him. "I wasn't sure there for a while. But I really do think I am going to be," I told him.

We sat in silence for a long time. Neither of us really knew what to say after I'd made such a confession. "Oh. I almost forgot," I told him, and reached into my pocket. "I bought you this graduation present." I gave him the small box that contained a cross on a necklace with a graduate's mortarboard as part of its design.

"Cool," Brandon said.

He unclasped the necklace and handed it to me to put around his neck.

He held the cross in his hand and looked down at it. "I like this graduation hat on it," he said.

"I'm sorry, Brandon, for disappearing. Do you forgive me?" I asked him.

He looked shocked by the question. "Come on, man. There's nothing to forgive," he said, the echo of all the love I'd ever felt in my life there in those words he hadn't even realized had been spoken to me before and he was now repeating with so much grown-up grace.

After saying good-bye to Brandon that morning I still had some time to kill before the fellowship meeting I always attended at 12:30. So I stopped off at the Strand Book Store on Broadway to browse its stacks and kill some time. I had wished Weiser Antiquarian Books was still open, since I had been thinking of all the hallucinations lost to me in my sobriety. Weiser's specialized in mysticism and the occult and especially works by Aleister Crowley, which I discovered when I looked up the company on my computer to see if it still had an online version. So many of my drug visions had involved astral projections and someone had told me that Crowley had created much of his following by promoting such visions himself. I'll go ahead and say it: I missed my visits from the Angel of Light and thought if I read about such visions by others then my loneliness for him could be sated.

At the Strand I found references in the books I was browsing through to many of the things I have written about in this one. Others had seemed to have had the same visions I had had. That was comforting in its way even as it made me feel less special. Then I found a poem by Crowley that shocked and comforted me all at the same time. It was called "Hymn to Lucifer." That was one hymn that Diane Sawyer and I had never sung from the Cokesbury. I cocked an eyebrow like that Australian professor had cocked hers at me when discussing Emily Dickinson, a much better poet than Crowley from what I could tell from reading those first few lines—and an even much more spiritual and visionary one in her way. I certainly didn't have any Crowley lines crawling across my flesh as I had hers. But I read on. When I got to the last sentence contained in the poem's last five lines—"The Key of Joy is disobedience"—I slammed the book shut and shoved it back onto the shelf at the Strand as a cold chill ran down my spine and then just as quickly raced back up it in a rush of warmth that I could only equate with a momentary slam of meth in my veins.

That line is what I had heard spoken to me in one of my own visions except it was slightly different. I had distinctly heard "The key TO joy is disobedience." Had I been visited by Lucifer or by the spirit of Aleister Crowley? Did Crowley rewrite himself in death? I laughed. It must have amused Crowley too—or Lucifer—for the book fell off the shelf onto my foot.

I got to the meeting early and hung around outside talking to new friends and old ones. One of the latter was a woman I had met when I first moved to New York in the mid-1970s. She was part of Henry Geldzahler's drove and had even married one of Henry's young boyfriends—with Henry's blessing—who fell in love with her. I was so happy and surprised to see her on the second floor where the fellowship took place, since I was so apprehensive to be attending new meetings in New York when I first got back to town. We were standing on the corner of 10th and University that day when another of our friends from the meeting came up to talk and asked how we knew each other. We went into our routine about how old we now were and how we'd met at the Ninth Circle gay bar in the 1970s when everybody hung out there and smoked joints in the back garden.

"I hadn't seen her in ages until I walked into the meeting a month ago," I said.

"That's not quite true, Kevin," she said. "I saw you at Perry Moore's funeral."

"You did?"

"Kevin, I sat next to you," she said, rubbing my shoulder.

"God. Now that you mention it, I sort of remember you being there next to me. I was having one of my out-of-body experiences during that funeral," I said.

"Yeah. You were sobbing all the way through it. I was concerned for you. You were in rough shape."

"Do you think he really died from an overdose?" I asked her, still having a hard time believing that he had been a drug addict.

"Kevin," she said. "How do you think I knew Perry? He was a regular at the meeting we're about to go to."

"I never even knew he did drugs, much less went to meetings," I said.

"He not only went to that meeting, but you know how we all stake out our chairs and sit in the same ones all the time? Well, you've been sitting in Perry's chair ever since you got here."

I thought of that day a month before when I had put my hand on Perry's book and asked for him to guide me and help me stay sober. He had led me to his very chair.

"Oh, honey," said my friend, giving me a hug. "I thought you knew Perry went there and that's why you were coming. I'm so sorry. I didn't mean to upset you."

"I'm not upset," I said. "I'm just amazed how prayers are answered."

I was beginning to recognize that not only was my ongoing recovery a spiritually based one, but the intervention, still taking place in my life, was as well. The intervention had not been conducted by family members and friends but by a marshaling of the spirit world.

By the first of October, still sober, I was back in Provincetown. I picked up Archie and Teddy on my way back up to the Cape to a tiny inexpensive 120-square-foot apartment I'd found for the winter. It was on the bay and had a big picture window, so if I turned my gaze outward I, at least, had a less cramped view. In fact, the view was magnificent. But there was no stove. I kept my clothes in garbage bags in the bathroom. I slept on a tattered twin mattress on the floor. The mattress was so old—its springs so worn out—that some nights I felt as if I was still trying to fall asleep lying atop the rocks back on Mount Kilimanjaro.

I attempted to find work but was having no luck. Again, I was running out of money. I was beginning to become paranoid that everyone in the small world of publishing and magazines knew of my meth addiction and my fall and was scared of offering me a hand up even for old times' sake. I did get two writing assignments out of the blue. One was for *Country Living* magazine, interviewing actor Corbin Bernsen and his wife, Amanda Pays, about their Studio City home. That one I could do by looking at the research photos and calling them on Skype from my tiny place on the bay.

The other was for *LA Confidential* magazine. Its editor in chief, Spencer Beck, had been the managing editor at Andy Warhol's *Interview* when I was the executive editor. I had not heard from him in years but got an e-mail from him asking if I'd like to do a cover story for him on Mary J. Blige. For that one, I had to go to New York.

He offered me a bit more money if I'd get myself down there from Provincetown and put myself up. I didn't let him know how broke I was. Hell, I could barely swing round-trip bus fare. Luckily, a friend down in New York let me stay at his place for a few nights. Spencer told me he thought I'd be a good match with Mary J. because he remembered that I had always said I was a black woman in a former life. "Even though sometimes I think you can pass for one in this one," he joked. I knew, though, that Mary J. Blige and I had a much deeper connection than that—addiction—and that's what I wanted to talk to her about.

I knew Mary J. Blige had also had a hardscrabble life. And I admired how she bore her own emotional scars with such dignity. This was more than a professional gig for me. It was a personal one. We met at a loft in lower Manhattan and curled up on a sofa together. As she sank into the cushions—giving the brim of the newsboy cap she was wearing a jauntier tilt as she did so—we dug into just how hard-won her dignity had been for her. We talked about a lot of things that day—her childhood, her upbringing in the church, her career, her molestation, her marriage, her mother, and, yes, her own struggle with drugs.

"There seems to be a lot of forgiveness in your story, Mary J. Have you finally forgiven yourself?" I asked.

"Yes. I have. Just lately I have been saying that to myself a lot. 'I forgive you, Mary. I forgive you.' I've been saying that a lot to myself. Out loud. And I've been praying to God to show me how to forgive myself. Because maybe that's the thing I've been searching for."

I did that interview with Mary J. Blige in November of 2012 and turned it in that December. But as of New Year's Eve I had still not been paid. That night I had $1.23 in my bank account and a five-dollar bill in my pocket. That was all the money I had in the world, and yet I felt blessed to have a little more than six months of sobriety. It was the longest I'd been sober since I started smoking pot when I was fifteen years old. I walked down to the beach beneath my tiny apartment on the bay in Provincetown and looked up into the star-filled sky that New Year's Eve. I waited for midnight. When it came, I got down on my knees and said a prayer of gratitude as 2013 arrived.

My checks for the stories arrived the next week to tide me over. On

February 23, I had almost eight months of sobriety. It was also the date of John Keats's death. To commemorate it I went to the tattoo parlor in town and had a tattoo written onto my left forearm so that I would now have a matching pair. I had a line from John Keats's letter on "The Vale of Soul-Making" already picked out.

I went back to my tiny apartment and began to clean it a bit. Since I had already been inked once that day, I took a Bic pen I found on the floor and headed for the bathroom mirror. I stood atop one of the garbage bags that contained my clothes. Balancing myself, I carefully pointed the Bic (my Honey West ritual) beneath my lower lip, inking on a beauty mark as perfect as a period, the punctuation on the two sentences—one by Keats, one by Dickinson—now written on my flesh.

I went and stood at the window gazing outward. Archie and Teddy lay curled up next to each other on a pair of sweatpants. I hummed "The Church's One Foundation" to them as they watched me rearrange the objects on the windowsill. I lined up the lone rock I brought home from Mount Kilimanjaro with the two I had carried in my pocket all the way across the Camino. Ganesha's mantra, "Om Gam Ganapataye Namaha," alighted in my mind and replaced the refrain I could no longer recall from the Cokesbury hymnal. I stood my armless altarpiece of Christ in a corner of the windowsill. I looked for any sign of Lucifer in the light streaming all about me.

I touched my arms.

I read the Dickinson tattoo:

HOPE IS THE THING WITH FEATHERS THAT PERCHES IN THE SOUL.

I then read my new one by Keats:

EVEN A PROVERB IS NO PROVERB TO YOU TILL YOUR LIFE HAS ILLUSTRATED IT.

Now, I am stirring like a seed in China.

Sobriety is my empyrean.

This.

This.

This.

"I forgive you, Kevin," I said out loud.

ACKNOWLEDGMENTS

I could not have finished this book without the encouragement, belief, talent, and friendship of my remarkable editor, Michael Flamini. His presence in my life is a blessing. He has not only made me a better writer, but also—dare I say it?—a better man.

I would also like to thank others at St. Martin's Press whose help has been invaluable: Steve Snider, John Murphy, John Karle, and Vicki Lame. Thank you also to my agent, Robert Guinsler, photographer Bill Miles, copyeditor Barbara Wild, and lawyer, Samuel Bayard.

And thank you to my fellows who, when I found you where you were waiting for me in those rooms, helped me to find myself.